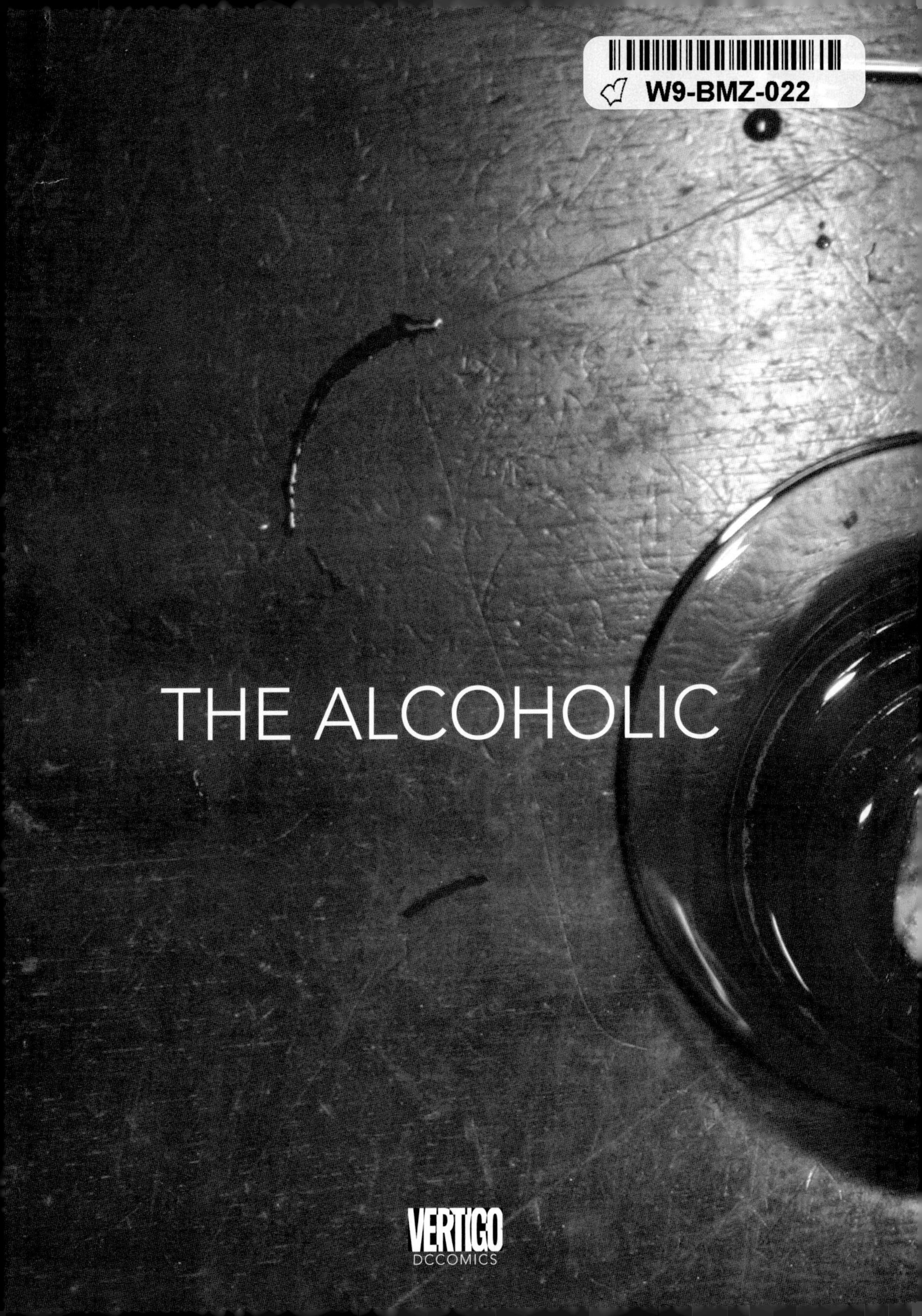

THE ALCOHOLIC

VERTIGO
DCCOMICS

"Last year I was at a storytelling event called The Moth, listening to Jonathan Ames telling a roomful of people a story from his life: funny and heartbreaking and much too personal for comfort. *The Alcoholic* is the comics equivalent of that: the kind of **odd, readable, painfully-honest**-even-if-we-don't-know-where-all-the-fictional-joins-are memoir-cum-fiction that could, a decade ago, only have been published somewhere out on the fringe of comics. Now it's right in the mainstream. I don't know how much Jonathan A is Jonathan Ames. I'm not sure I want to. But **I'm glad I read The Alcoholic."**

NEIL GAIMAN
author Sandman, American Gods

"*The Alcoholic* possesses that Amesian mixture of sexual and scatalogical hilarity with real horniness and also a tender humanity. **I went into a kind of spell reading this book.** I couldn't put it down. **Dean Haspiel's drawings are terrific, funny and immediate.** "

THOMAS BELLER
author The Sleep-Over Artist

"I fucking loved *The Alcoholic*! Ames has clearly researched his subject, and the result is **sometimes debauched, sometimes heartbreaking, hysterical and weirdly wholesome**. So good, it should be required reading at rehabs everywhere."

JERRY STAHL
author Permanent Midnight, I Fatty

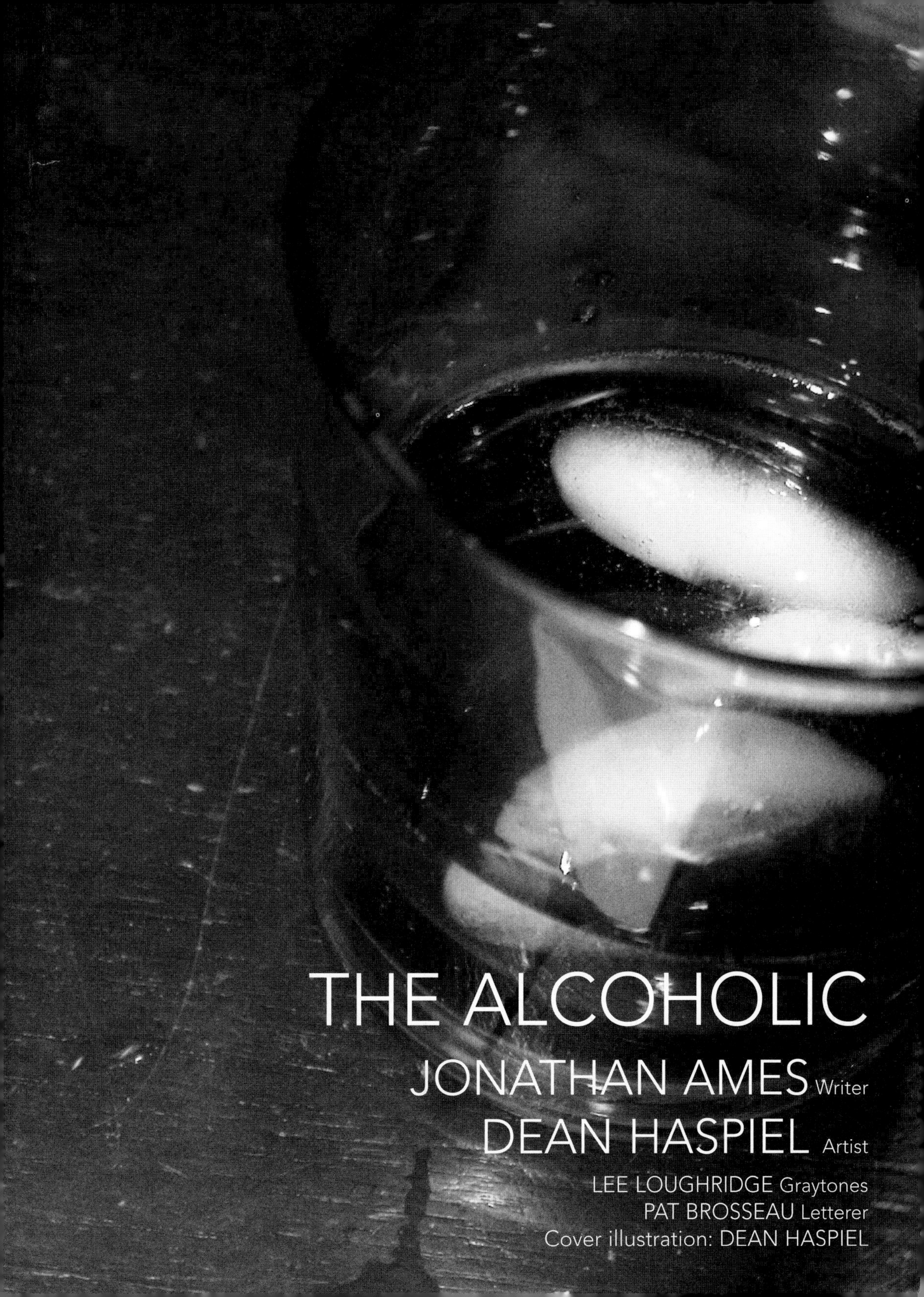

THE ALCOHOLIC

JONATHAN AMES Writer
DEAN HASPIEL Artist
LEE LOUGHRIDGE Graytones
PAT BROSSEAU Letterer
Cover illustration: DEAN HASPIEL

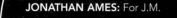

JONATHAN AMES: For J.M.

Dean Haspiel would like to thank
Michel Fiffe, Sarah Butterworth,
Pedro Camargo, Kat Roberts,
and DEEP6 Studios.

Karen Berger Sr. VP-Executive Editor   Jonathan Vankin
Editor   Mark Doyle Assistant Editor   Louis Prandi Art
Director   Paul Levitz President & Publisher Georg Brewer
VP-Design & DC Direct Creative   Richard Bruning Sr. VP-
Creative Director   Patrick Caldon Exec. VP-Finance &
Operations Chris Caramalis VP-Finance John Cunningham
VP-Marketing   Terri Cunningham VP-Managing Editor
Alison Gill VP-Manufacturing   Hank Kanalz VP-General
Manager, WildStorm Jim Lee, Editorial Director-WildStorm
Paula Lowitt Sr. VP-Business & Legal Affairs   MaryEllen
McLaughlin VP-Advertising & Custom Publishing John Nee
VP-Business Development Gregory Noveck Sr. VP-Creative
Affairs Sue Pohja VP-Book Trade Sales Cheryl Rubin Sr. VP-
Brand Management   Jeff Trojan VP-Business Development,
DC Direct   Bob Wayne VP-Sales

THE ALCOHOLIC

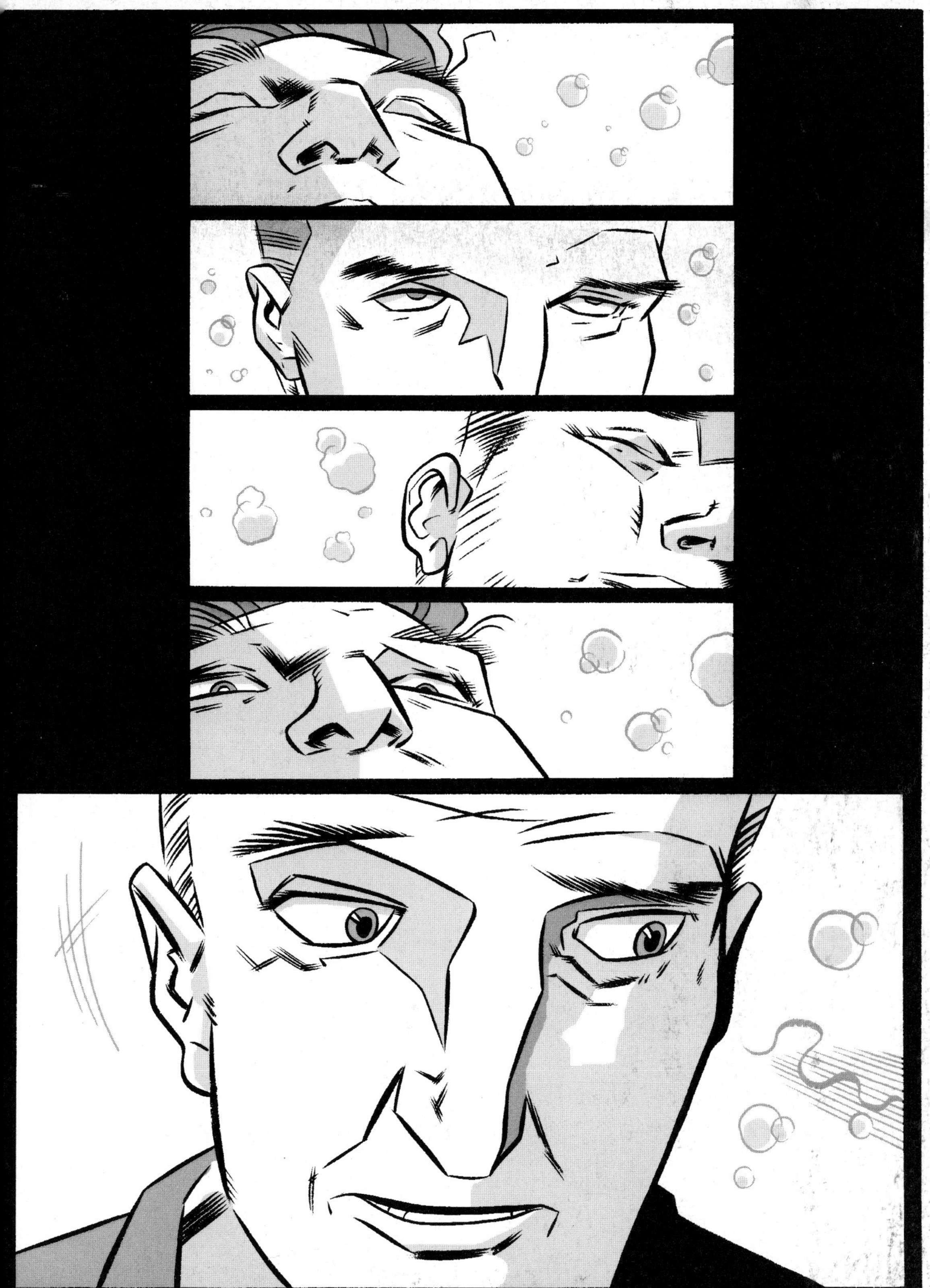

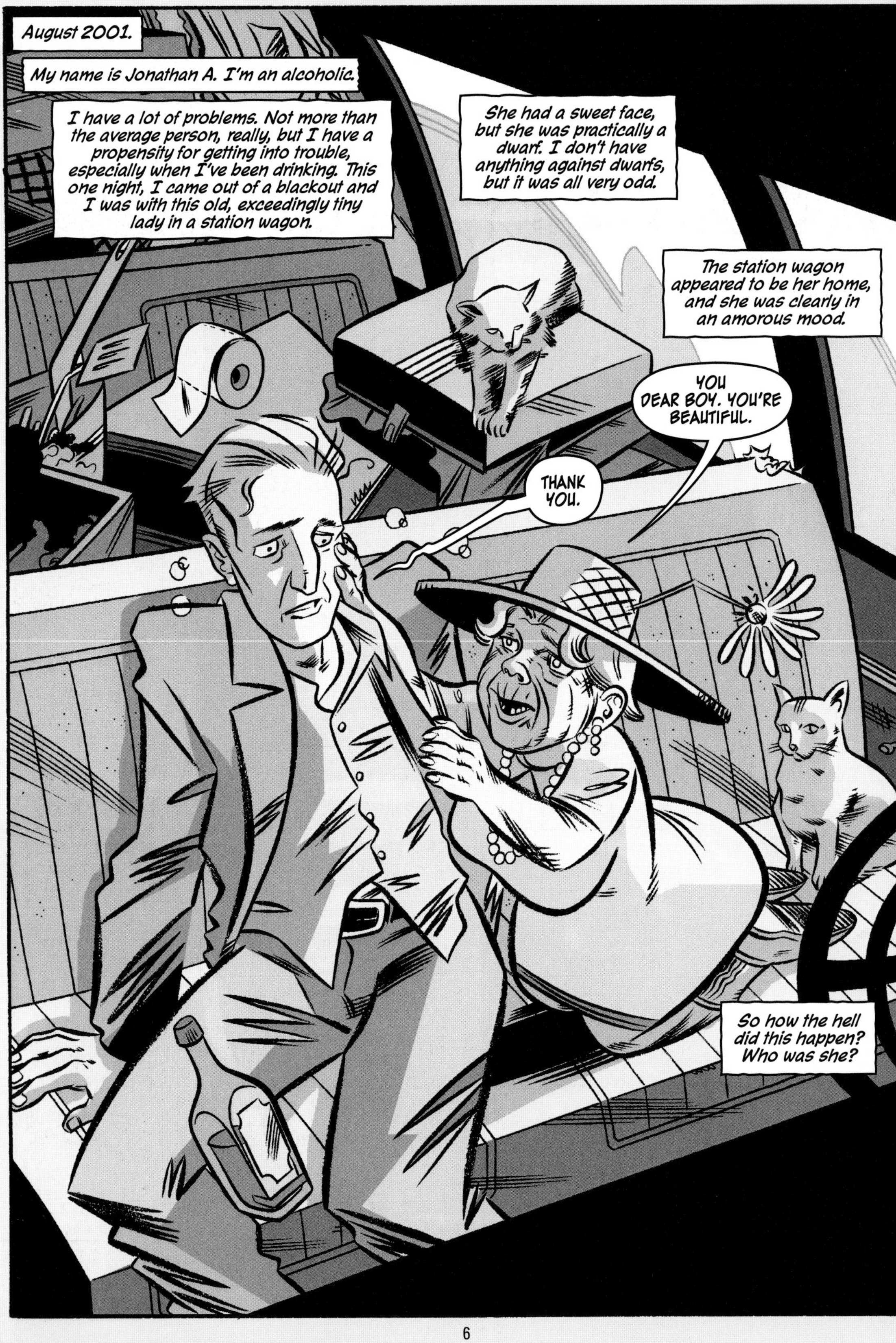
August 2001.
My name is Jonathan A. I'm an alcoholic.
I have a lot of problems. Not more than the average person, really, but I have a propensity for getting into trouble, especially when I've been drinking. This one night, I came out of a blackout and I was with this old, exceedingly tiny lady in a station wagon.
She had a sweet face, but she was practically a dwarf. I don't have anything against dwarfs, but it was all very odd.
The station wagon appeared to be her home, and she was clearly in an amorous mood.
YOU DEAR BOY. YOU'RE BEAUTIFUL.
THANK YOU.
So how the hell did this happen? Who was she?

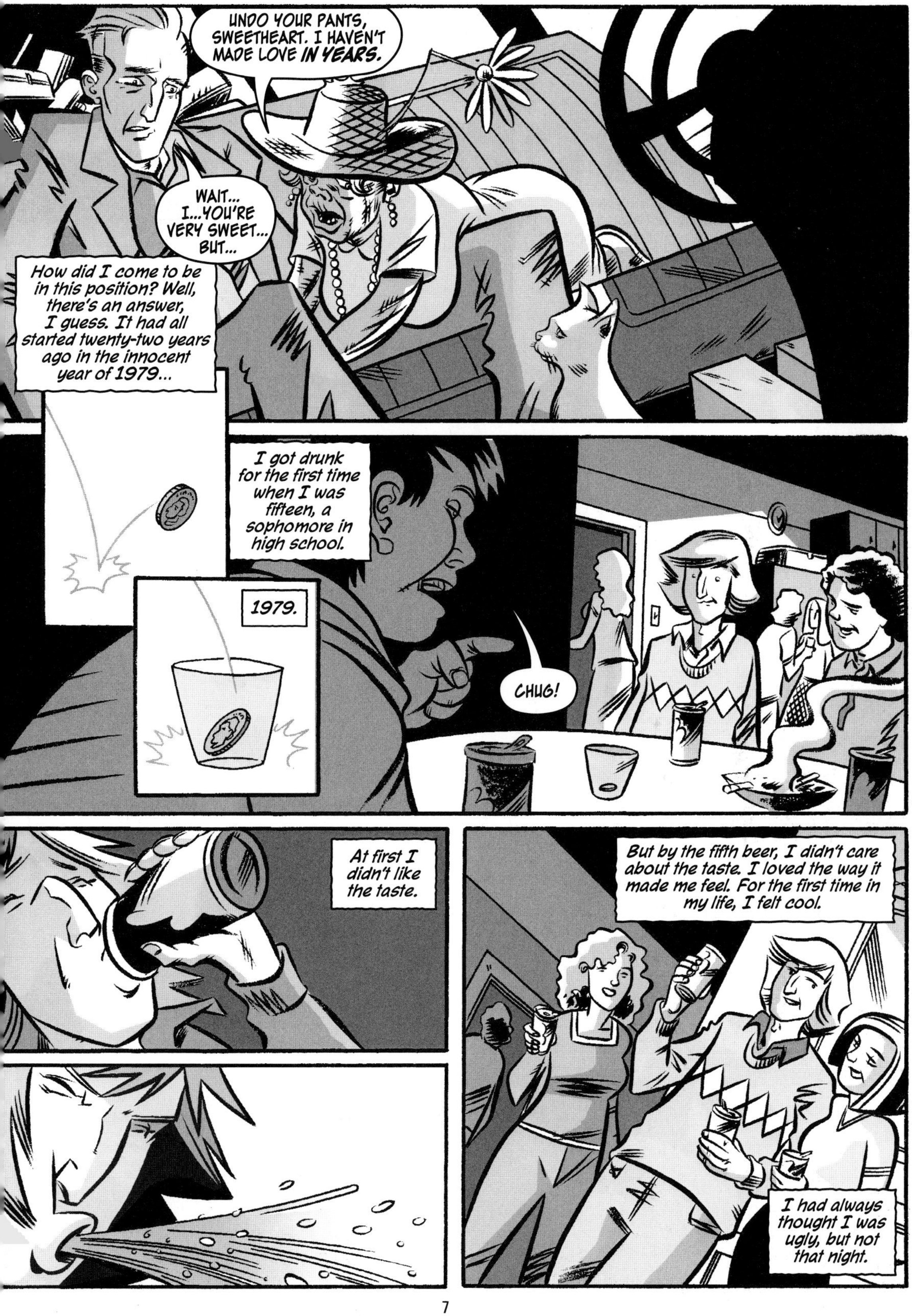
UNDO YOUR PANTS, SWEETHEART. I HAVEN'T MADE LOVE IN YEARS.
WAIT... I...YOU'RE VERY SWEET... BUT...
How did I come to be in this position? Well, there's an answer, I guess. It had all started twenty-two years ago in the innocent year of 1979...
I got drunk for the first time when I was fifteen, a sophomore in high school.
1979.
CHUG!
At first I didn't like the taste.
But by the fifth beer, I didn't care about the taste. I loved the way it made me feel. For the first time in my life, I felt cool.
I had always thought I was ugly, but not that night.

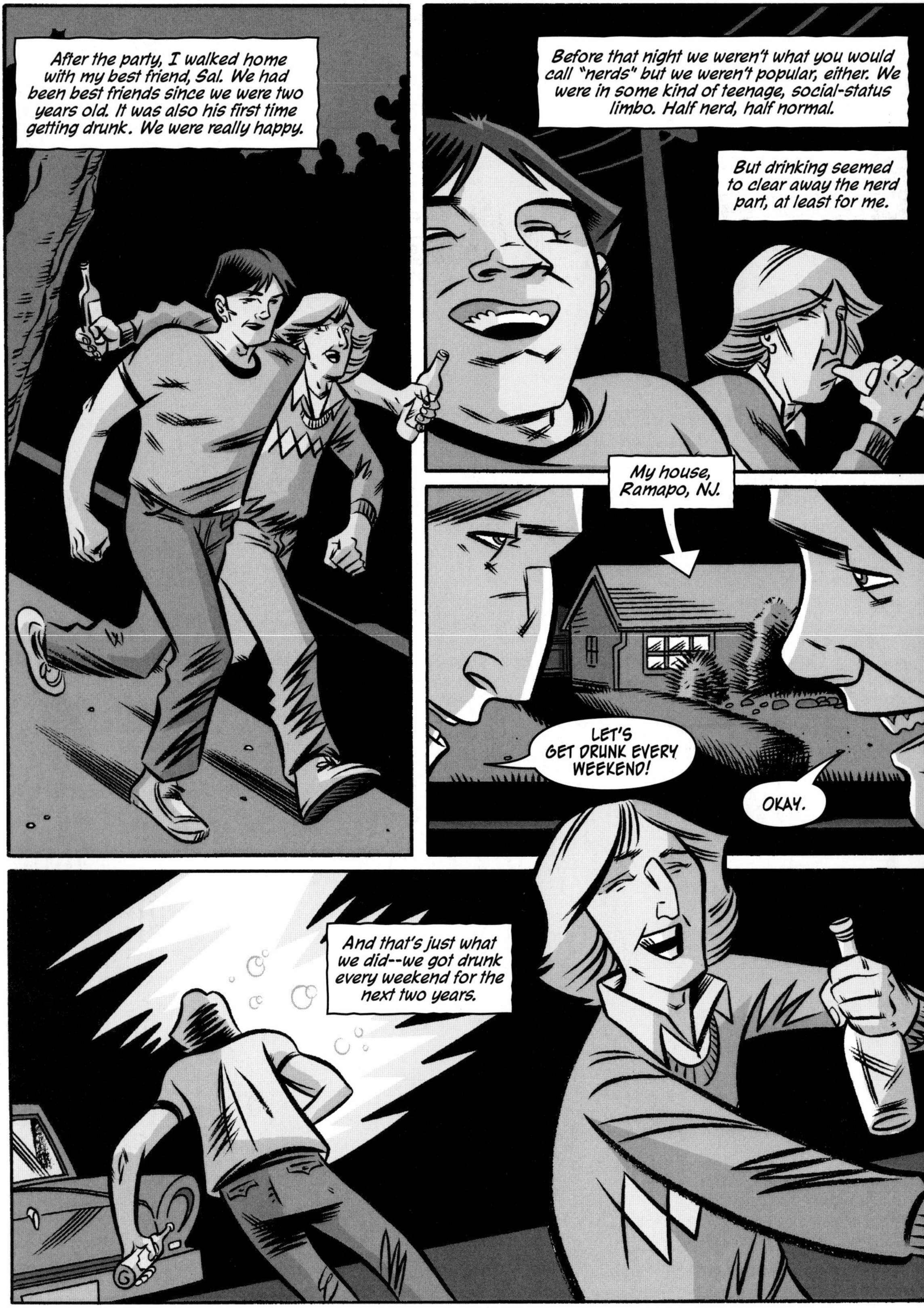
After the party, I walked home with my best friend, Sal. We had been best friends since we were two years old. It was also his first time getting drunk. We were really happy.
Before that night we weren't what you would call "nerds" but we weren't popular, either. We were in some kind of teenage, social-status limbo. Half nerd, half normal.
But drinking seemed to clear away the nerd part, at least for me.
My house, Ramapo, NJ.
LET'S GET DRUNK EVERY WEEKEND!
OKAY.
And that's just what we did--we got drunk every weekend for the next two years.

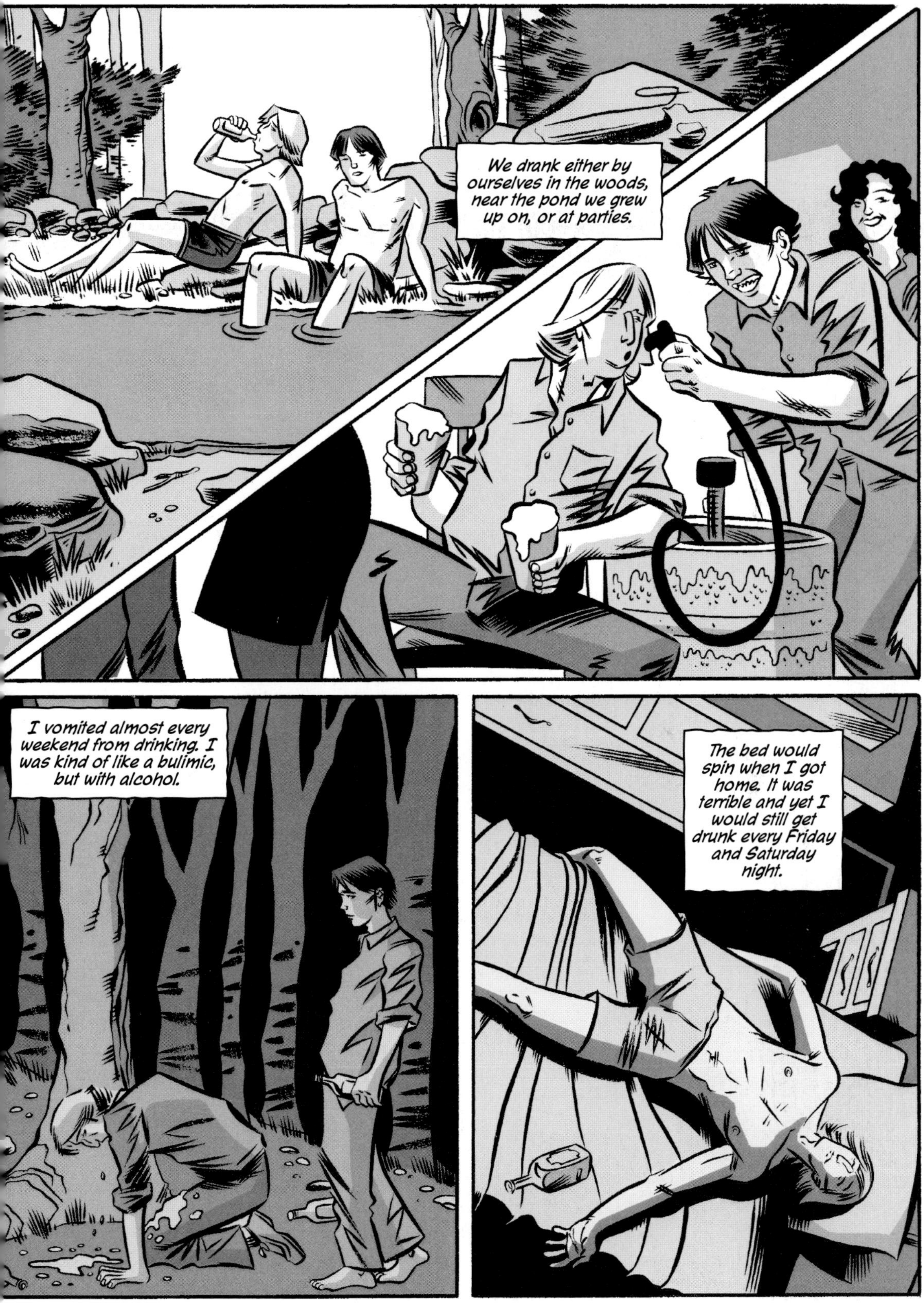
We drank either by ourselves in the woods, near the pond we grew up on, or at parties.
I vomited almost every weekend from drinking. I was kind of like a bulimic, but with alcohol.
The bed would spin when I got home. It was terrible and yet I would still get drunk every Friday and Saturday night.

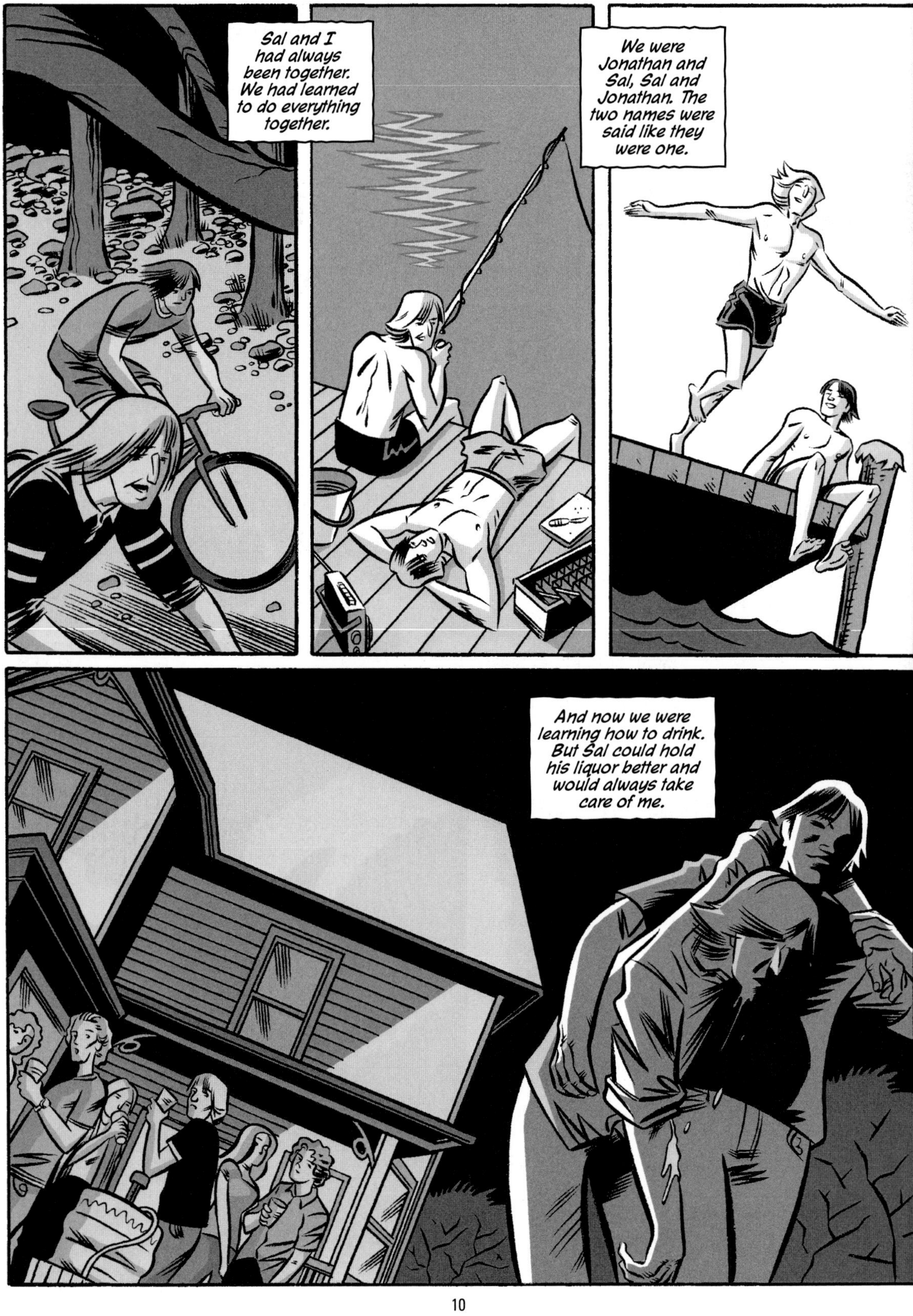
Sal and I had always been together. We had learned to do everything together.
We were Jonathan and Sal, Sal and Jonathan. The two names were said like they were one.
And now we were learning how to drink. But Sal could hold his liquor better and would always take care of me.

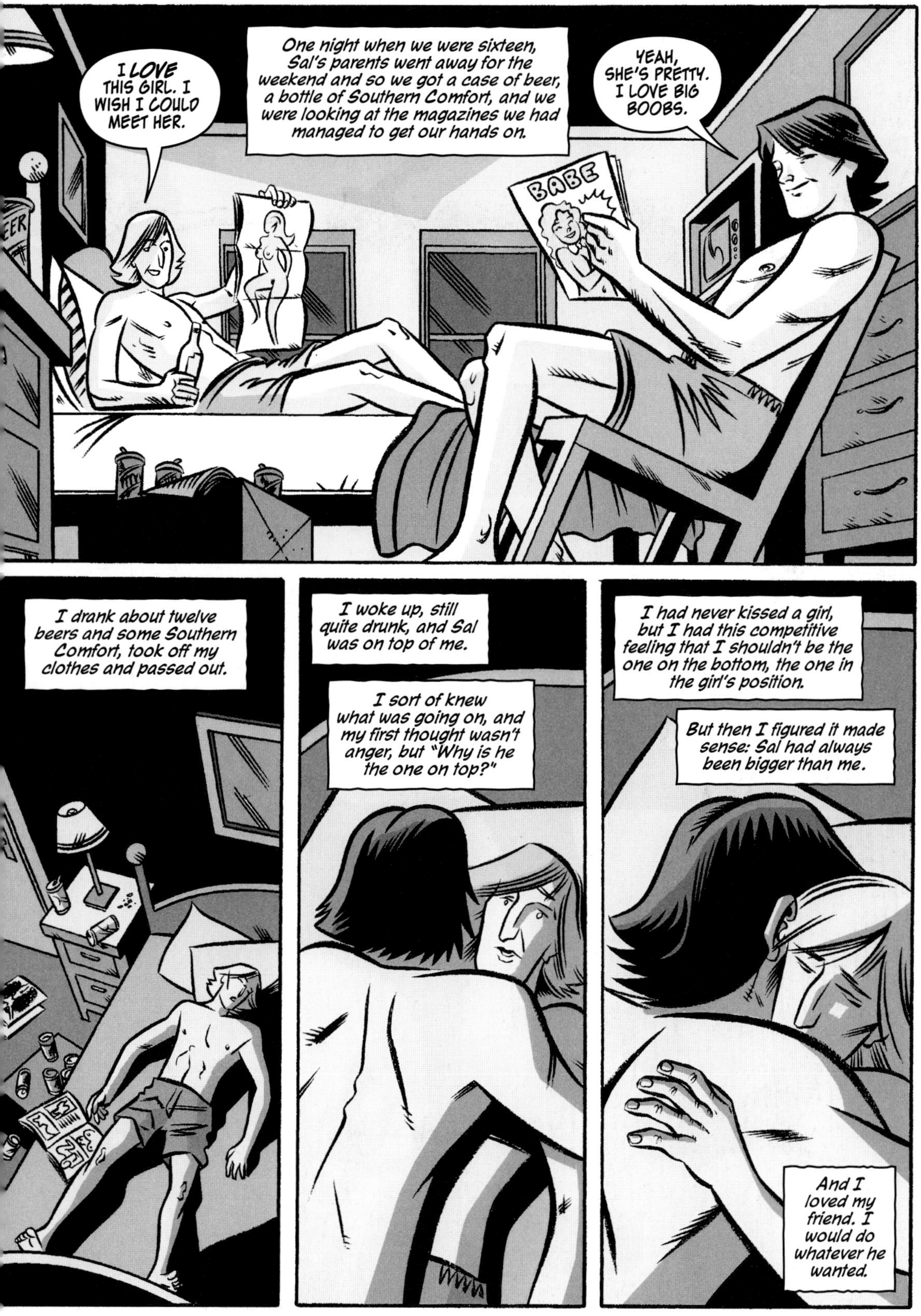
One night when we were sixteen, Sal's parents went away for the weekend and so we got a case of beer, a bottle of Southern Comfort, and we were looking at the magazines we had managed to get our hands on.
I LOVE THIS GIRL. I WISH I COULD MEET HER.
YEAH, SHE'S PRETTY. I LOVE BIG BOOBS.
BABE
I drank about twelve beers and some Southern Comfort, took off my clothes and passed out.
I woke up, still quite drunk, and Sal was on top of me.
I sort of knew what was going on, and my first thought wasn't anger, but "Why is he the one on top?"
I had never kissed a girl, but I had this competitive feeling that I shouldn't be the one on the bottom, the one in the girl's position.
But then I figured it made sense: Sal had always been bigger than me.
And I loved my friend. I would do whatever he wanted.

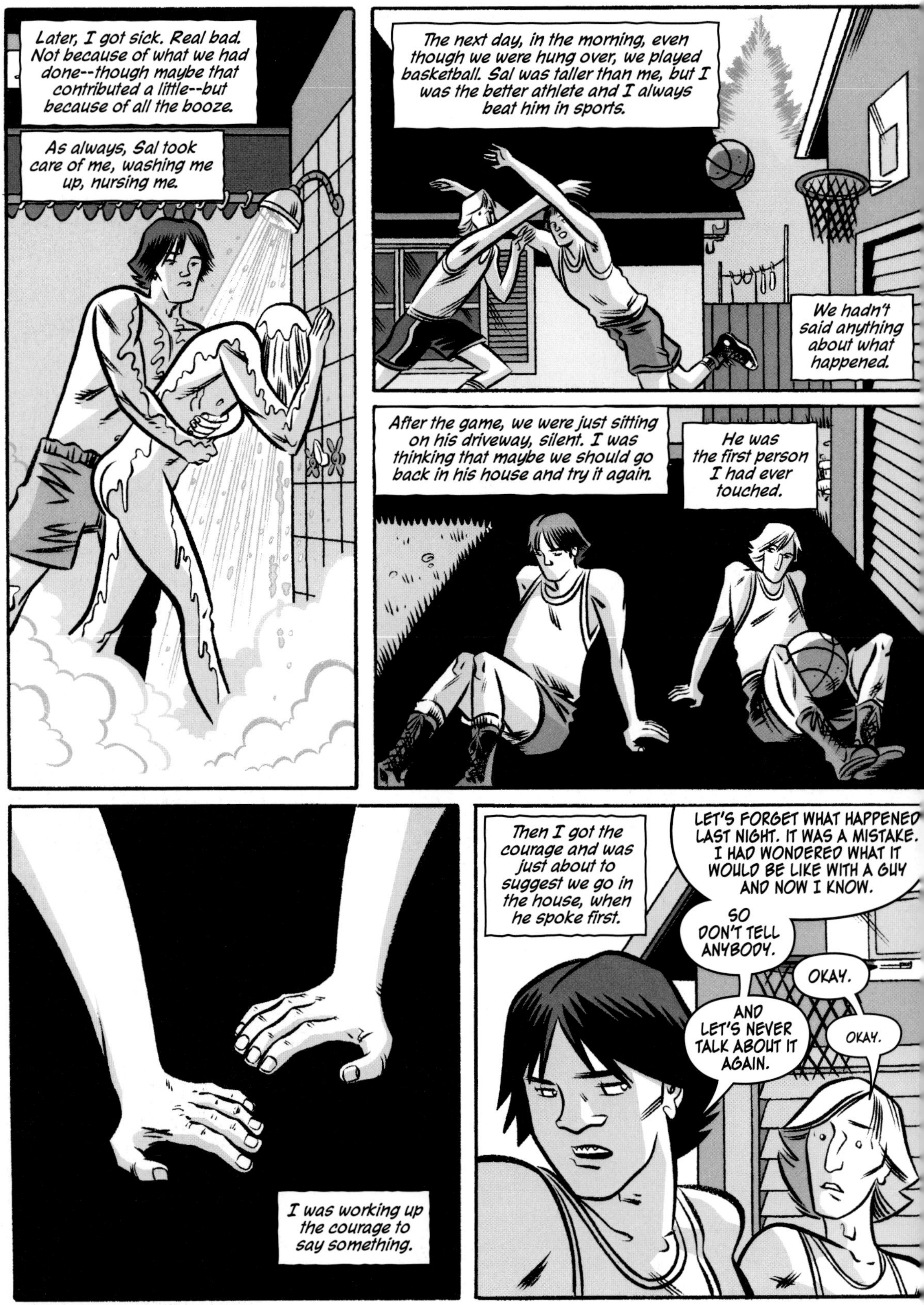

Later, I got sick. Real bad. Not because of what we had done--though maybe that contributed a little--but because of all the booze.
As always, Sal took care of me, washing me up, nursing me.
The next day, in the morning, even though we were hung over, we played basketball. Sal was taller than me, but I was the better athlete and I always beat him in sports.
We hadn't said anything about what happened.
After the game, we were just sitting on his driveway, silent. I was thinking that maybe we should go back in his house and try it again.
He was the first person I had ever touched.
I was working up the courage to say something.
Then I got the courage and was just about to suggest we go in the house, when he spoke first.
LET'S FORGET WHAT HAPPENED LAST NIGHT. IT WAS A MISTAKE. I HAD WONDERED WHAT IT WOULD BE LIKE WITH A GUY AND NOW I KNOW.
SO DON'T TELL ANYBODY.
OKAY.
AND LET'S NEVER TALK ABOUT IT AGAIN.
OKAY.

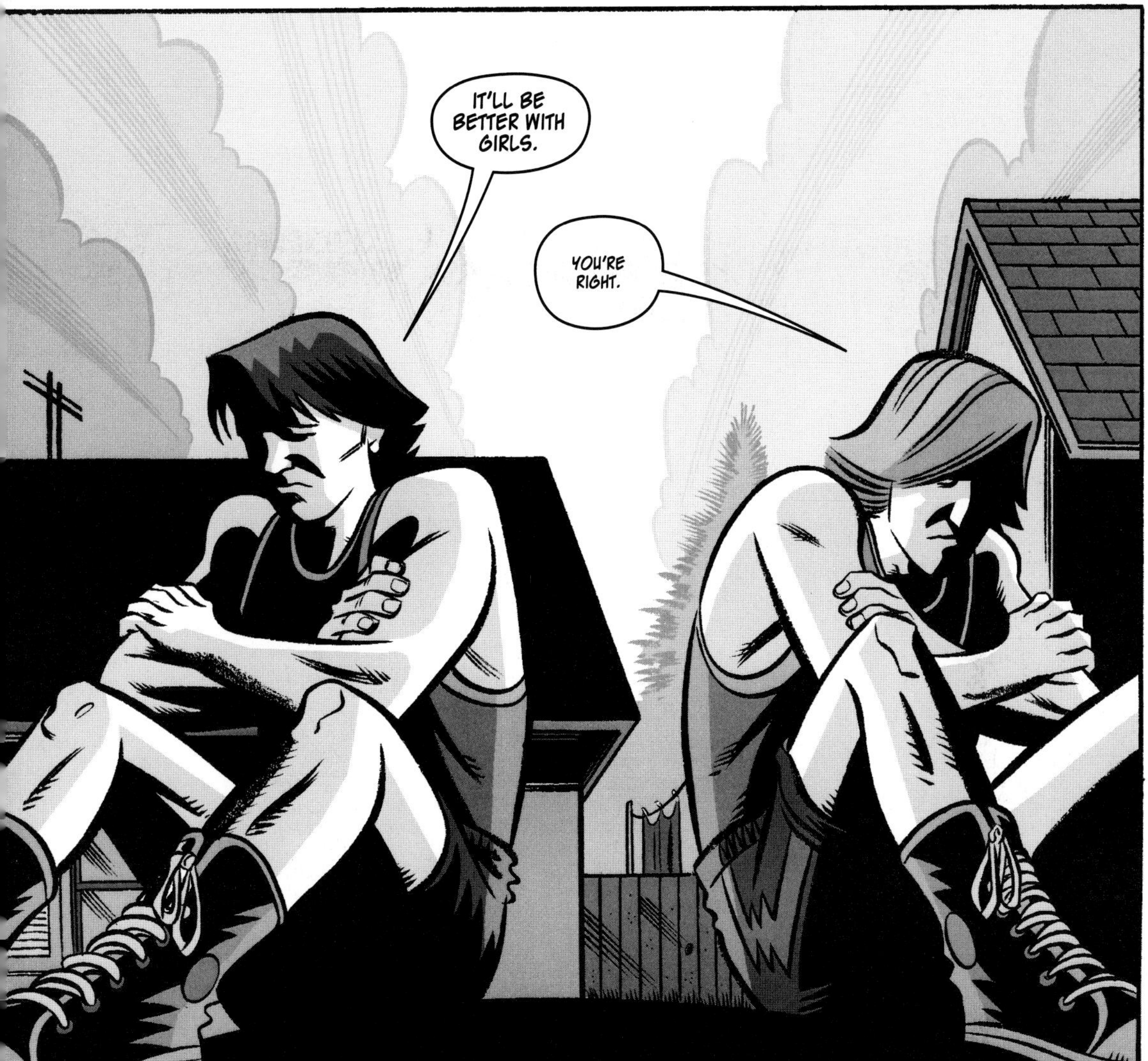
IT'LL BE BETTER WITH GIRLS.
YOU'RE RIGHT.

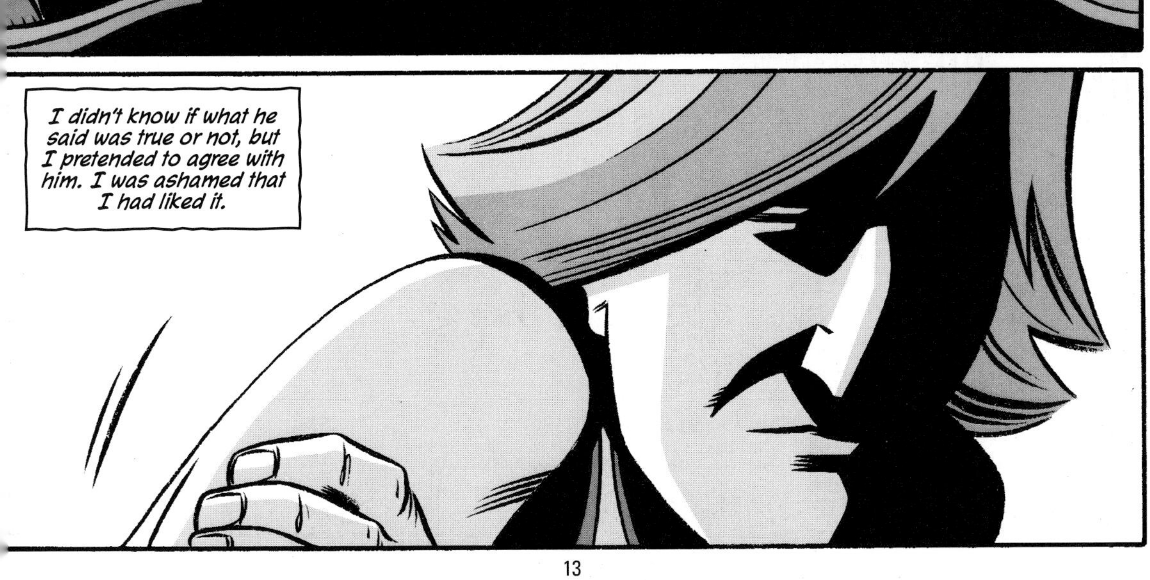
I didn't know if what he said was true or not, but I pretended to agree with him. I was ashamed that I had liked it.

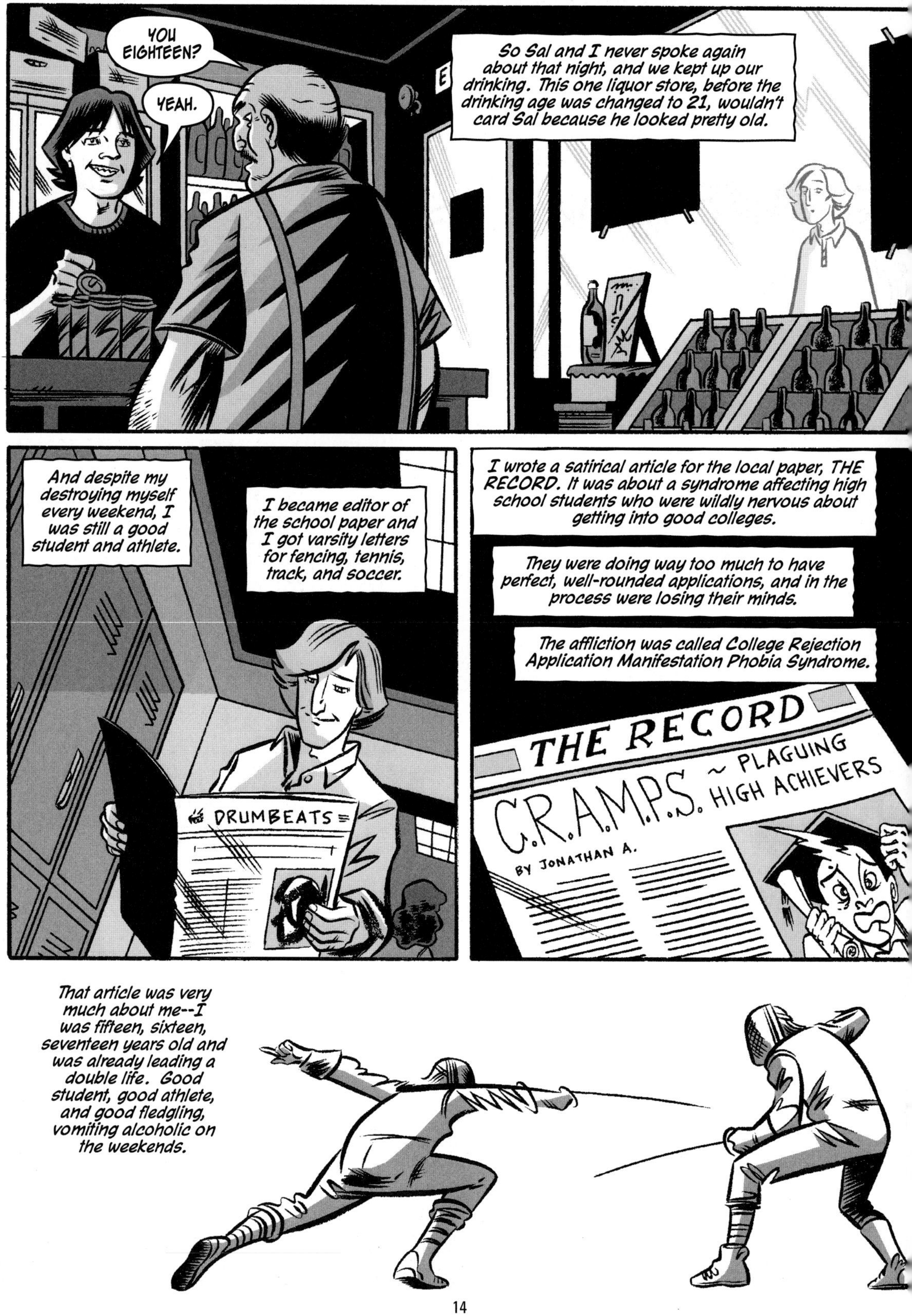
YOU EIGHTEEN?
YEAH.
So Sal and I never spoke again about that night, and we kept up our drinking. This one liquor store, before the drinking age was changed to 21, wouldn't card Sal because he looked pretty old.
And despite my destroying myself every weekend, I was still a good student and athlete.
I became editor of the school paper and I got varsity letters for fencing, tennis, track, and soccer.
DRUMBEATS
I wrote a satirical article for the local paper, THE RECORD. It was about a syndrome affecting high school students who were wildly nervous about getting into good colleges.
They were doing way too much to have perfect, well-rounded applications, and in the process were losing their minds.
The affliction was called College Rejection Application Manifestation Phobia Syndrome.
THE RECORD
C.R.A.M.P.S. ~ PLAGUING HIGH ACHIEVERS
BY JONATHAN A.
That article was very much about me--I was fifteen, sixteen, seventeen years old and was already leading a double life. Good student, good athlete, and good fledgling, vomiting alcoholic on the weekends.

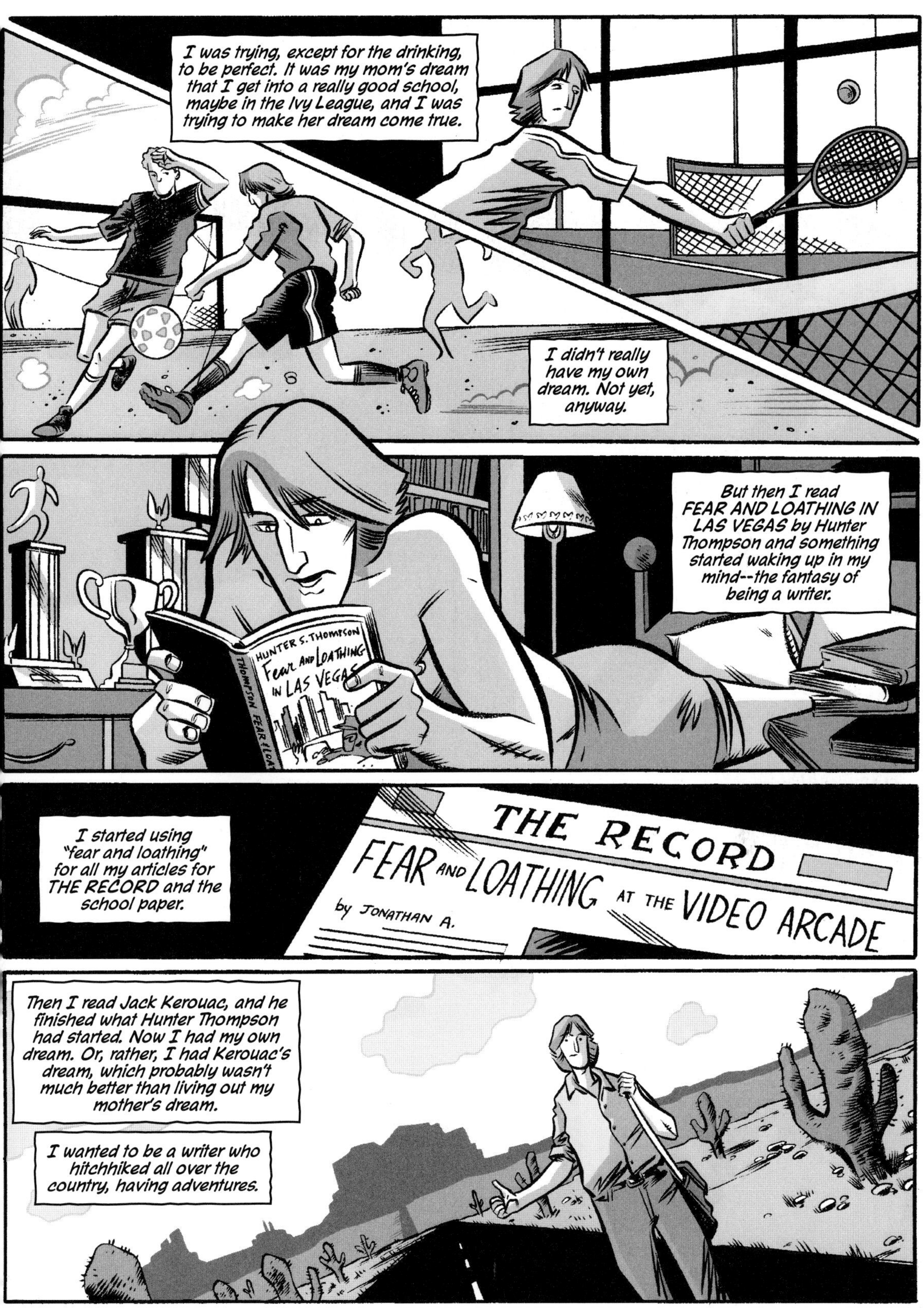
I was trying, except for the drinking, to be perfect. It was my mom's dream that I get into a really good school, maybe in the Ivy League, and I was trying to make her dream come true.
I didn't really have my own dream. Not yet, anyway.
But then I read FEAR AND LOATHING IN LAS VEGAS by Hunter Thompson and something started waking up in my mind--the fantasy of being a writer.
HUNTER S. THOMPSON
Fear and Loathing in Las Vegas
I started using "fear and loathing" for all my articles for THE RECORD and the school paper.
THE RECORD
FEAR AND LOATHING AT THE VIDEO ARCADE
by JONATHAN A.
Then I read Jack Kerouac, and he finished what Hunter Thompson had started. Now I had my own dream. Or, rather, I had Kerouac's dream, which probably wasn't much better than living out my mother's dream.
I wanted to be a writer who hitchhiked all over the country, having adventures.

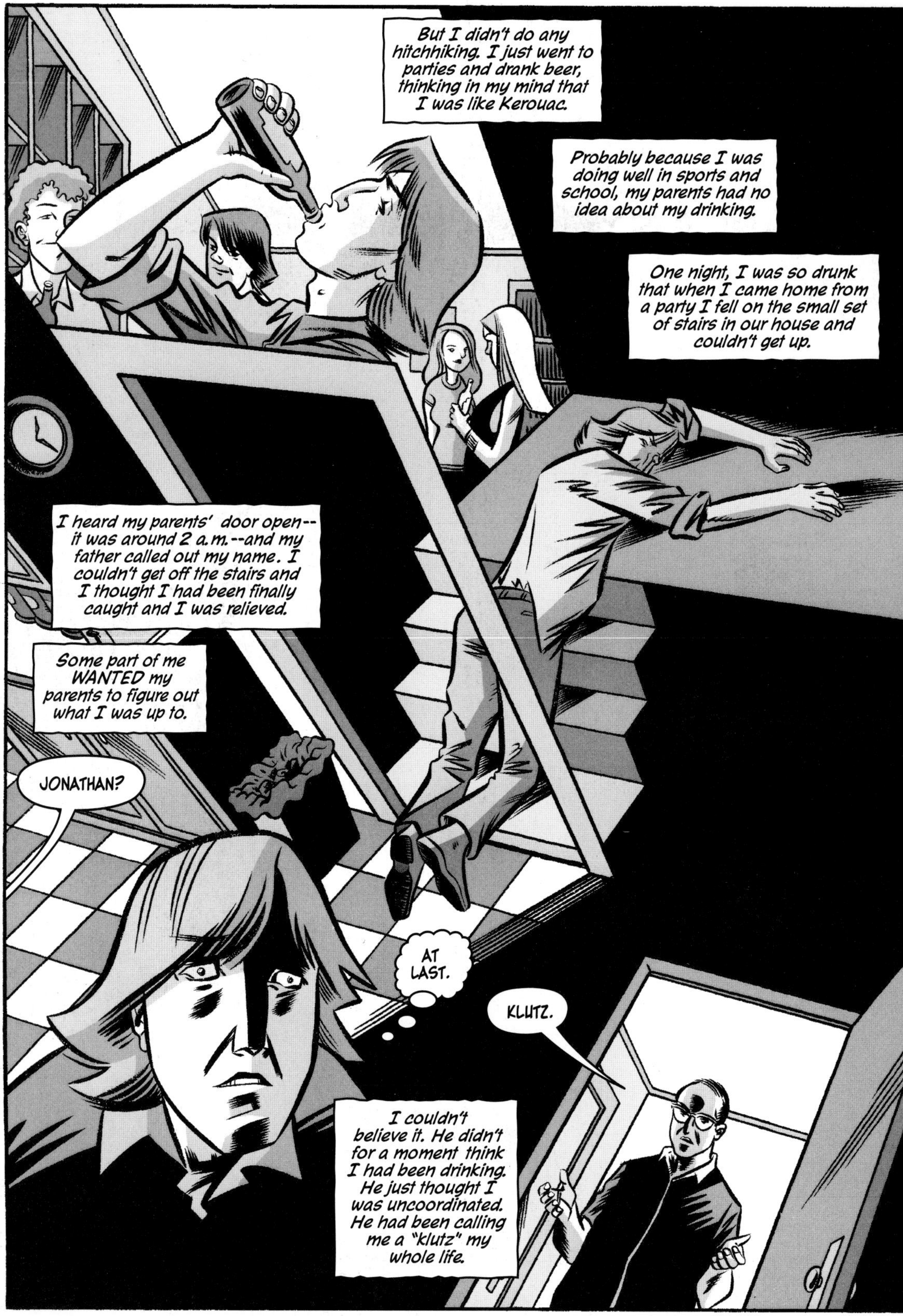

But I didn't do any hitchhiking. I just went to parties and drank beer, thinking in my mind that I was like Kerouac.
Probably because I was doing well in sports and school, my parents had no idea about my drinking.
One night, I was so drunk that when I came home from a party I fell on the small set of stairs in our house and couldn't get up.
I heard my parents' door open--it was around 2 a.m.--and my father called out my name. I couldn't get off the stairs and I thought I had been finally caught and I was relieved.
Some part of me WANTED my parents to figure out what I was up to.
JONATHAN?
AT LAST.
KLUTZ.
I couldn't believe it. He didn't for a moment think I had been drinking. He just thought I was uncoordinated. He had been calling me a "klutz" my whole life.

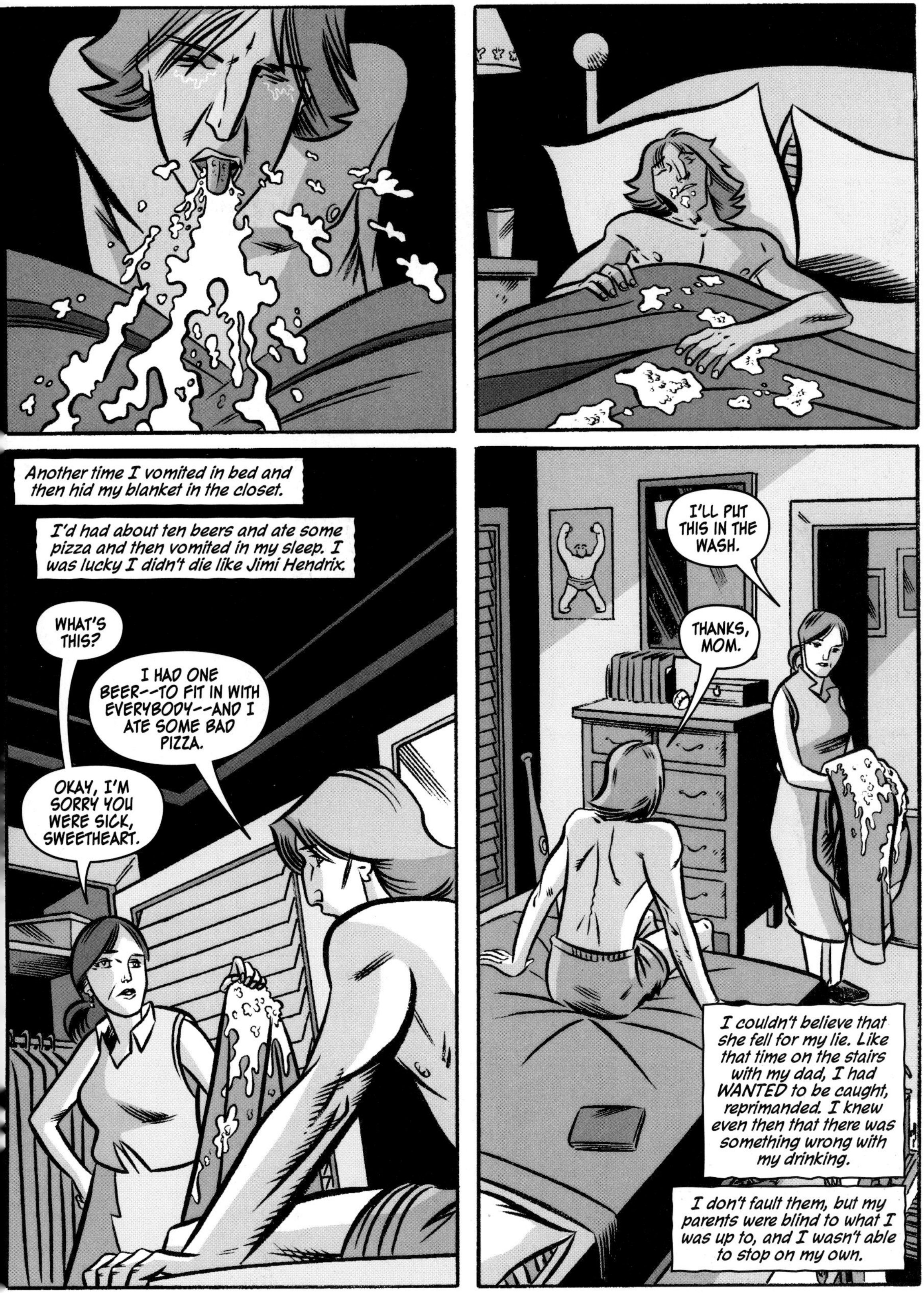
Another time I vomited in bed and then hid my blanket in the closet.
I'd had about ten beers and ate some pizza and then vomited in my sleep. I was lucky I didn't die like Jimi Hendrix.
WHAT'S THIS?
I HAD ONE BEER--TO FIT IN WITH EVERYBODY--AND I ATE SOME BAD PIZZA.
OKAY, I'M SORRY YOU WERE SICK, SWEETHEART.
I'LL PUT THIS IN THE WASH.
THANKS, MOM.
I couldn't believe that she fell for my lie. Like that time on the stairs with my dad, I had WANTED to be caught, reprimanded. I knew even then that there was something wrong with my drinking.
I don't fault them, but my parents were blind to what I was up to, and I wasn't able to stop on my own.

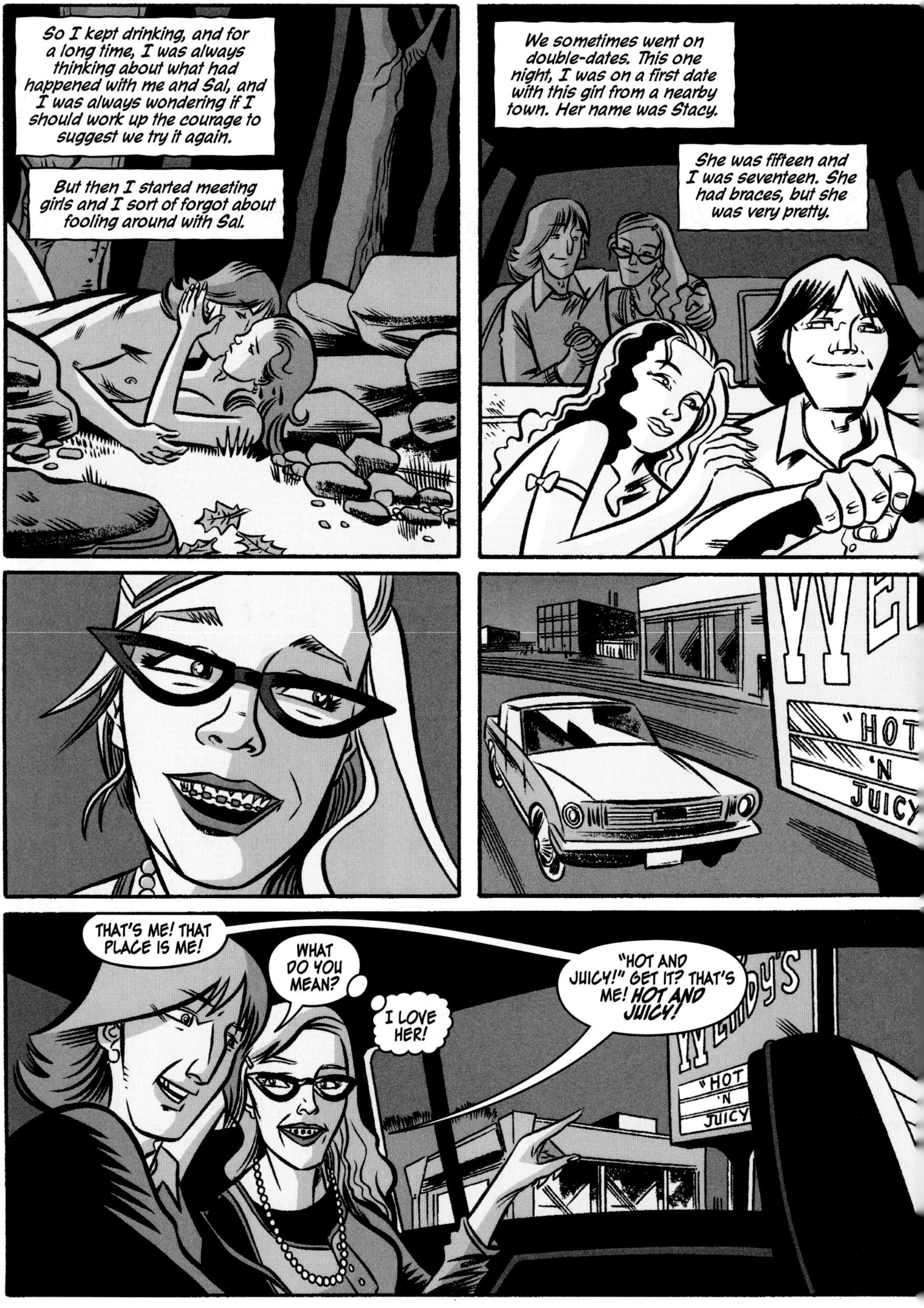
So I kept drinking, and for a long time, I was always thinking about what had happened with me and Sal, and I was always wondering if I should work up the courage to suggest we try it again.
But then I started meeting girls and I sort of forgot about fooling around with Sal.
We sometimes went on double-dates. This one night, I was on a first date with this girl from a nearby town. Her name was Stacy.
She was fifteen and I was seventeen. She had braces, but she was very pretty.
"HOT 'N JUICY
THAT'S ME! THAT PLACE IS ME!
WHAT DO YOU MEAN?
I LOVE HER!
"HOT AND JUICY!" GET IT? THAT'S ME! HOT AND JUICY!
"HOT 'N JUICY

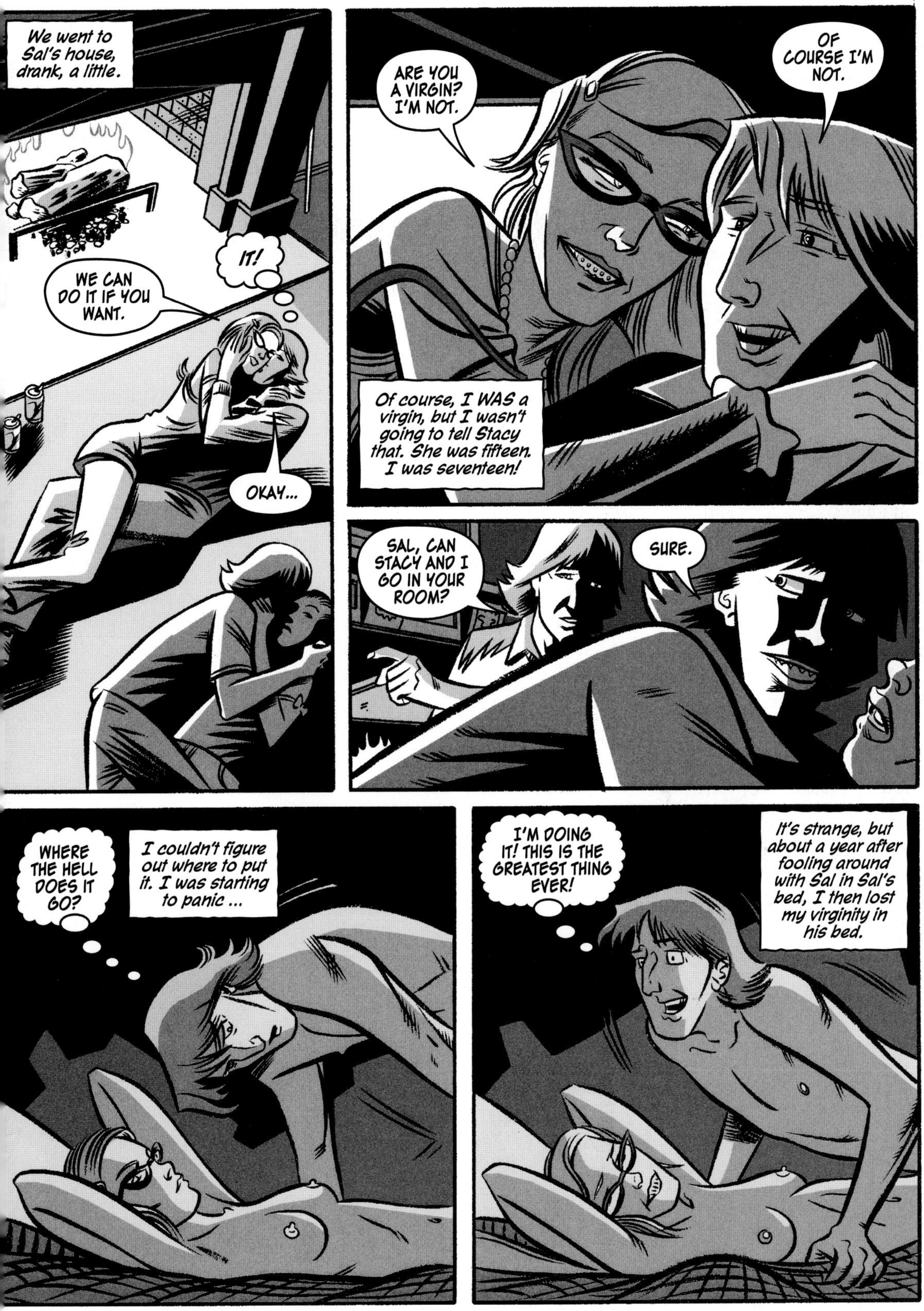
We went to Sal's house, drank, a little.
WE CAN DO IT IF YOU WANT.
IT!
OKAY...
ARE YOU A VIRGIN? I'M NOT.
OF COURSE I'M NOT.
Of course, I WAS a virgin, but I wasn't going to tell Stacy that. She was fifteen. I was seventeen!
SAL, CAN STACY AND I GO IN YOUR ROOM?
SURE.
WHERE THE HELL DOES IT GO?
I couldn't figure out where to put it. I was starting to panic ...
I'M DOING IT! THIS IS THE GREATEST THING EVER!
It's strange, but about a year after fooling around with Sal in Sal's bed, I then lost my virginity in his bed.

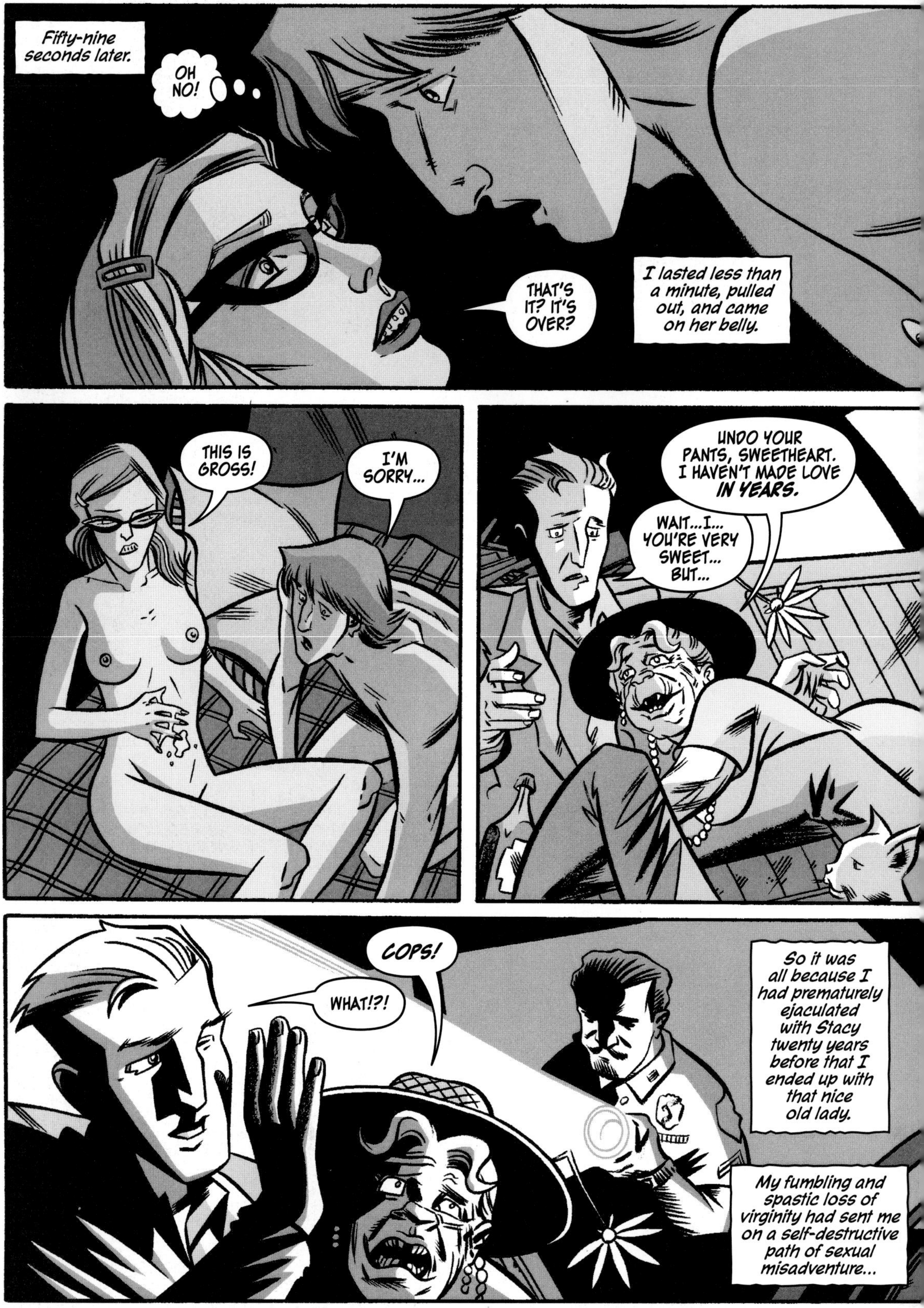

Fifty-nine seconds later.
OH NO!
THAT'S IT? IT'S OVER?
I lasted less than a minute, pulled out, and came on her belly.
THIS IS GROSS!
I'M SORRY...
UNDO YOUR PANTS, SWEETHEART. I HAVEN'T MADE LOVE IN YEARS.
WAIT...I... YOU'RE VERY SWEET... BUT...
COPS!
WHAT!?!
So it was all because I had prematurely ejaculated with Stacy twenty years before that I ended up with that nice old lady.
My fumbling and spastic loss of virginity had sent me on a self-destructive path of sexual misadventure...

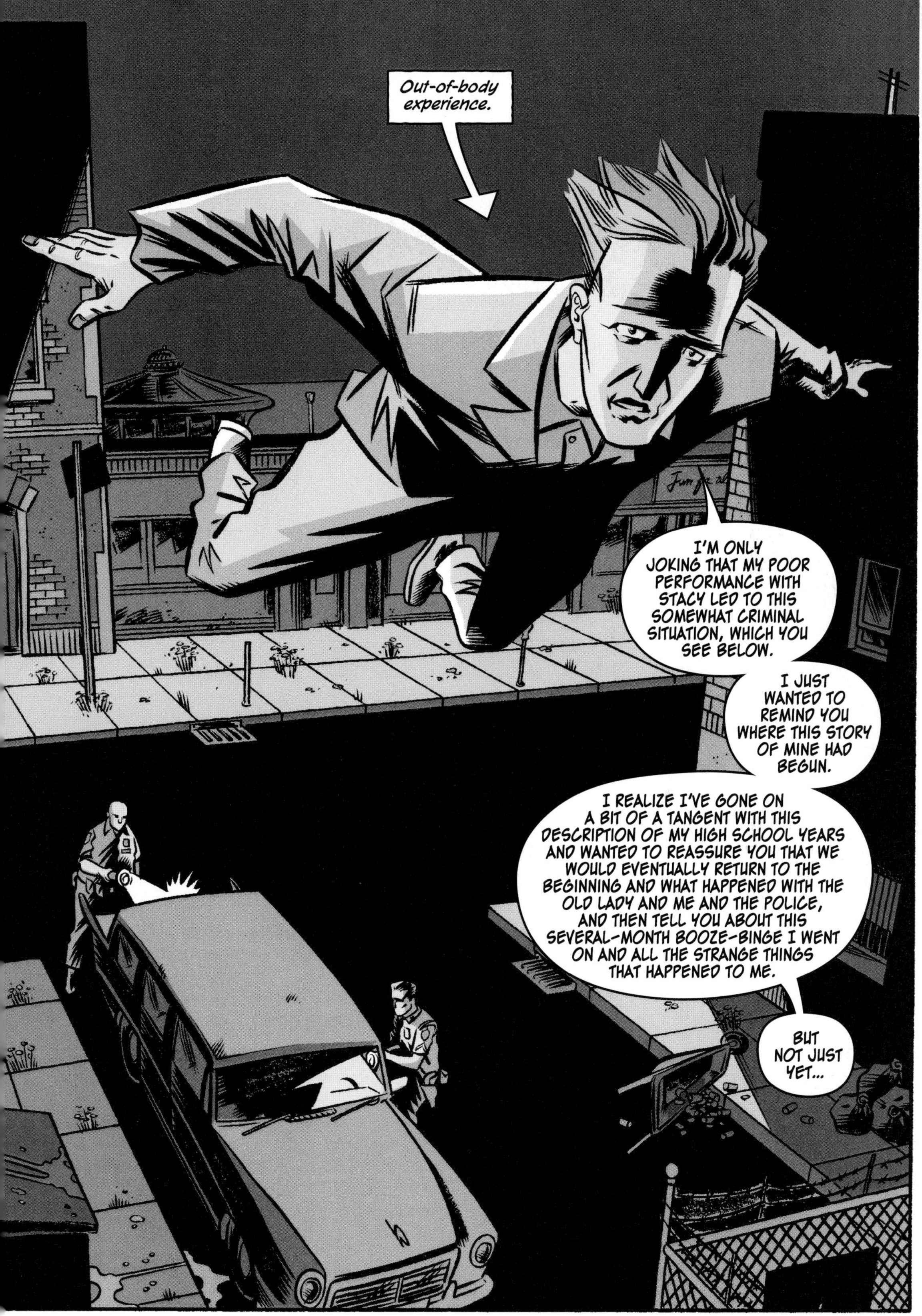
Out-of-body experience.
I'M ONLY JOKING THAT MY POOR PERFORMANCE WITH STACY LED TO THIS SOMEWHAT CRIMINAL SITUATION, WHICH YOU SEE BELOW.
I JUST WANTED TO REMIND YOU WHERE THIS STORY OF MINE HAD BEGUN.
I REALIZE I'VE GONE ON A BIT OF A TANGENT WITH THIS DESCRIPTION OF MY HIGH SCHOOL YEARS AND WANTED TO REASSURE YOU THAT WE WOULD EVENTUALLY RETURN TO THE BEGINNING AND WHAT HAPPENED WITH THE OLD LADY AND ME AND THE POLICE, AND THEN TELL YOU ABOUT THIS SEVERAL-MONTH BOOZE-BINGE I WENT ON AND ALL THE STRANGE THINGS THAT HAPPENED TO ME.
BUT NOT JUST YET...

Stacy and I, despite our less-than-perfect start, went out for almost two months. This was during my senior year of high school.

72 seconds.

37 seconds.

But I was a lousy lover. I was too overwhelmed by how good it felt.

11 seconds.

DON'T MOVE!

OKAY.

OH, SHOOT!

NOT AGAIN!

So then we tried oral sex. It was Stacy's idea.

But she didn't hurt me--she was very gentle.

Naturally, I was a little scared because of her braces.

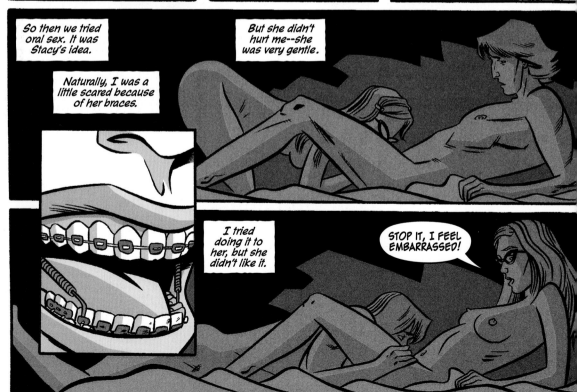

I tried doing it to her, but she didn't like it.

STOP IT, I FEEL EMBARRASSED!

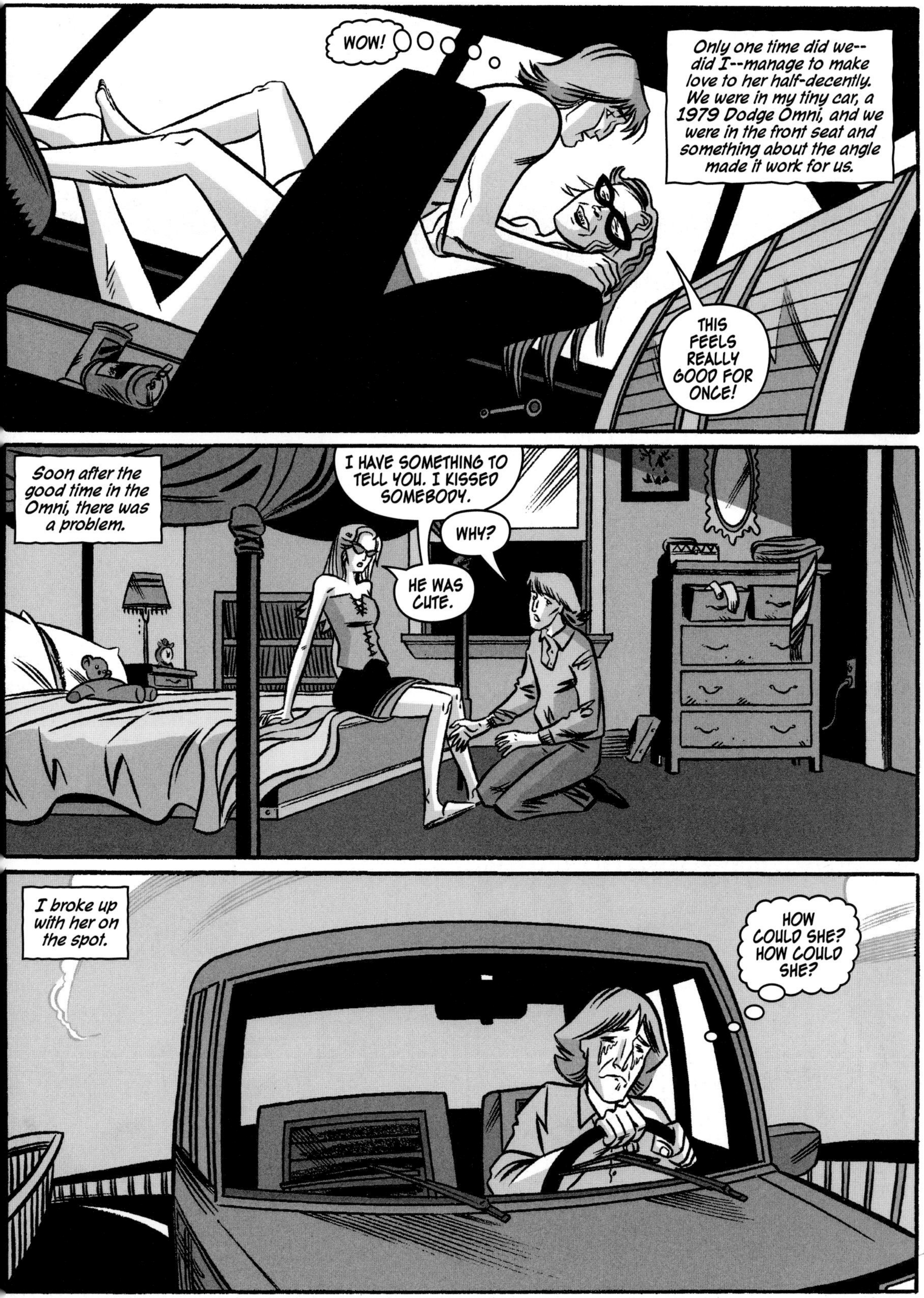
WOW!
Only one time did we--did I--manage to make love to her half-decently. We were in my tiny car, a 1979 Dodge Omni, and we were in the front seat and something about the angle made it work for us.
THIS FEELS REALLY GOOD FOR ONCE!
Soon after the good time in the Omni, there was a problem.
I HAVE SOMETHING TO TELL YOU. I KISSED SOMEBODY.
WHY?
HE WAS CUTE.
I broke up with her on the spot.
HOW COULD SHE? HOW COULD SHE?

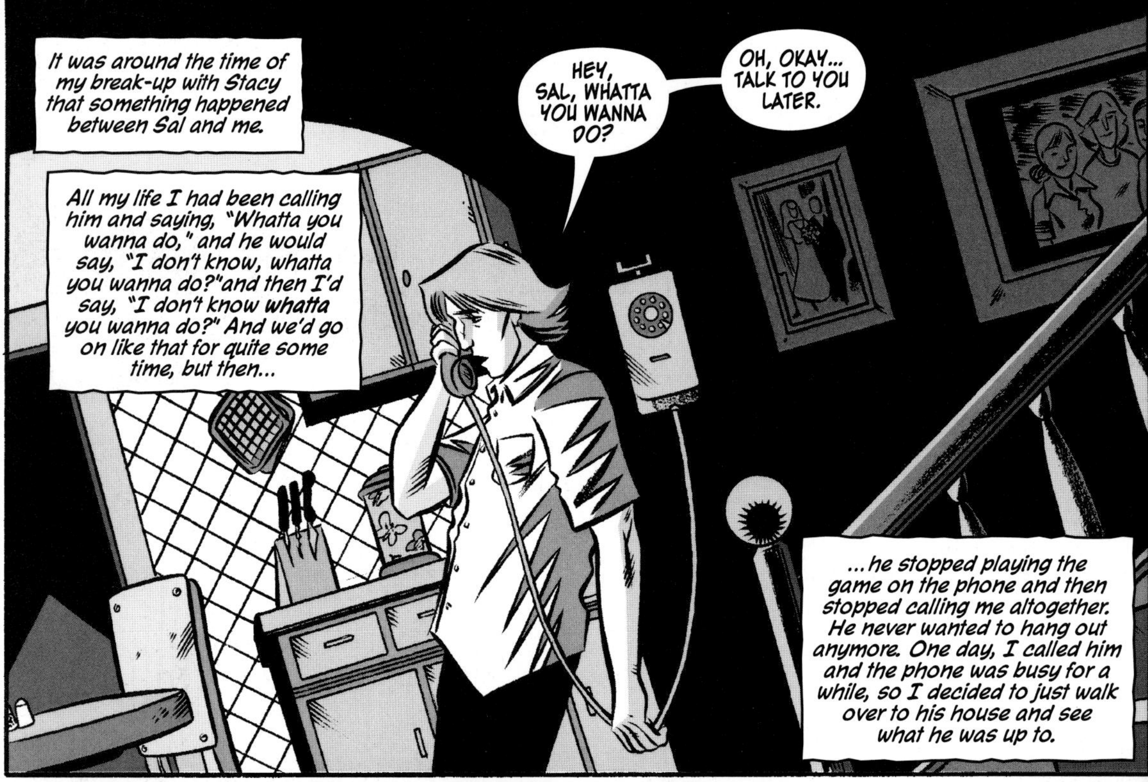
It was around the time of my break-up with Stacy that something happened between Sal and me.
All my life I had been calling him and saying, "Whatta you wanna do," and he would say, "I don't know, whatta you wanna do?"and then I'd say, "I don't know whatta you wanna do?" And we'd go on like that for quite some time, but then...
HEY, SAL, WHATTA YOU WANNA DO?
OH, OKAY... TALK TO YOU LATER.
...he stopped playing the game on the phone and then stopped calling me altogether. He never wanted to hang out anymore. One day, I called him and the phone was busy for a while, so I decided to just walk over to his house and see what he was up to.

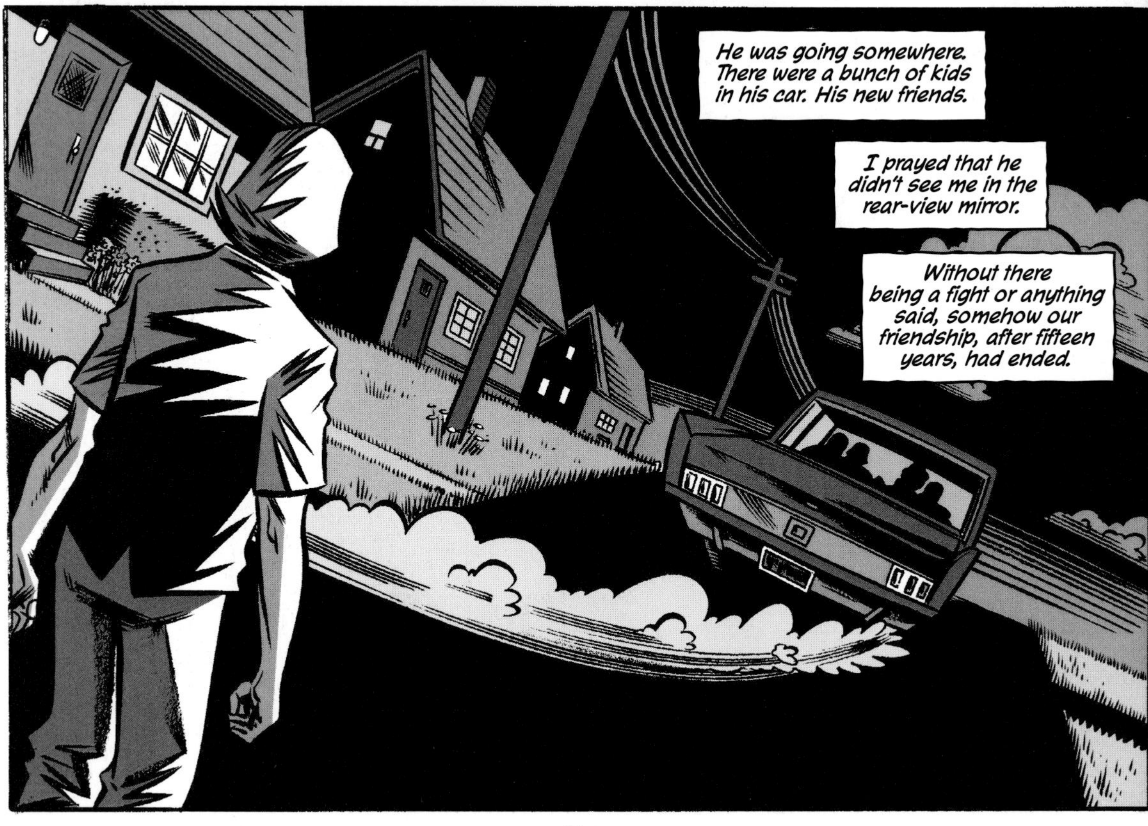
He was going somewhere. There were a bunch of kids in his car. His new friends.
I prayed that he didn't see me in the rear-view mirror.
Without there being a fight or anything said, somehow our friendship, after fifteen years, had ended.

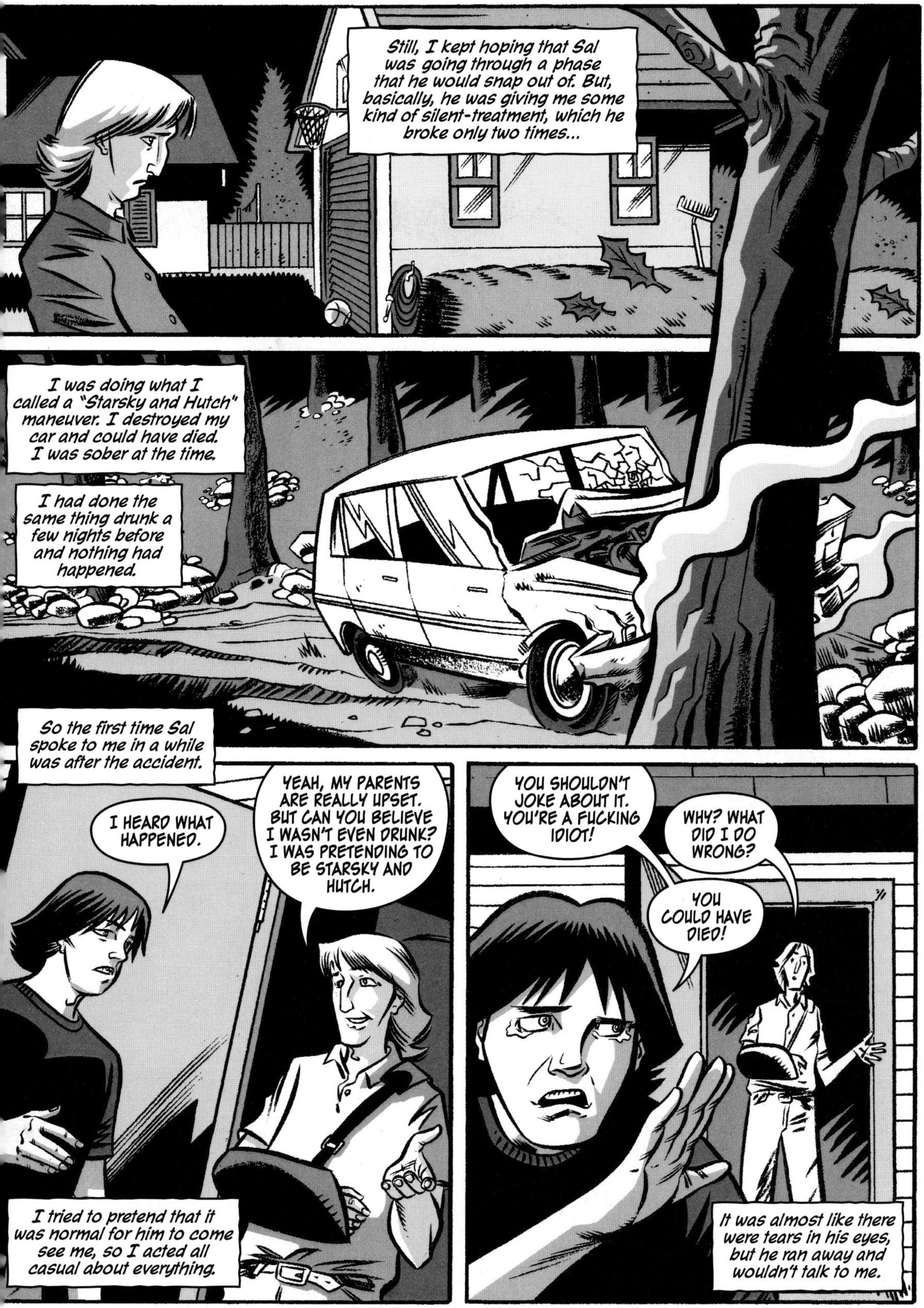
Still, I kept hoping that Sal was going through a phase that he would snap out of. But, basically, he was giving me some kind of silent-treatment, which he broke only two times...
I was doing what I called a "Starsky and Hutch" maneuver. I destroyed my car and could have died. I was sober at the time.
I had done the same thing drunk a few nights before and nothing had happened.
So the first time Sal spoke to me in a while was after the accident.
I HEARD WHAT HAPPENED.
YEAH, MY PARENTS ARE REALLY UPSET. BUT CAN YOU BELIEVE I WASN'T EVEN DRUNK? I WAS PRETENDING TO BE STARSKY AND HUTCH.
I tried to pretend that it was normal for him to come see me, so I acted all casual about everything.
YOU SHOULDN'T JOKE ABOUT IT. YOU'RE A FUCKING IDIOT!
WHY? WHAT DID I DO WRONG?
YOU COULD HAVE DIED!
It was almost like there were tears in his eyes, but he ran away and wouldn't talk to me.

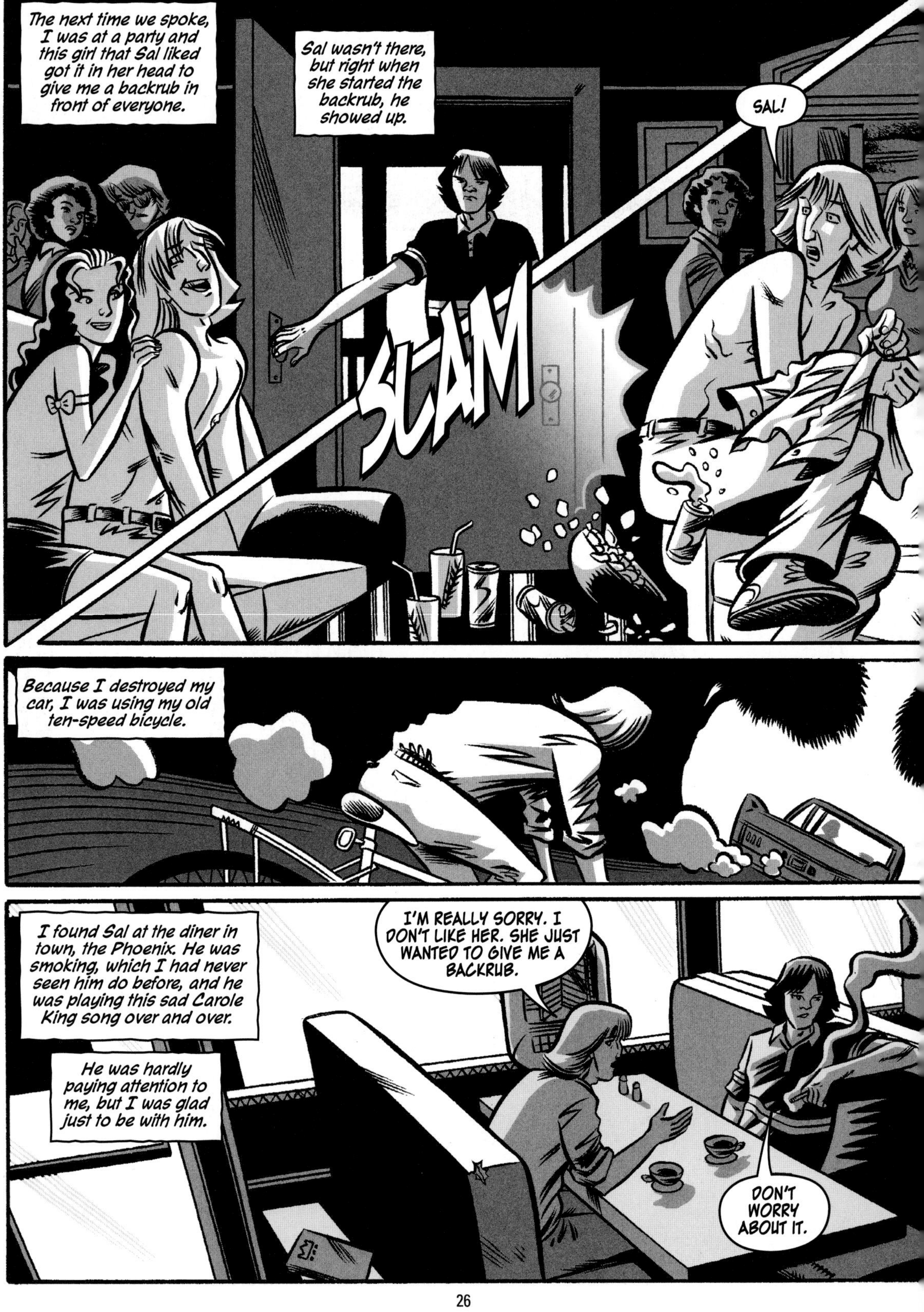
The next time we spoke, I was at a party and this girl that Sal liked got it in her head to give me a backrub in front of everyone.
Sal wasn't there, but right when she started the backrub, he showed up.
SAL!
SLAM
Because I destroyed my car, I was using my old ten-speed bicycle.
I found Sal at the diner in town, the Phoenix. He was smoking, which I had never seen him do before, and he was playing this sad Carole King song over and over.
He was hardly paying attention to me, but I was glad just to be with him.
I'M REALLY SORRY. I DON'T LIKE HER. SHE JUST WANTED TO GIVE ME A BACKRUB.
DON'T WORRY ABOUT IT.

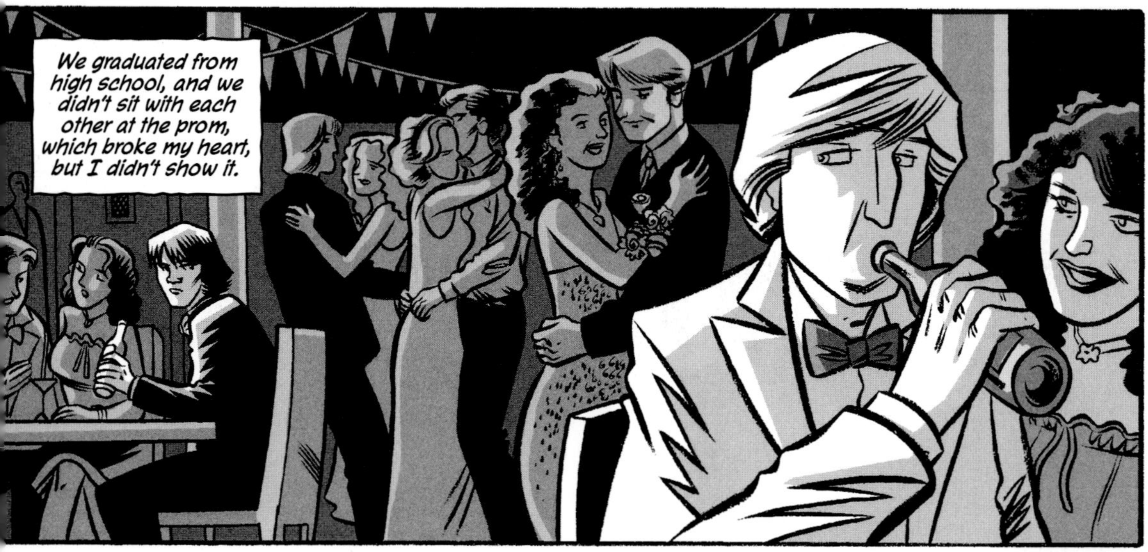
We graduated from high school, and we didn't sit with each other at the prom, which broke my heart, but I didn't show it.

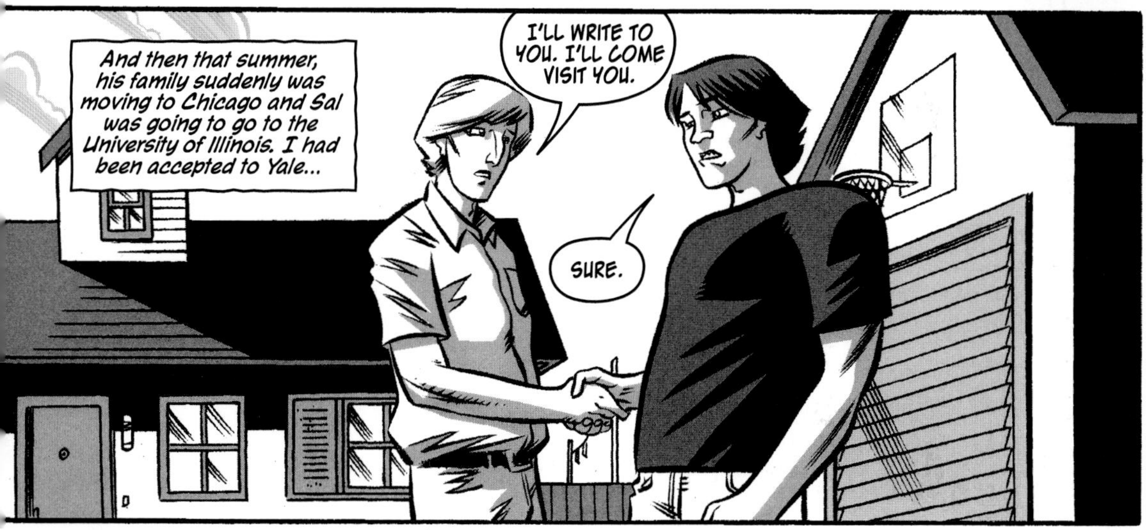
And then that summer, his family suddenly was moving to Chicago and Sal was going to go to the University of Illinois. I had been accepted to Yale...
I'LL WRITE TO YOU. I'LL COME VISIT YOU.
SURE.

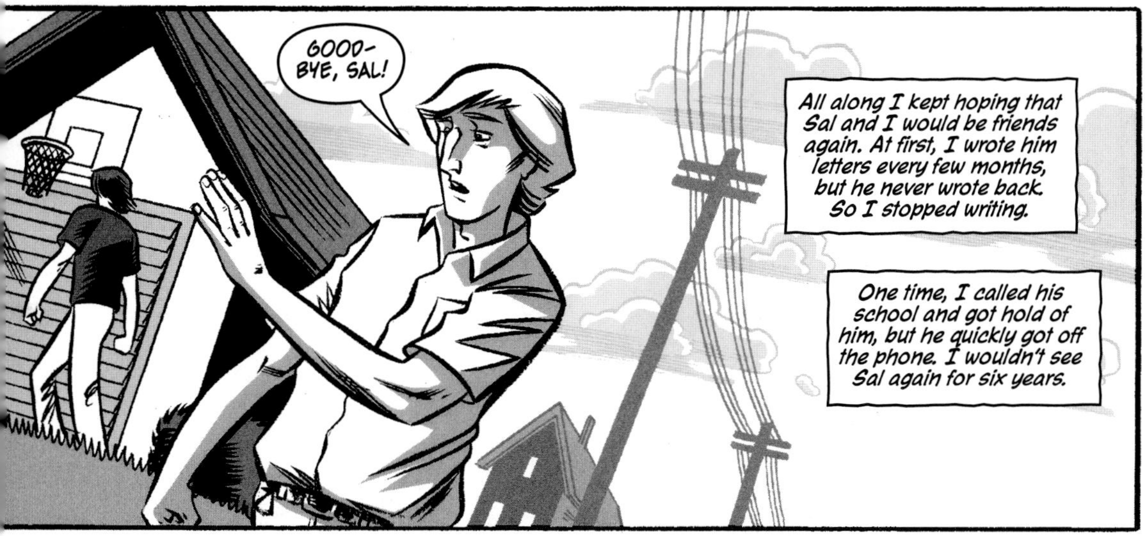
GOOD-BYE, SAL!
All along I kept hoping that Sal and I would be friends again. At first, I wrote him letters every few months, but he never wrote back. So I stopped writing.
One time, I called his school and got hold of him, but he quickly got off the phone. I wouldn't see Sal again for six years.

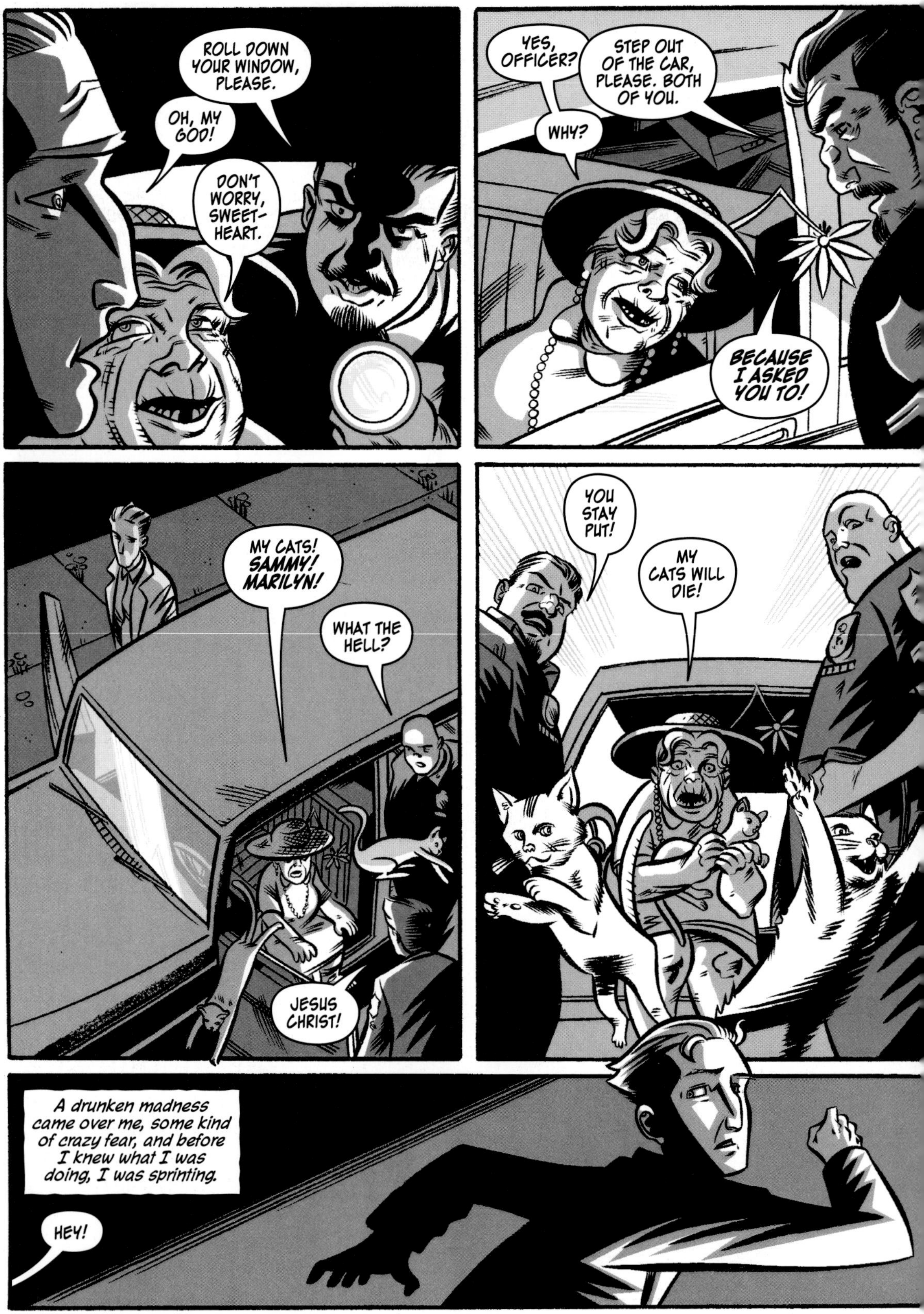
ROLL DOWN YOUR WINDOW, PLEASE.
OH, MY GOD!
DON'T WORRY, SWEET-HEART.
YES, OFFICER?
STEP OUT OF THE CAR, PLEASE. BOTH OF YOU.
WHY?
BECAUSE I ASKED YOU TO!
MY CATS! SAMMY! MARILYN!
WHAT THE HELL?
JESUS CHRIST!
YOU STAY PUT!
MY CATS WILL DIE!
A drunken madness came over me, some kind of crazy fear, and before I knew what I was doing, I was sprinting.
HEY!

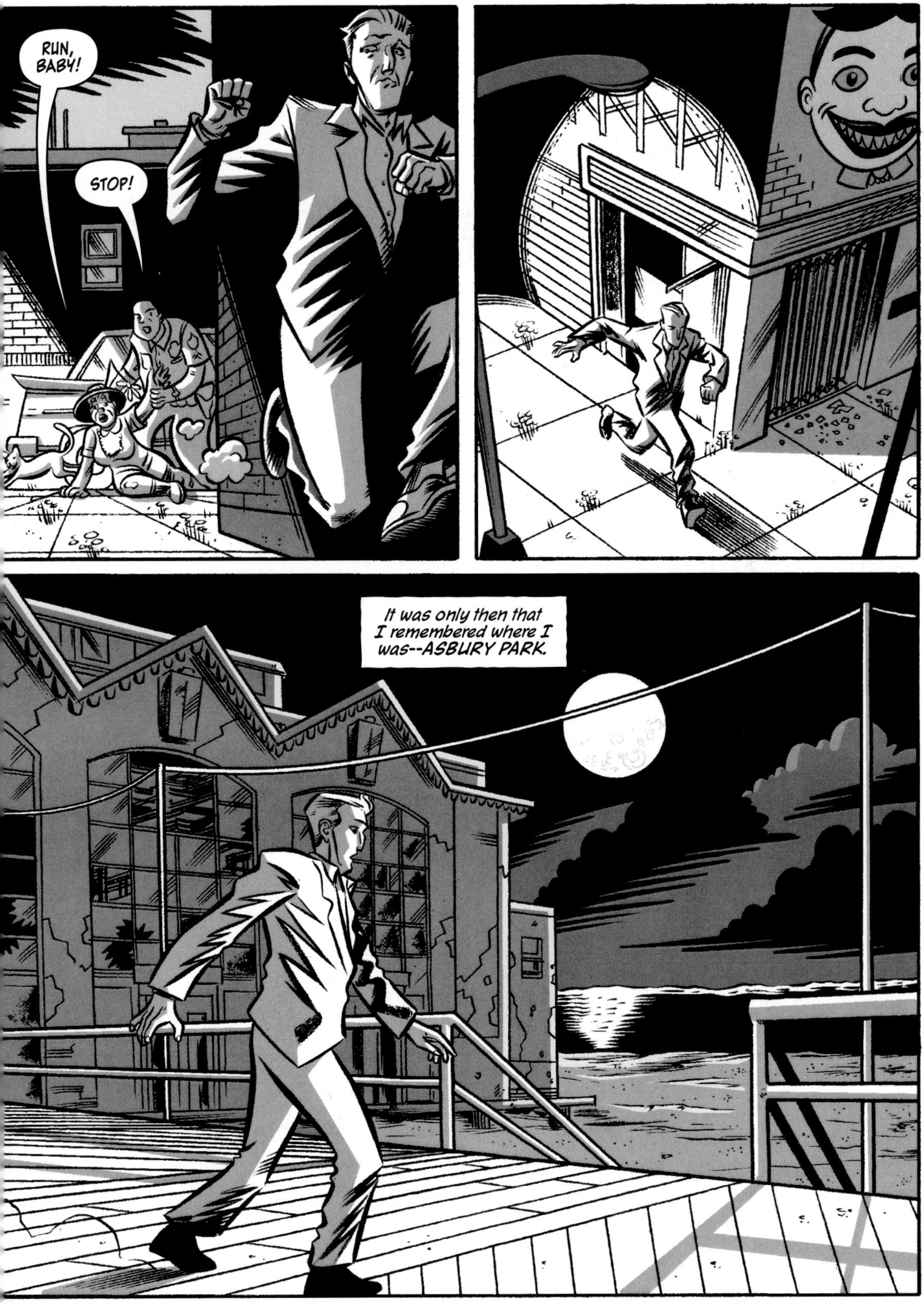
RUN, BABY!
STOP!
It was only then that I remembered where I was--ASBURY PARK.

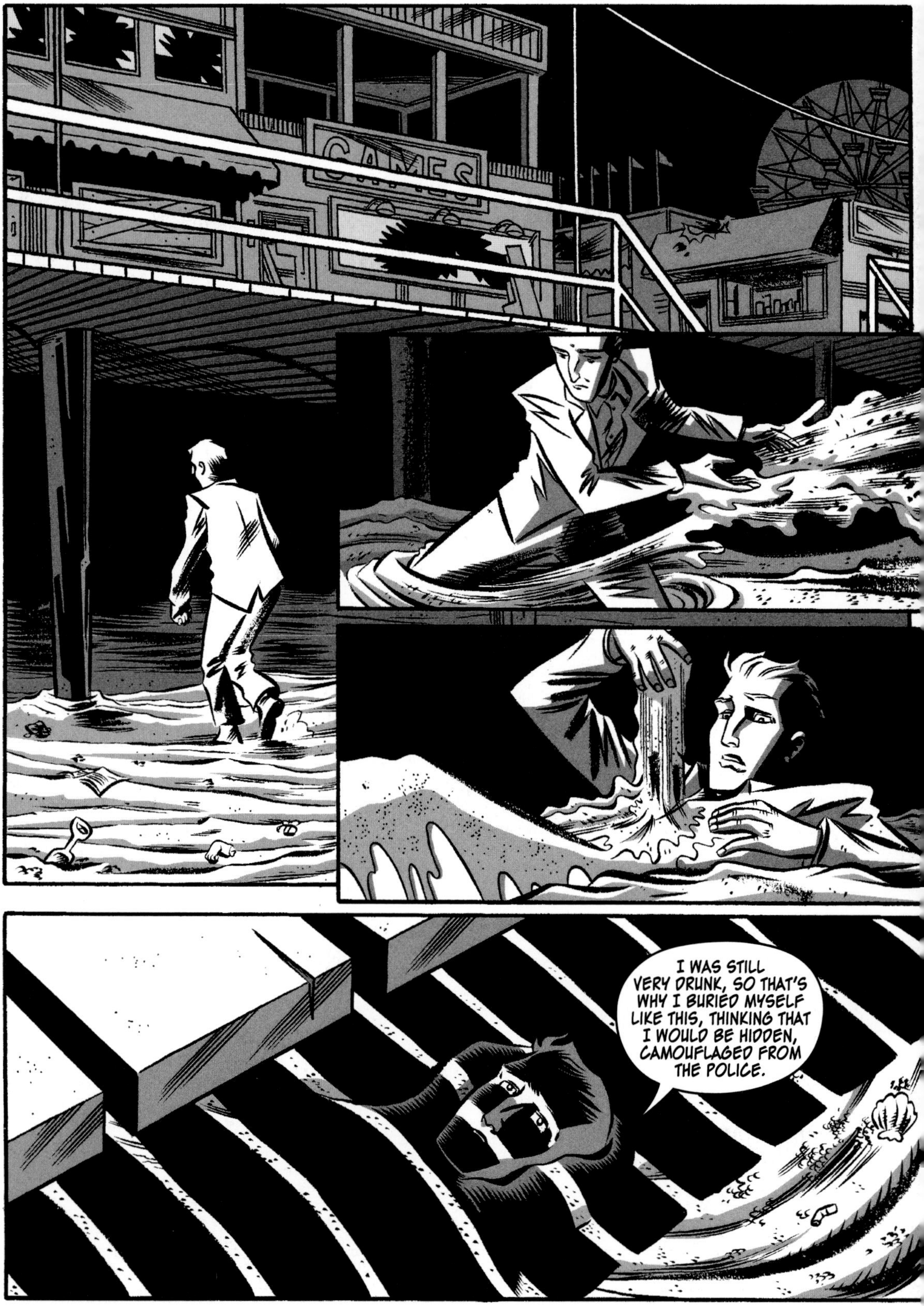
GAMES
I WAS STILL VERY DRUNK, SO THAT'S WHY I BURIED MYSELF LIKE THIS, THINKING THAT I WOULD BE HIDDEN, CAMOUFLAGED FROM THE POLICE.

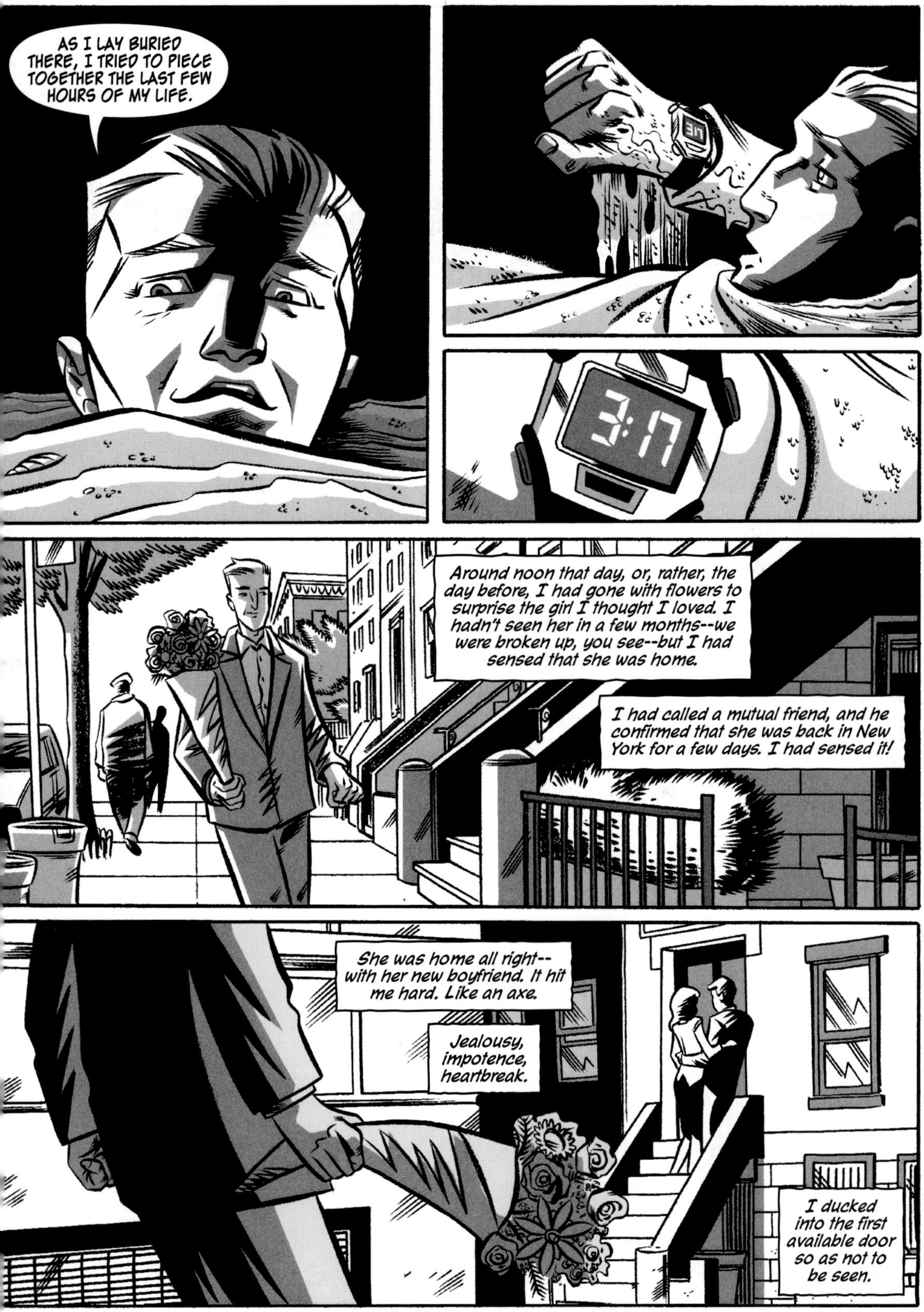
AS I LAY BURIED THERE, I TRIED TO PIECE TOGETHER THE LAST FEW HOURS OF MY LIFE.
3:17
Around noon that day, or, rather, the day before, I had gone with flowers to surprise the girl I thought I loved. I hadn't seen her in a few months--we were broken up, you see--but I had sensed that she was home.
I had called a mutual friend, and he confirmed that she was back in New York for a few days. I had sensed it!
She was home all right--with her new boyfriend. It hit me hard. Like an axe.
Jealousy, impotence, heartbreak.
I ducked into the first available door so as not to be seen.

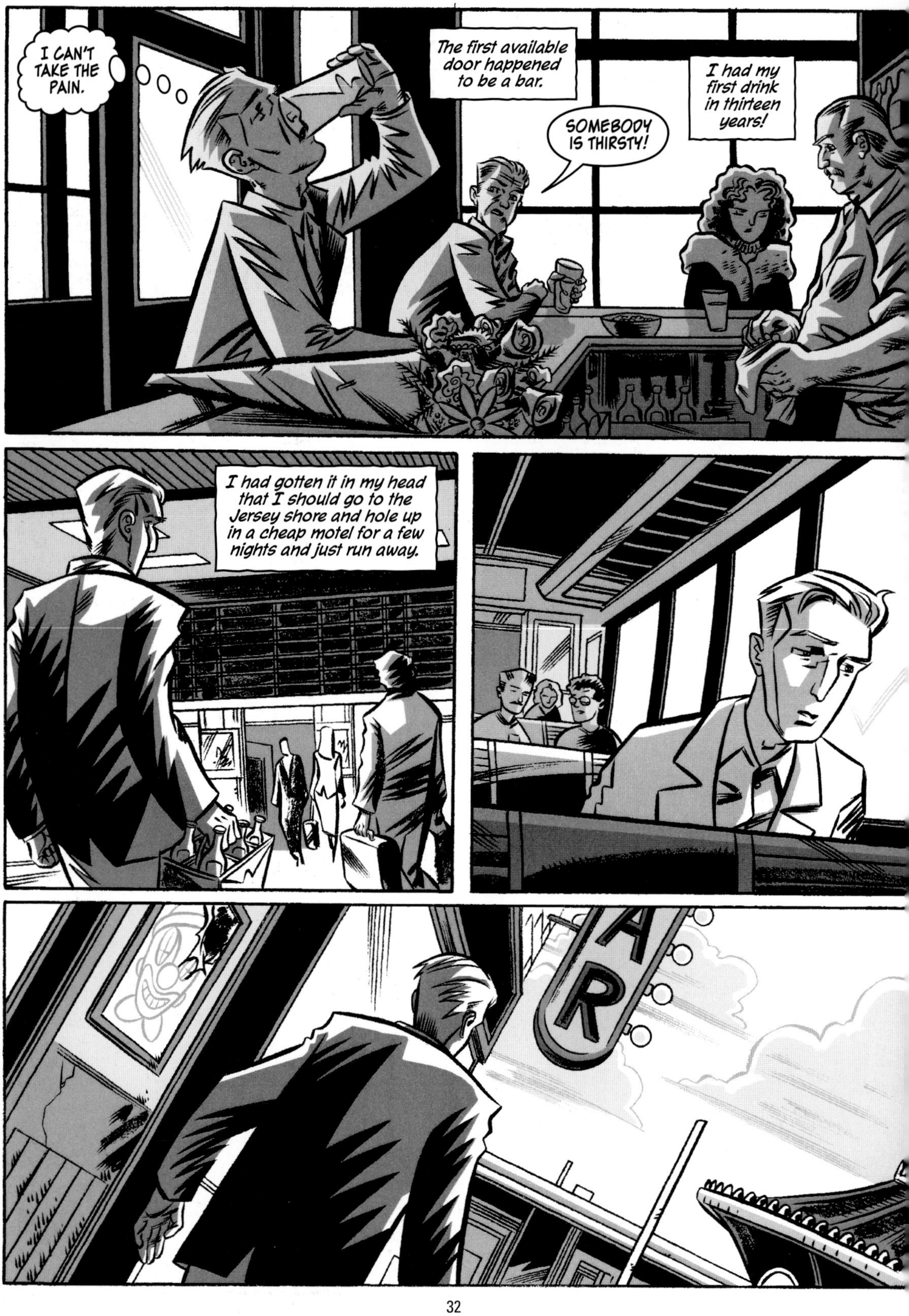
I CAN'T TAKE THE PAIN.
The first available door happened to be a bar.
SOMEBODY IS THIRSTY!
I had my first drink in thirteen years!
I had gotten it in my head that I should go to the Jersey shore and hole up in a cheap motel for a few nights and just run away.
AR

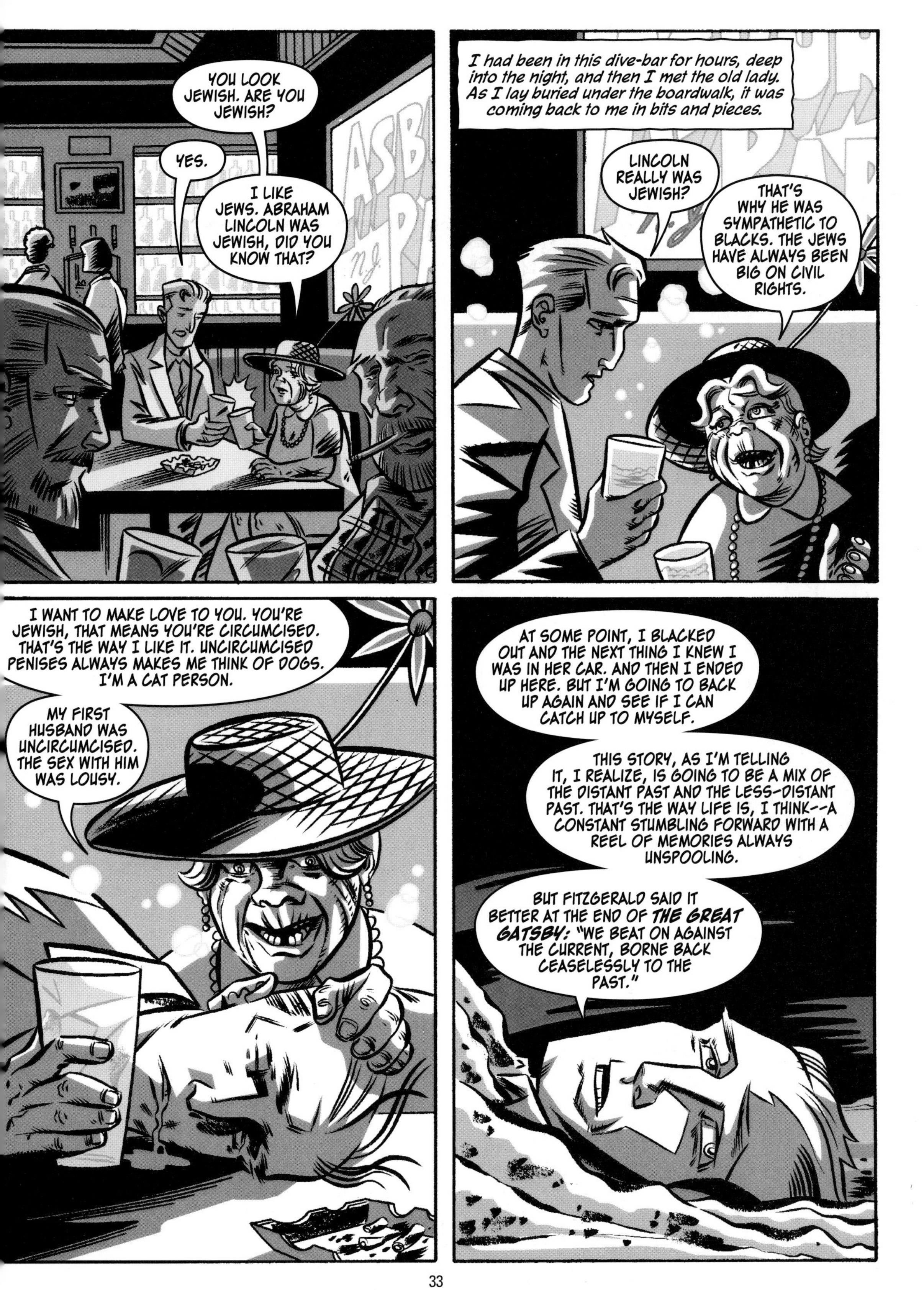
YOU LOOK JEWISH. ARE YOU JEWISH?
YES.
I LIKE JEWS. ABRAHAM LINCOLN WAS JEWISH, DID YOU KNOW THAT?
I had been in this dive-bar for hours, deep into the night, and then I met the old lady. As I lay buried under the boardwalk, it was coming back to me in bits and pieces.
LINCOLN REALLY WAS JEWISH?
THAT'S WHY HE WAS SYMPATHETIC TO BLACKS. THE JEWS HAVE ALWAYS BEEN BIG ON CIVIL RIGHTS.
I WANT TO MAKE LOVE TO YOU. YOU'RE JEWISH, THAT MEANS YOU'RE CIRCUMCISED. THAT'S THE WAY I LIKE IT. UNCIRCUMCISED PENISES ALWAYS MAKES ME THINK OF DOGS. I'M A CAT PERSON.
MY FIRST HUSBAND WAS UNCIRCUMCISED. THE SEX WITH HIM WAS LOUSY.
AT SOME POINT, I BLACKED OUT AND THE NEXT THING I KNEW I WAS IN HER CAR. AND THEN I ENDED UP HERE. BUT I'M GOING TO BACK UP AGAIN AND SEE IF I CAN CATCH UP TO MYSELF.
THIS STORY, AS I'M TELLING IT, I REALIZE, IS GOING TO BE A MIX OF THE DISTANT PAST AND THE LESS-DISTANT PAST. THAT'S THE WAY LIFE IS, I THINK--A CONSTANT STUMBLING FORWARD WITH A REEL OF MEMORIES ALWAYS UNSPOOLING.
BUT FITZGERALD SAID IT BETTER AT THE END OF *THE GREAT GATSBY:* "WE BEAT ON AGAINST THE CURRENT, BORNE BACK CEASELESSLY TO THE PAST."

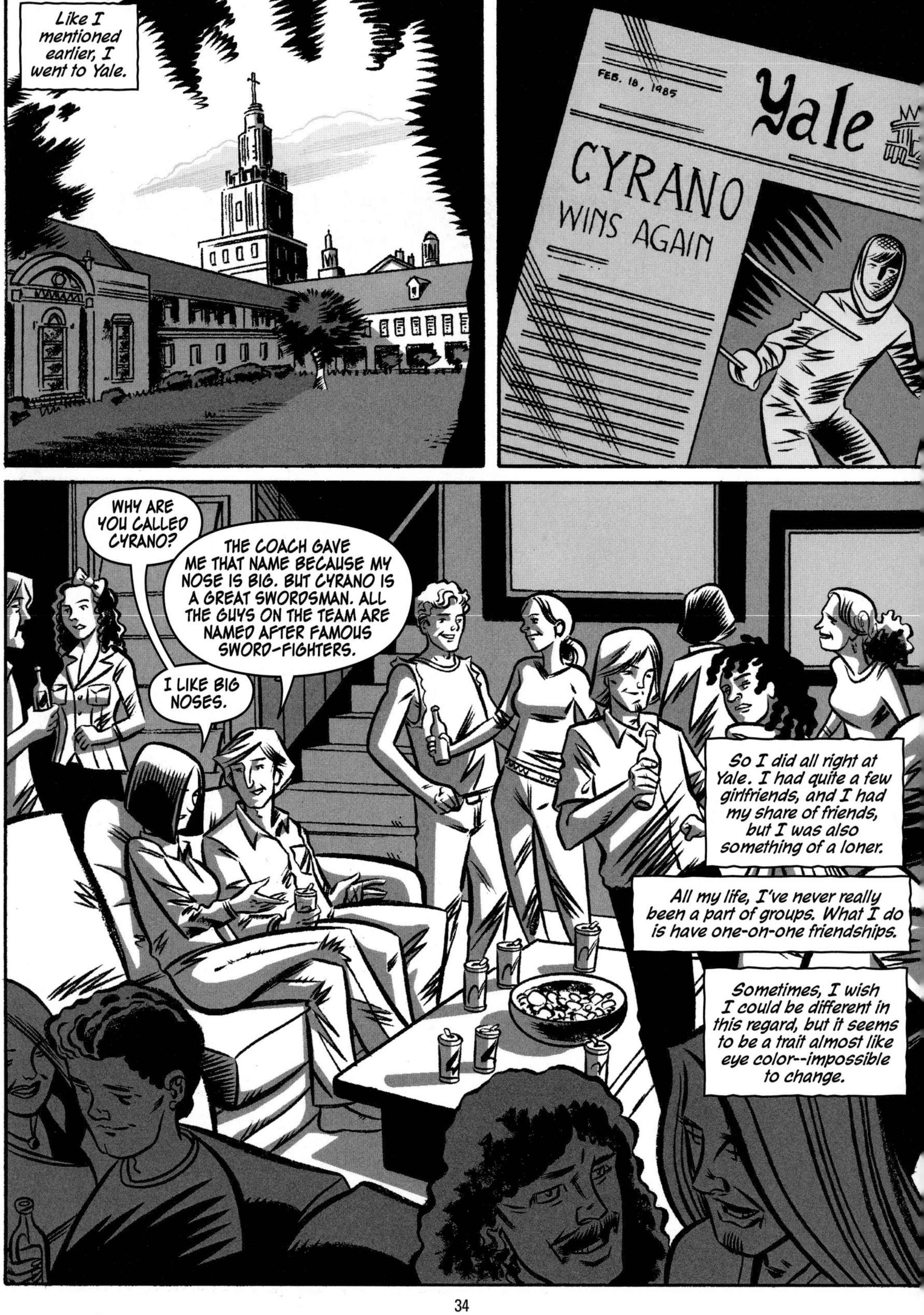
Like I mentioned earlier, I went to Yale.
FEB. 18, 1985
Yale
CYRANO
WINS AGAIN
WHY ARE YOU CALLED CYRANO?
THE COACH GAVE ME THAT NAME BECAUSE MY NOSE IS BIG. BUT CYRANO IS A GREAT SWORDSMAN. ALL THE GUYS ON THE TEAM ARE NAMED AFTER FAMOUS SWORD-FIGHTERS.
I LIKE BIG NOSES.
So I did all right at Yale. I had quite a few girlfriends, and I had my share of friends, but I was also something of a loner.
All my life, I've never really been a part of groups. What I do is have one-on-one friendships.
Sometimes, I wish I could be different in this regard, but it seems to be a trait almost like eye color--impossible to change.

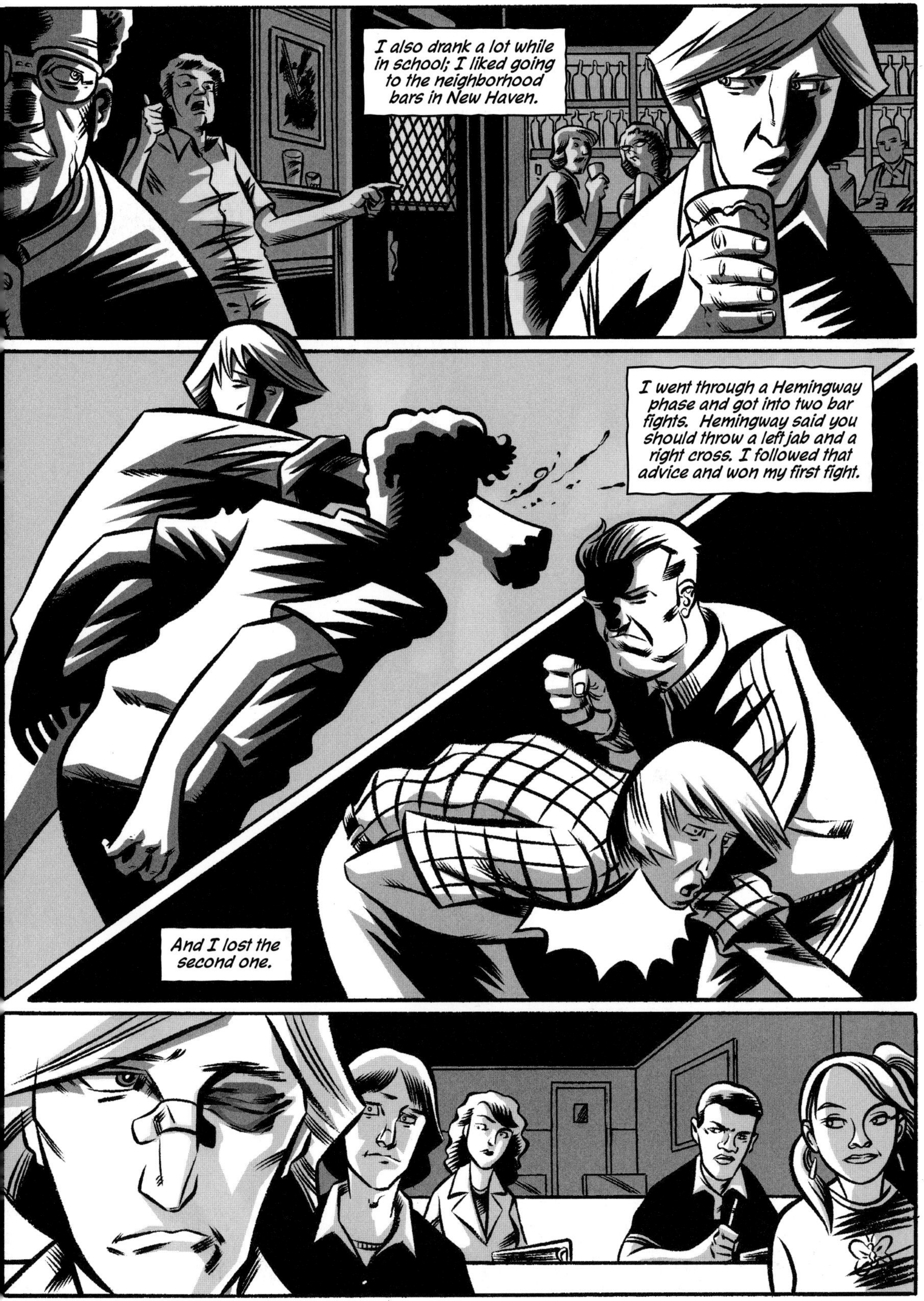
I also drank a lot while in school; I liked going to the neighborhood bars in New Haven.
I went through a Hemingway phase and got into two bar fights. Hemingway said you should throw a left jab and a right cross. I followed that advice and won my first fight.
And I lost the second one.

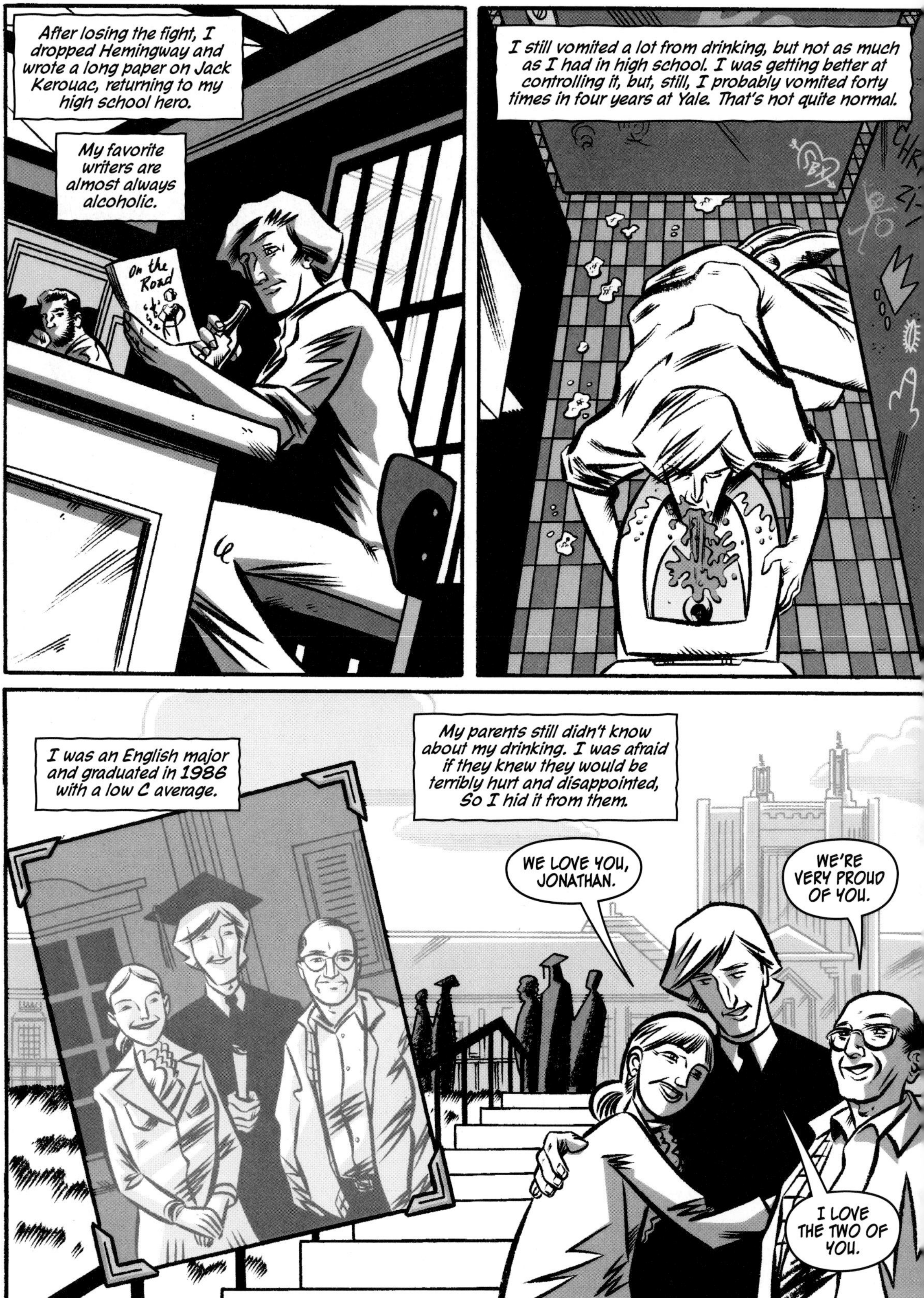

After losing the fight, I dropped Hemingway and wrote a long paper on Jack Kerouac, returning to my high school hero.
My favorite writers are almost always alcoholic.
On the Road
I still vomited a lot from drinking, but not as much as I had in high school. I was getting better at controlling it, but, still, I probably vomited forty times in four years at Yale. That's not quite normal.
I was an English major and graduated in 1986 with a low C average.
My parents still didn't know about my drinking. I was afraid if they knew they would be terribly hurt and disappointed, So I hid it from them.
WE LOVE YOU, JONATHAN.
WE'RE VERY PROUD OF YOU.
I LOVE THE TWO OF YOU.

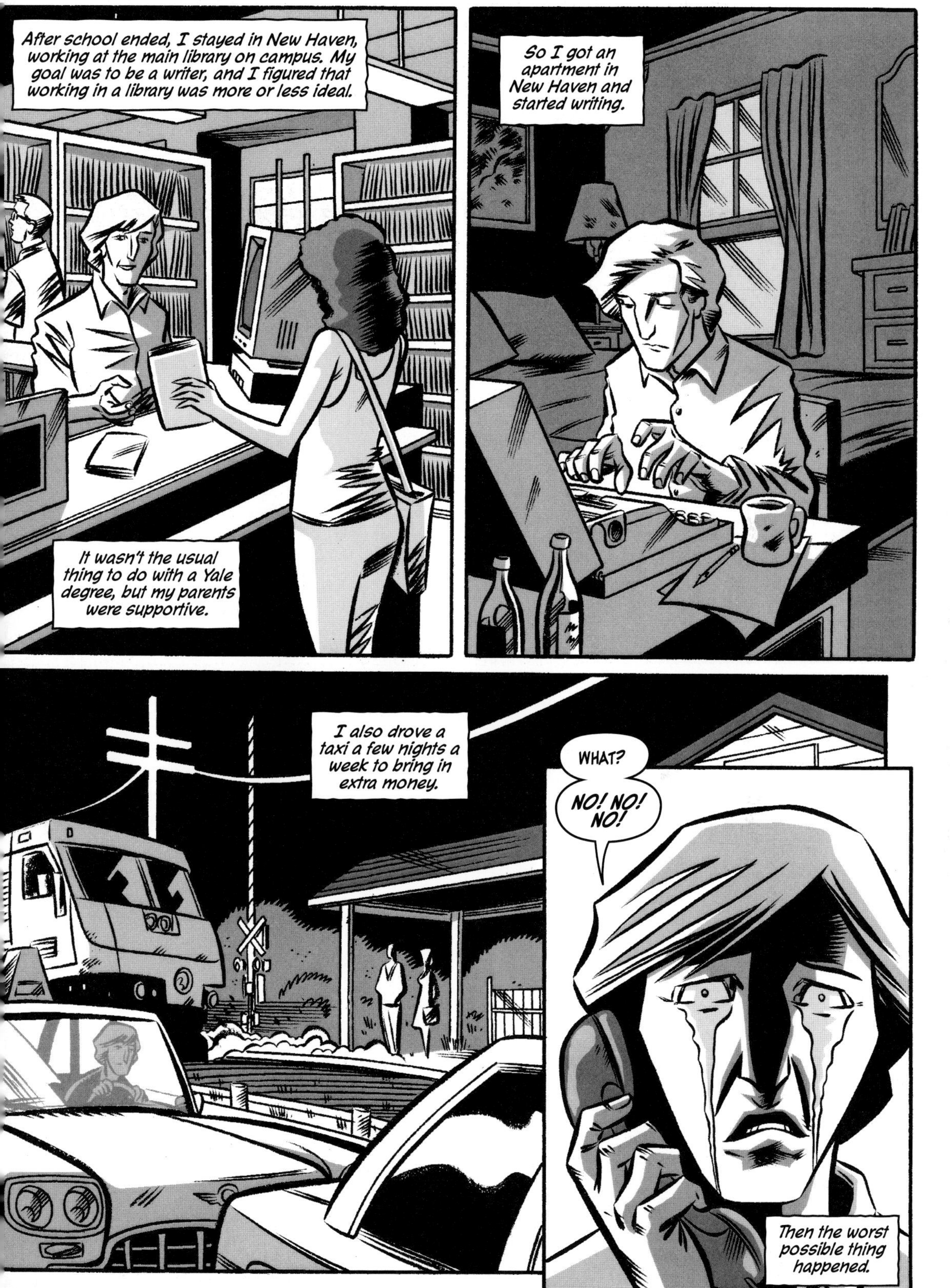
After school ended, I stayed in New Haven, working at the main library on campus. My goal was to be a writer, and I figured that working in a library was more or less ideal.
It wasn't the usual thing to do with a Yale degree, but my parents were supportive.
So I got an apartment in New Haven and started writing.
I also drove a taxi a few nights a week to bring in extra money.
WHAT?
NO! NO! NO!
Then the worst possible thing happened.

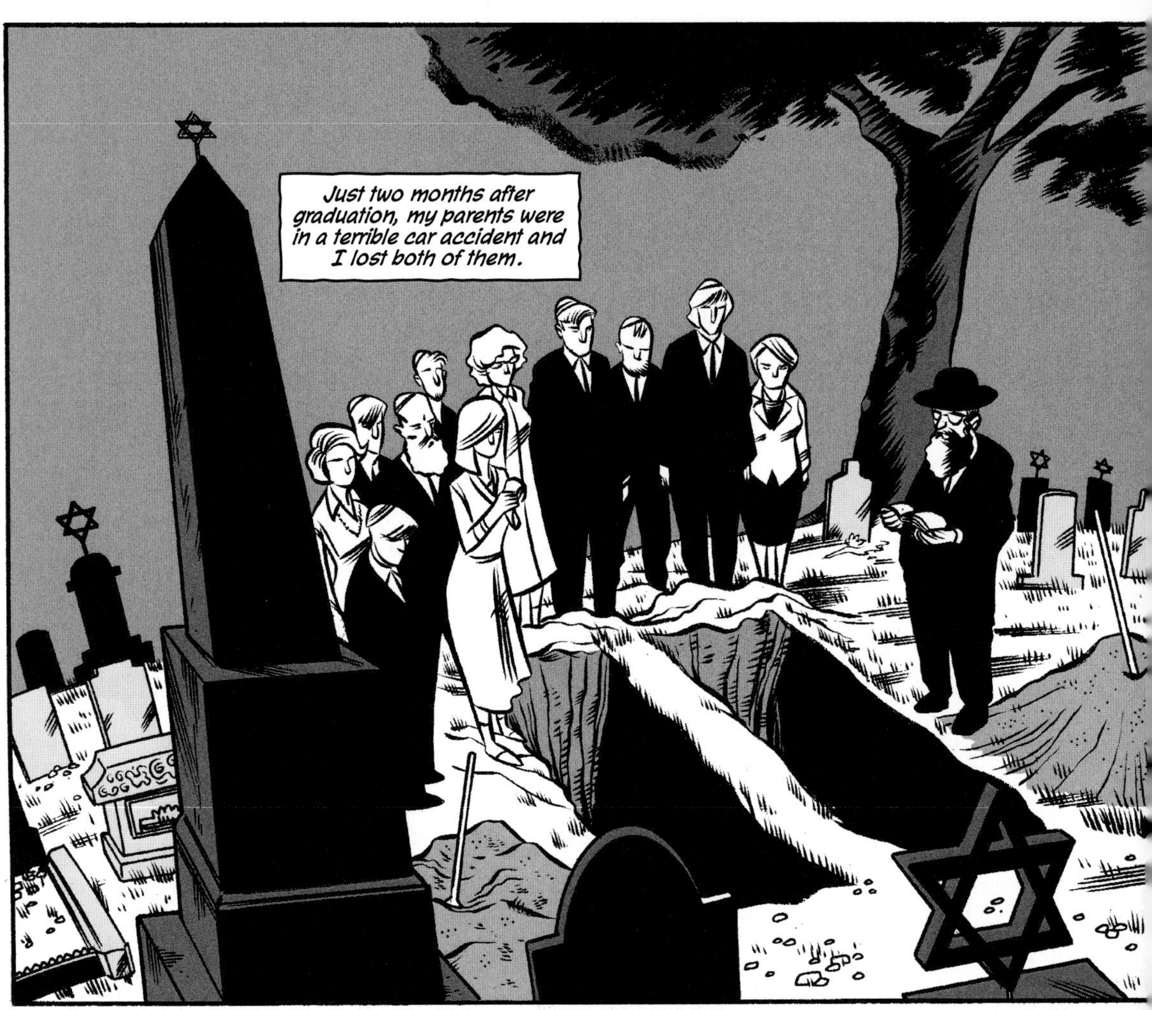
Just two months after graduation, my parents were in a terrible car accident and I lost both of them.

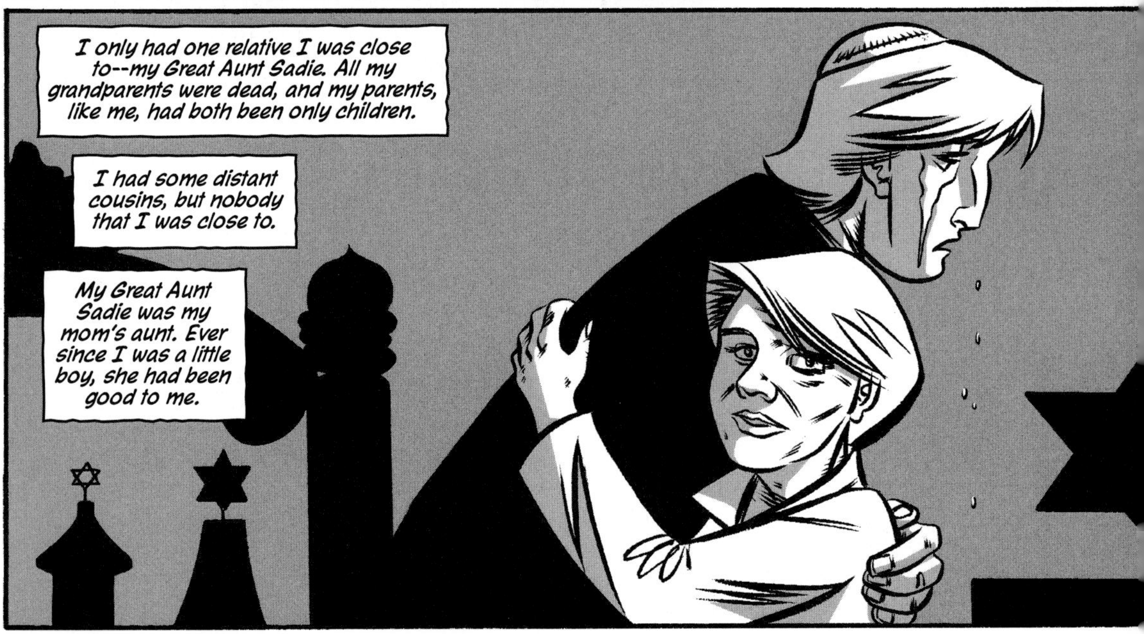
I only had one relative I was close to--my Great Aunt Sadie. All my grandparents were dead, and my parents, like me, had both been only children.
I had some distant cousins, but nobody that I was close to.
My Great Aunt Sadie was my mom's aunt. Ever since I was a little boy, she had been good to me.

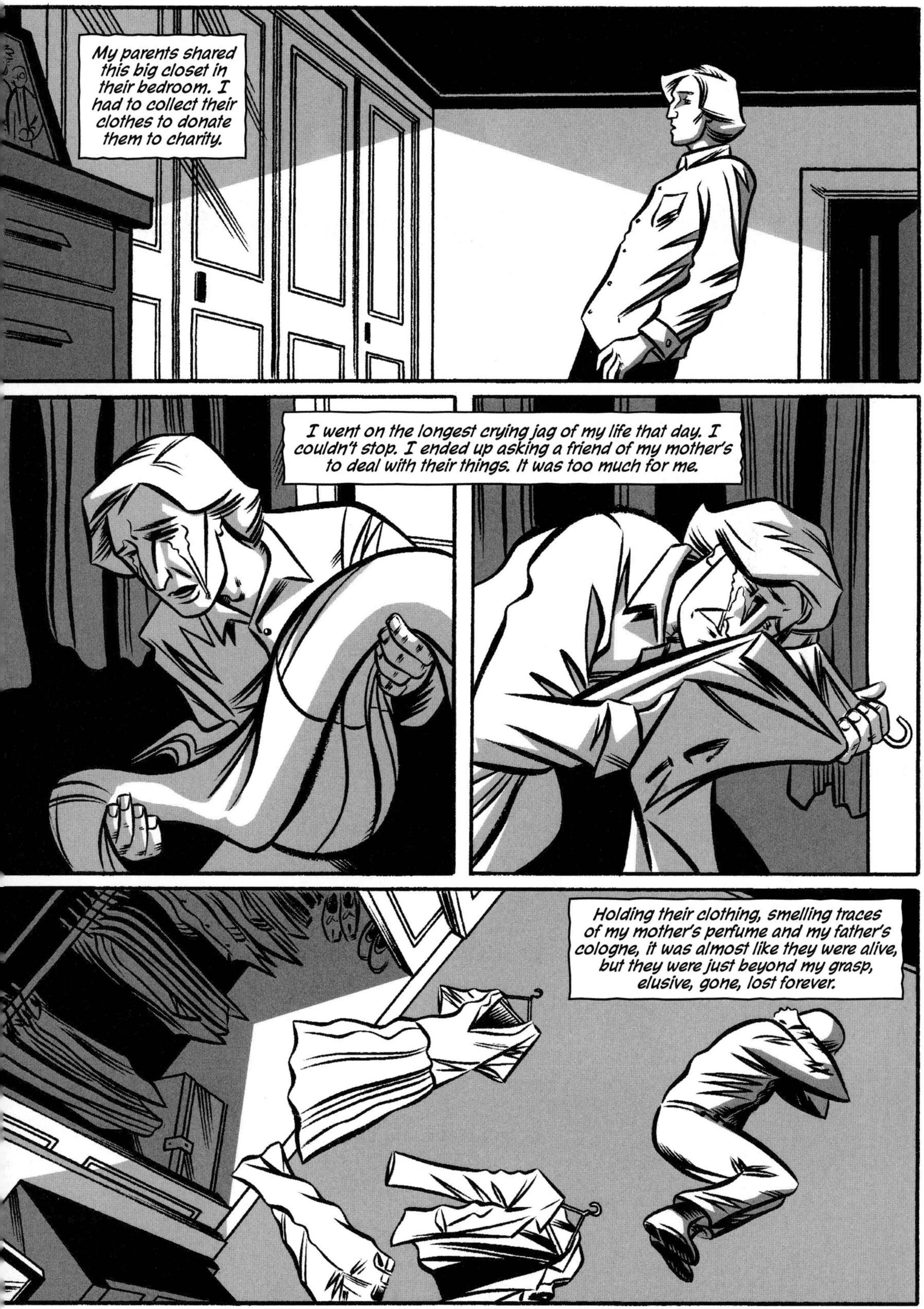
My parents shared this big closet in their bedroom. I had to collect their clothes to donate them to charity.
I went on the longest crying jag of my life that day. I couldn't stop. I ended up asking a friend of my mother's to deal with their things. It was too much for me.
Holding their clothing, smelling traces of my mother's perfume and my father's cologne, it was almost like they were alive, but they were just beyond my grasp, elusive, gone, lost forever.

At first I kept on with my life, as if nothing had changed.

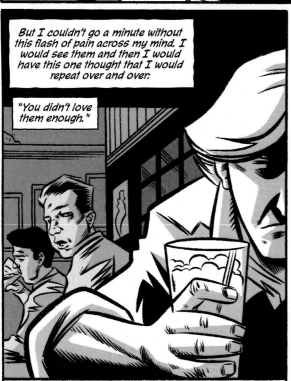

But I couldn't go a minute without this flash of pain across my mind. I would see them and then I would have this one thought that I would repeat over and over:

"You didn't love them enough."

It was sort of like OCD. The other thought I'd have is imagining their horrible pain right at the end, that their last thoughts were filled with terror.

I started driving down from New Haven to Queens on Sundays to visit my Great Aunt.

YOU SHOULD GO TO PARIS. I DID THAT WHEN MY FIRST MARRIAGE FELL APART. YOU'VE GOT TO PUT THIS BEHIND YOU.

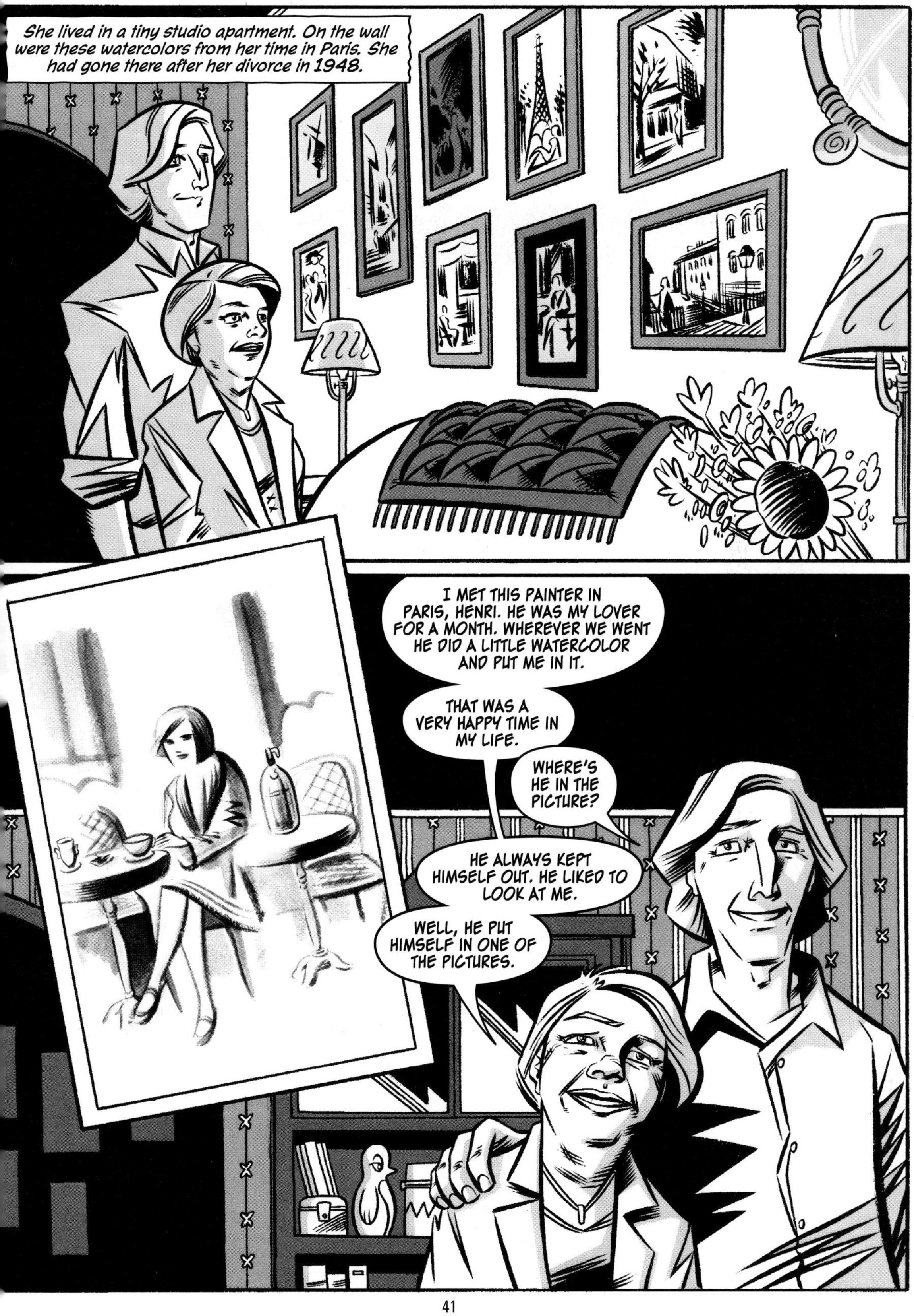

She lived in a tiny studio apartment. On the wall were these watercolors from her time in Paris. She had gone there after her divorce in 1948.
I MET THIS PAINTER IN PARIS, HENRI. HE WAS MY LOVER FOR A MONTH. WHEREVER WE WENT HE DID A LITTLE WATERCOLOR AND PUT ME IN IT.
THAT WAS A VERY HAPPY TIME IN MY LIFE.
WHERE'S HE IN THE PICTURE?
HE ALWAYS KEPT HIMSELF OUT. HE LIKED TO LOOK AT ME.
WELL, HE PUT HIMSELF IN ONE OF THE PICTURES.

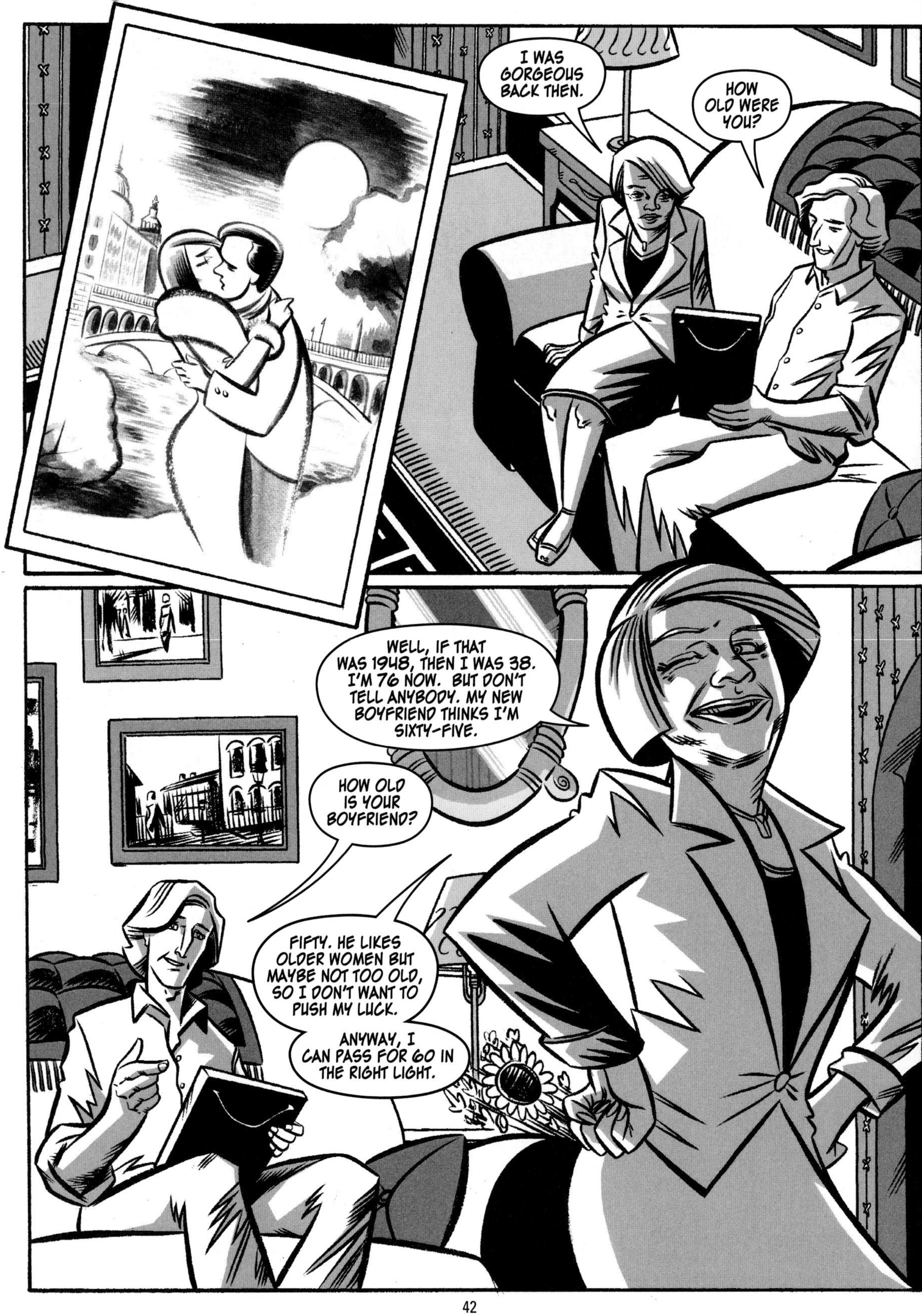

I WAS GORGEOUS BACK THEN.
HOW OLD WERE YOU?
WELL, IF THAT WAS 1948, THEN I WAS 38. I'M 76 NOW. BUT DON'T TELL ANYBODY. MY NEW BOYFRIEND THINKS I'M SIXTY-FIVE.
HOW OLD IS YOUR BOYFRIEND?
FIFTY. HE LIKES OLDER WOMEN BUT MAYBE NOT TOO OLD, SO I DON'T WANT TO PUSH MY LUCK.
ANYWAY, I CAN PASS FOR 60 IN THE RIGHT LIGHT.

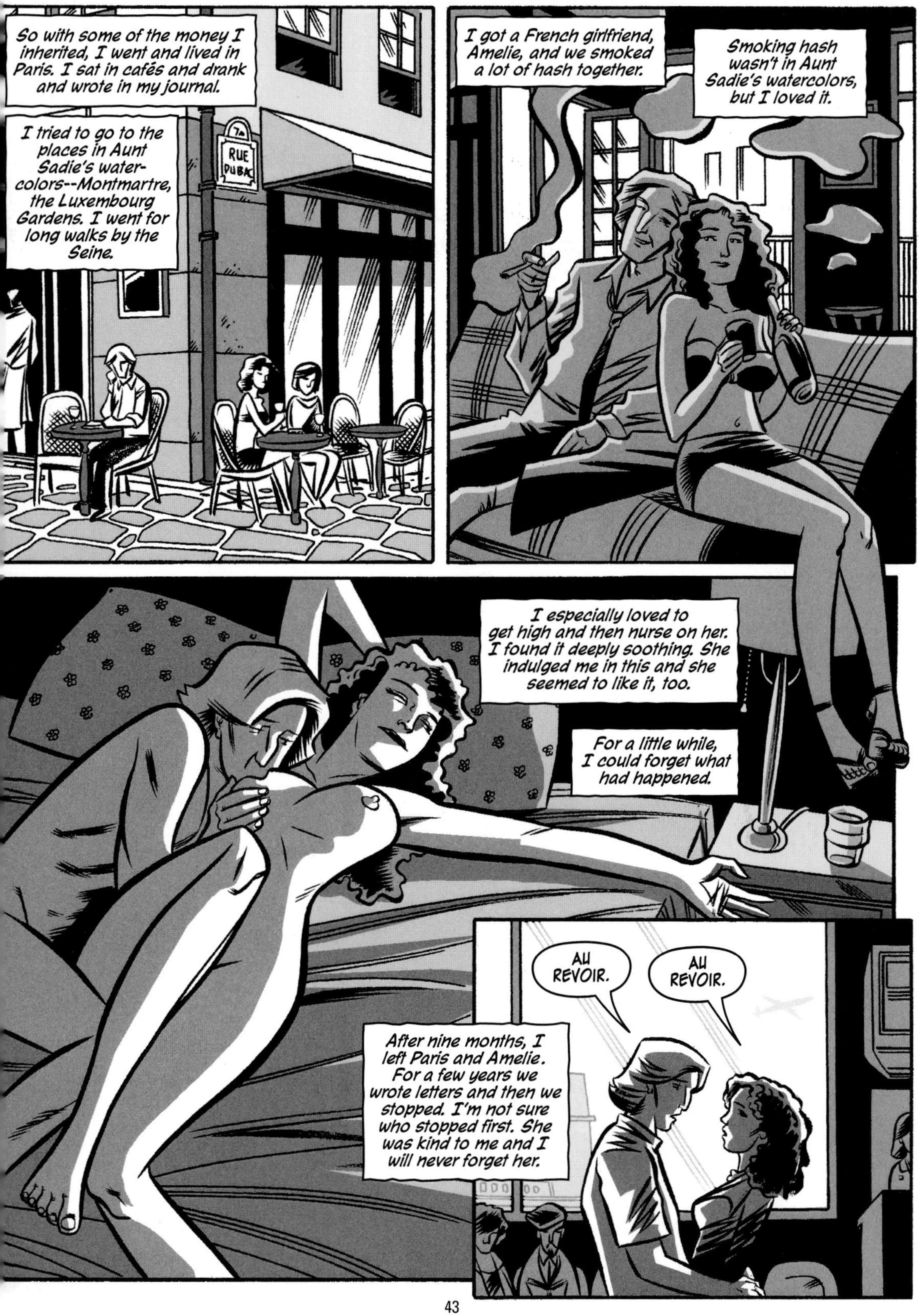
So with some of the money I inherited, I went and lived in Paris. I sat in cafés and drank and wrote in my journal.
I tried to go to the places in Aunt Sadie's water-colors--Montmartre, the Luxembourg Gardens. I went for long walks by the Seine.
RUE DU BAC
I got a French girlfriend, Amelie, and we smoked a lot of hash together.
Smoking hash wasn't in Aunt Sadie's watercolors, but I loved it.
I especially loved to get high and then nurse on her. I found it deeply soothing. She indulged me in this and she seemed to like it, too.
For a little while, I could forget what had happened.
AU REVOIR.
AU REVOIR.
After nine months, I left Paris and Amelie. For a few years we wrote letters and then we stopped. I'm not sure who stopped first. She was kind to me and I will never forget her.

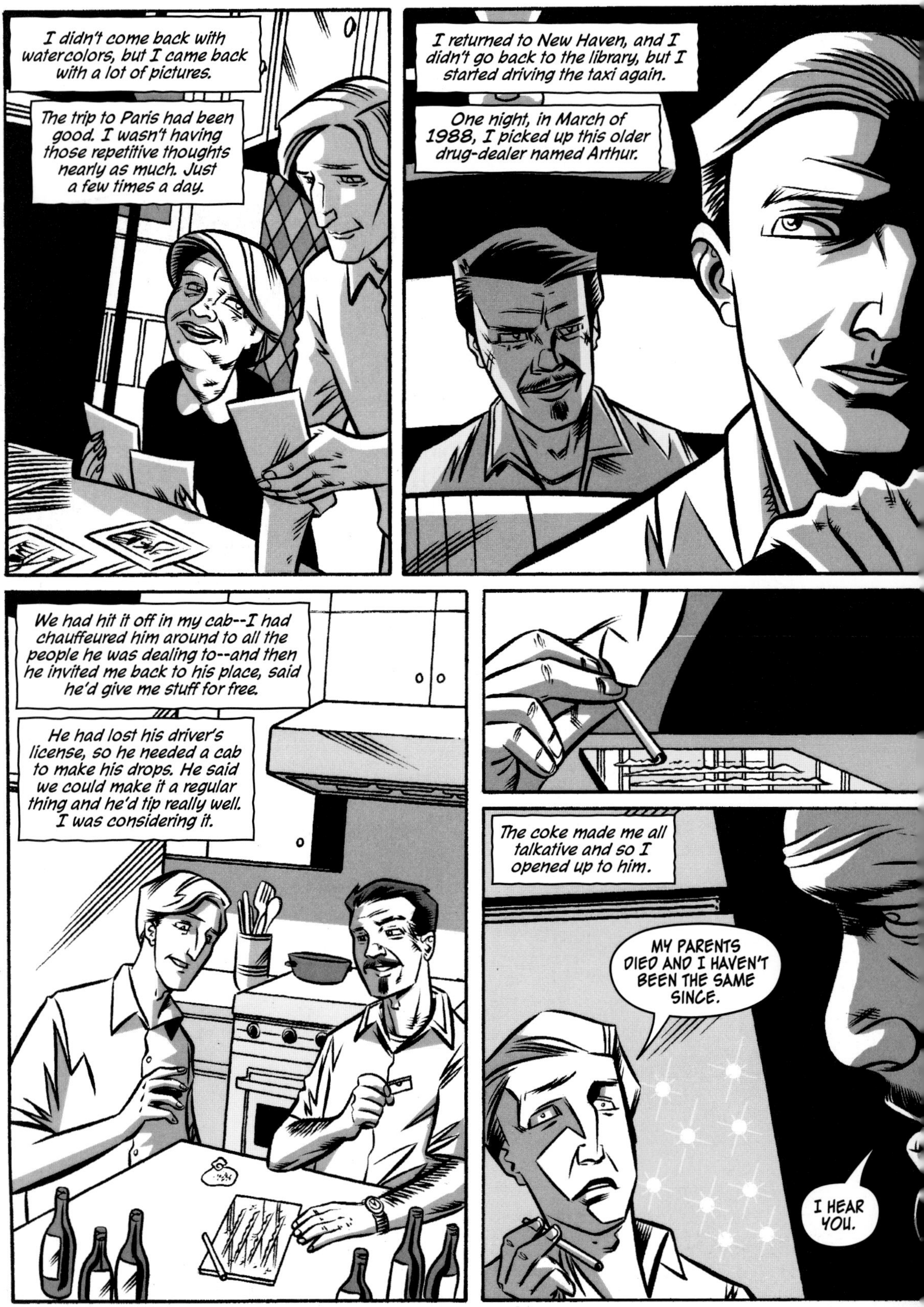
I didn't come back with watercolors, but I came back with a lot of pictures.
The trip to Paris had been good. I wasn't having those repetitive thoughts nearly as much. Just a few times a day.
I returned to New Haven, and I didn't go back to the library, but I started driving the taxi again.
One night, in March of 1988, I picked up this older drug-dealer named Arthur.
We had hit it off in my cab--I had chauffeured him around to all the people he was dealing to--and then he invited me back to his place, said he'd give me stuff for free.
He had lost his driver's license, so he needed a cab to make his drops. He said we could make it a regular thing and he'd tip really well. I was considering it.
The coke made me all talkative and so I opened up to him.
MY PARENTS DIED AND I HAVEN'T BEEN THE SAME SINCE.
I HEAR YOU.

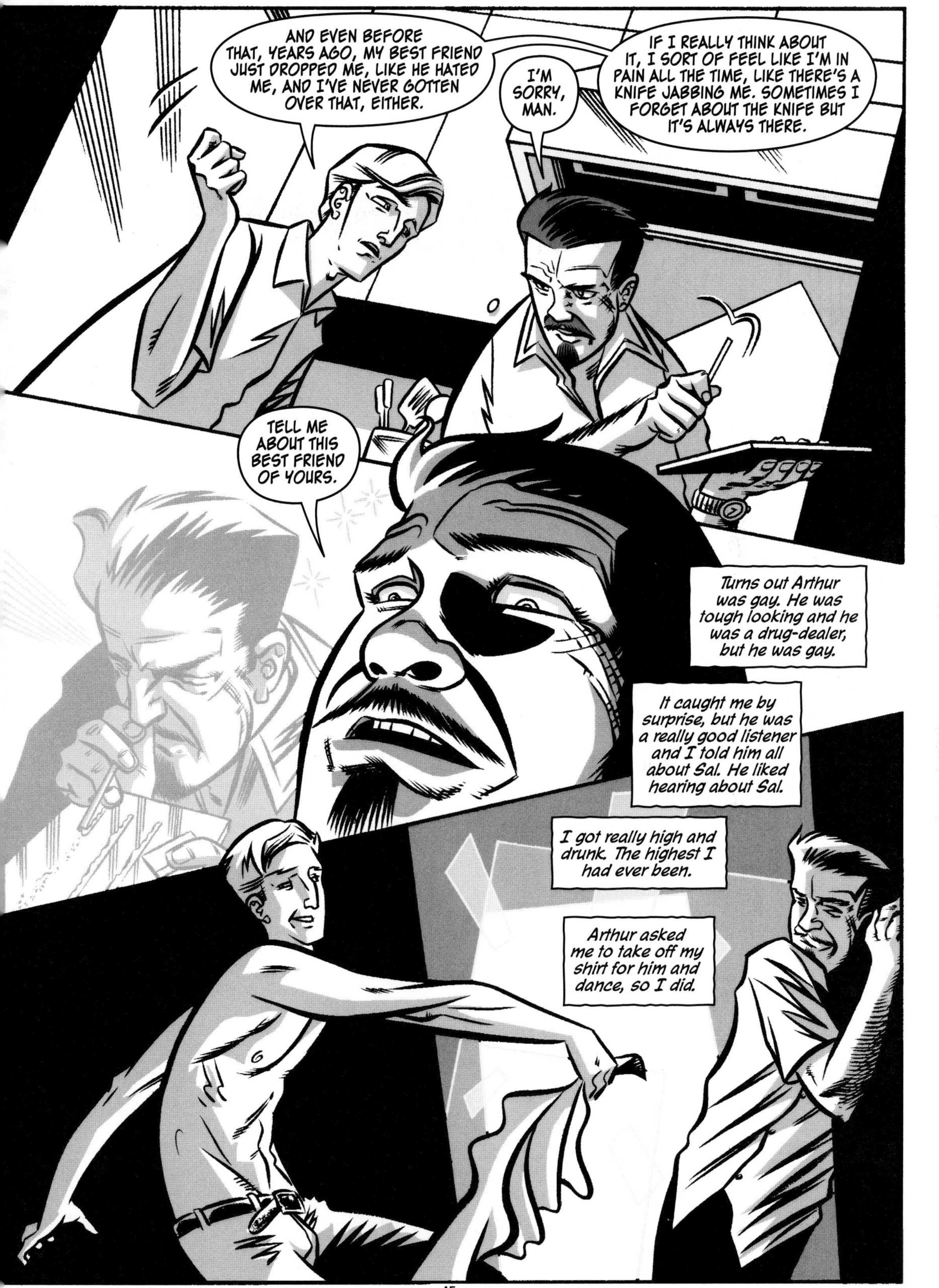
AND EVEN BEFORE THAT, YEARS AGO, MY BEST FRIEND JUST DROPPED ME, LIKE HE HATED ME, AND I'VE NEVER GOTTEN OVER THAT, EITHER.
I'M SORRY, MAN.
IF I REALLY THINK ABOUT IT, I SORT OF FEEL LIKE I'M IN PAIN ALL THE TIME, LIKE THERE'S A KNIFE JABBING ME. SOMETIMES I FORGET ABOUT THE KNIFE BUT IT'S ALWAYS THERE.
TELL ME ABOUT THIS BEST FRIEND OF YOURS.
Turns out Arthur was gay. He was tough looking and he was a drug-dealer, but he was gay.
It caught me by surprise, but he was a really good listener and I told him all about Sal. He liked hearing about Sal.
I got really high and drunk. The highest I had ever been.
Arthur asked me to take off my shirt for him and dance, so I did.

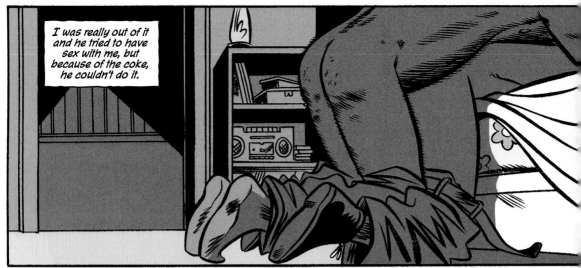

I was really out of it and he tried to have sex with me, but because of the coke, he couldn't do it.

I woke up in a garbage can. He had put me in there because at some point I had started vomiting.

Arthur wasn't a bad guy--he had tried to help me when I was throwing up--but waking up naked in that garbage can was a terrible thing.

When I got back to my place, I was incredibly frightened. I felt like if I didn't get some kind of help I would die.

On some level, I wanted to die, but another part of me, some survival instinct, was also kicking in.

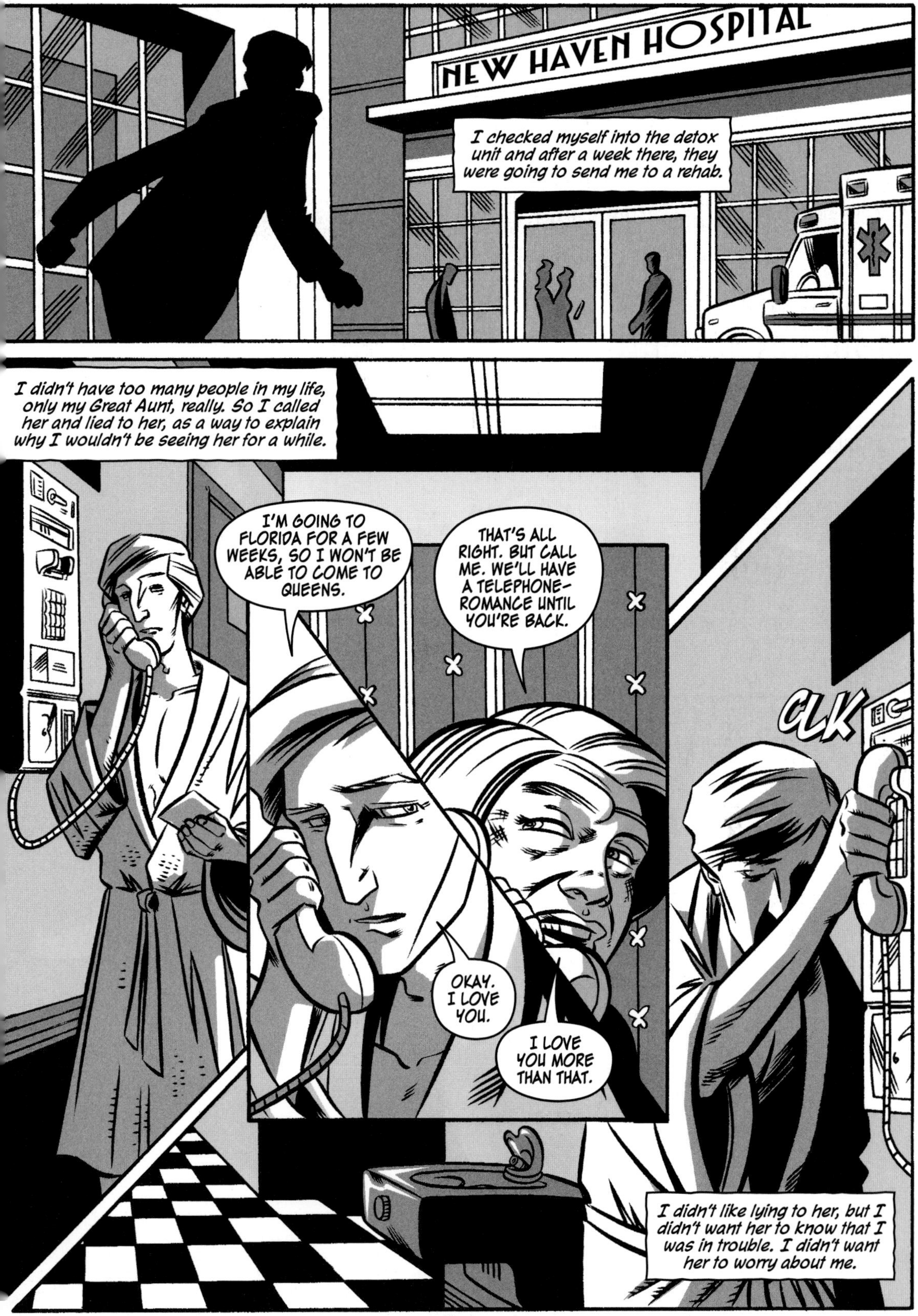
NEW HAVEN HOSPITAL
I checked myself into the detox unit and after a week there, they were going to send me to a rehab.
I didn't have too many people in my life, only my Great Aunt, really. So I called her and lied to her, as a way to explain why I wouldn't be seeing her for a while.
I'M GOING TO FLORIDA FOR A FEW WEEKS, SO I WON'T BE ABLE TO COME TO QUEENS.
THAT'S ALL RIGHT. BUT CALL ME. WE'LL HAVE A TELEPHONE-ROMANCE UNTIL YOU'RE BACK.
OKAY. I LOVE YOU.
I LOVE YOU MORE THAN THAT.
CLK
I didn't like lying to her, but I didn't want her to know that I was in trouble. I didn't want her to worry about me.

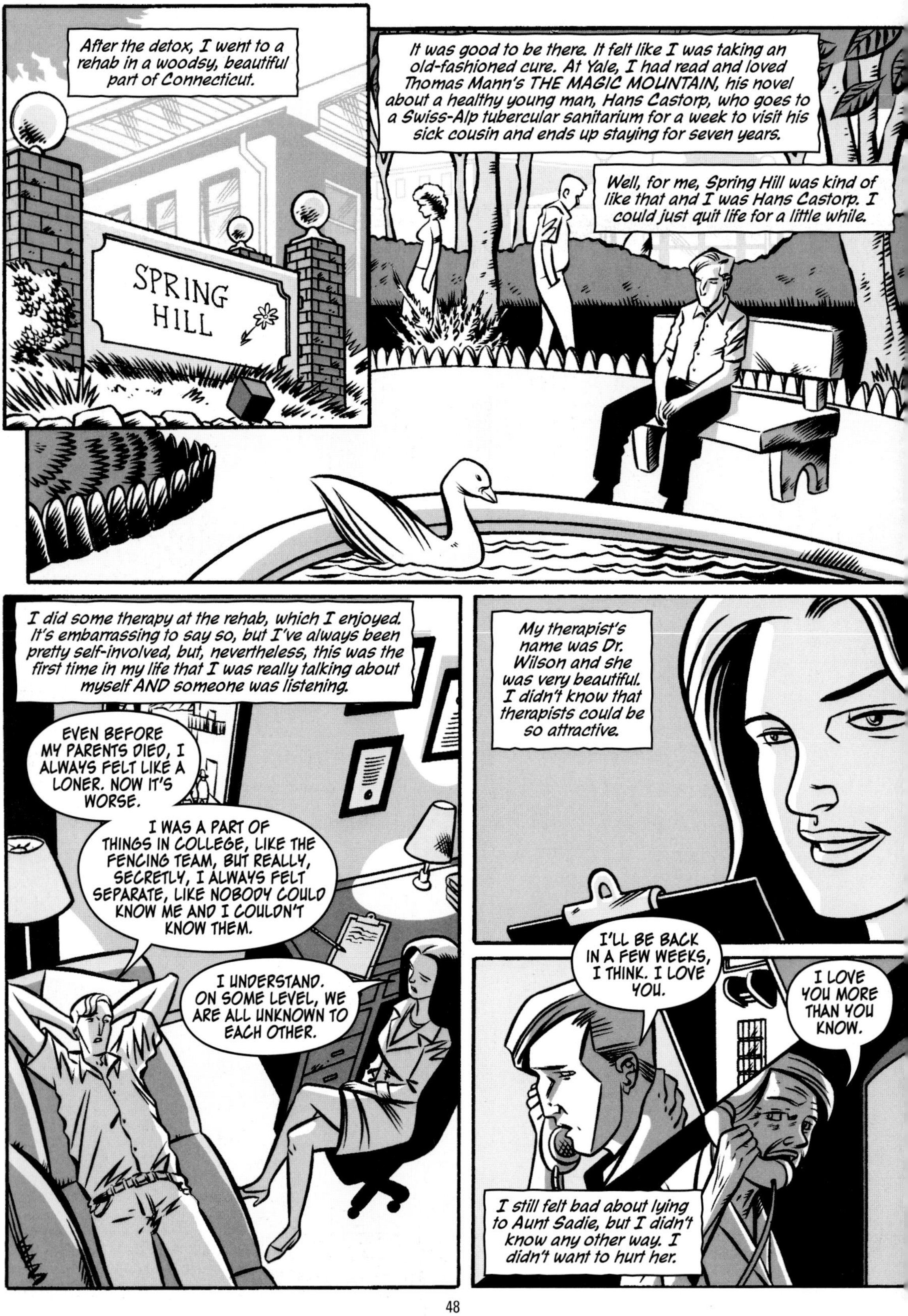
After the detox, I went to a rehab in a woodsy, beautiful part of Connecticut.
SPRING HILL
It was good to be there. It felt like I was taking an old-fashioned cure. At Yale, I had read and loved Thomas Mann's THE MAGIC MOUNTAIN, his novel about a healthy young man, Hans Castorp, who goes to a Swiss-Alp tubercular sanitarium for a week to visit his sick cousin and ends up staying for seven years.
Well, for me, Spring Hill was kind of like that and I was Hans Castorp. I could just quit life for a little while.
I did some therapy at the rehab, which I enjoyed. It's embarrassing to say so, but I've always been pretty self-involved, but, nevertheless, this was the first time in my life that I was really talking about myself AND someone was listening.
EVEN BEFORE MY PARENTS DIED, I ALWAYS FELT LIKE A LONER. NOW IT'S WORSE.
I WAS A PART OF THINGS IN COLLEGE, LIKE THE FENCING TEAM, BUT REALLY, SECRETLY, I ALWAYS FELT SEPARATE, LIKE NOBODY COULD KNOW ME AND I COULDN'T KNOW THEM.
I UNDERSTAND. ON SOME LEVEL, WE ARE ALL UNKNOWN TO EACH OTHER.
My therapist's name was Dr. Wilson and she was very beautiful. I didn't know that therapists could be so attractive.
I'LL BE BACK IN A FEW WEEKS, I THINK. I LOVE YOU.
I LOVE YOU MORE THAN YOU KNOW.
I still felt bad about lying to Aunt Sadie, but I didn't know any other way. I didn't want to hurt her.

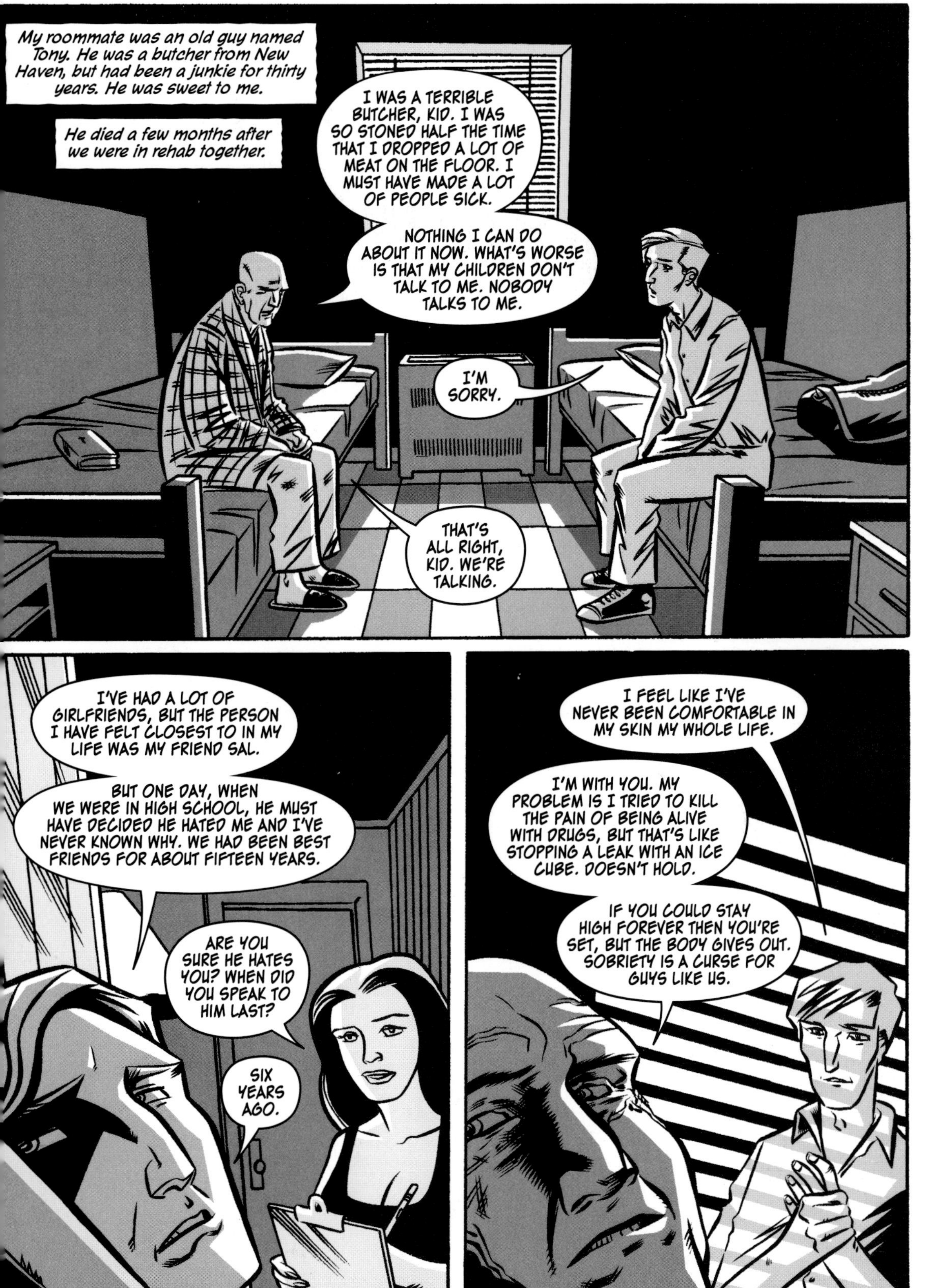
My roommate was an old guy named Tony. He was a butcher from New Haven, but had been a junkie for thirty years. He was sweet to me.
He died a few months after we were in rehab together.
I WAS A TERRIBLE BUTCHER, KID. I WAS SO STONED HALF THE TIME THAT I DROPPED A LOT OF MEAT ON THE FLOOR. I MUST HAVE MADE A LOT OF PEOPLE SICK.
NOTHING I CAN DO ABOUT IT NOW. WHAT'S WORSE IS THAT MY CHILDREN DON'T TALK TO ME. NOBODY TALKS TO ME.
I'M SORRY.
THAT'S ALL RIGHT, KID. WE'RE TALKING.
I'VE HAD A LOT OF GIRLFRIENDS, BUT THE PERSON I HAVE FELT CLOSEST TO IN MY LIFE WAS MY FRIEND SAL.
BUT ONE DAY, WHEN WE WERE IN HIGH SCHOOL, HE MUST HAVE DECIDED HE HATED ME AND I'VE NEVER KNOWN WHY. WE HAD BEEN BEST FRIENDS FOR ABOUT FIFTEEN YEARS.
ARE YOU SURE HE HATES YOU? WHEN DID YOU SPEAK TO HIM LAST?
SIX YEARS AGO.
I FEEL LIKE I'VE NEVER BEEN COMFORTABLE IN MY SKIN MY WHOLE LIFE.
I'M WITH YOU. MY PROBLEM IS I TRIED TO KILL THE PAIN OF BEING ALIVE WITH DRUGS, BUT THAT'S LIKE STOPPING A LEAK WITH AN ICE CUBE. DOESN'T HOLD.
IF YOU COULD STAY HIGH FOREVER THEN YOU'RE SET, BUT THE BODY GIVES OUT. SOBRIETY IS A CURSE FOR GUYS LIKE US.

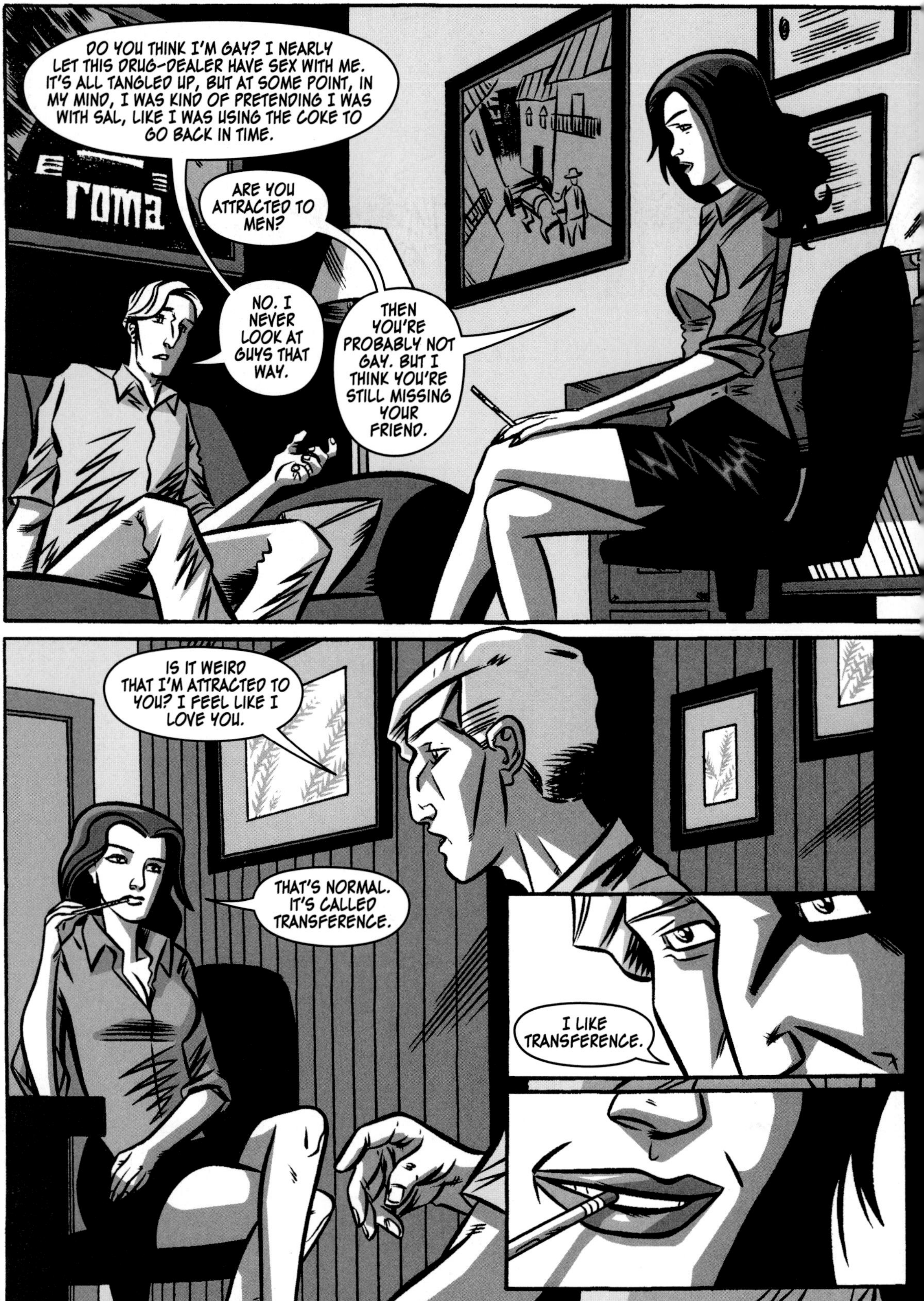
DO YOU THINK I'M GAY? I NEARLY LET THIS DRUG-DEALER HAVE SEX WITH ME. IT'S ALL TANGLED UP, BUT AT SOME POINT, IN MY MIND, I WAS KIND OF PRETENDING I WAS WITH SAL, LIKE I WAS USING THE COKE TO GO BACK IN TIME.
roma
ARE YOU ATTRACTED TO MEN?
NO. I NEVER LOOK AT GUYS THAT WAY.
THEN YOU'RE PROBABLY NOT GAY. BUT I THINK YOU'RE STILL MISSING YOUR FRIEND.
IS IT WEIRD THAT I'M ATTRACTED TO YOU? I FEEL LIKE I LOVE YOU.
THAT'S NORMAL. IT'S CALLED TRANSFERENCE.
I LIKE TRANSFERENCE.

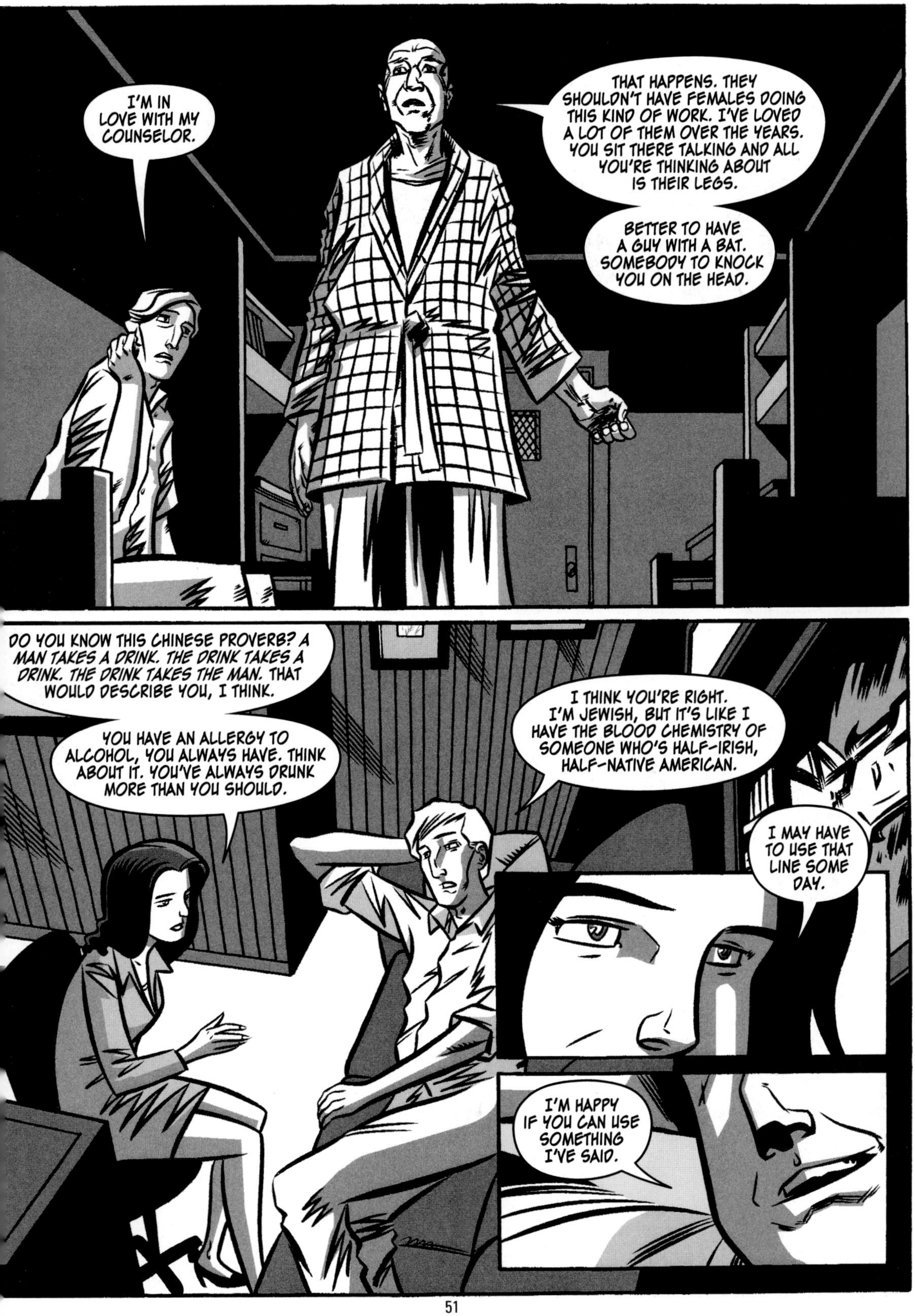
I'M IN LOVE WITH MY COUNSELOR.
THAT HAPPENS. THEY SHOULDN'T HAVE FEMALES DOING THIS KIND OF WORK. I'VE LOVED A LOT OF THEM OVER THE YEARS. YOU SIT THERE TALKING AND ALL YOU'RE THINKING ABOUT IS THEIR LEGS.
BETTER TO HAVE A GUY WITH A BAT. SOMEBODY TO KNOCK YOU ON THE HEAD.
DO YOU KNOW THIS CHINESE PROVERB? *A MAN TAKES A DRINK. THE DRINK TAKES A DRINK. THE DRINK TAKES THE MAN.* THAT WOULD DESCRIBE YOU, I THINK.
YOU HAVE AN ALLERGY TO ALCOHOL, YOU ALWAYS HAVE. THINK ABOUT IT. YOU'VE ALWAYS DRUNK MORE THAN YOU SHOULD.
I THINK YOU'RE RIGHT. I'M JEWISH, BUT IT'S LIKE I HAVE THE BLOOD CHEMISTRY OF SOMEONE WHO'S HALF-IRISH, HALF-NATIVE AMERICAN.
I MAY HAVE TO USE THAT LINE SOME DAY.
I'M HAPPY IF YOU CAN USE SOMETHING I'VE SAID.

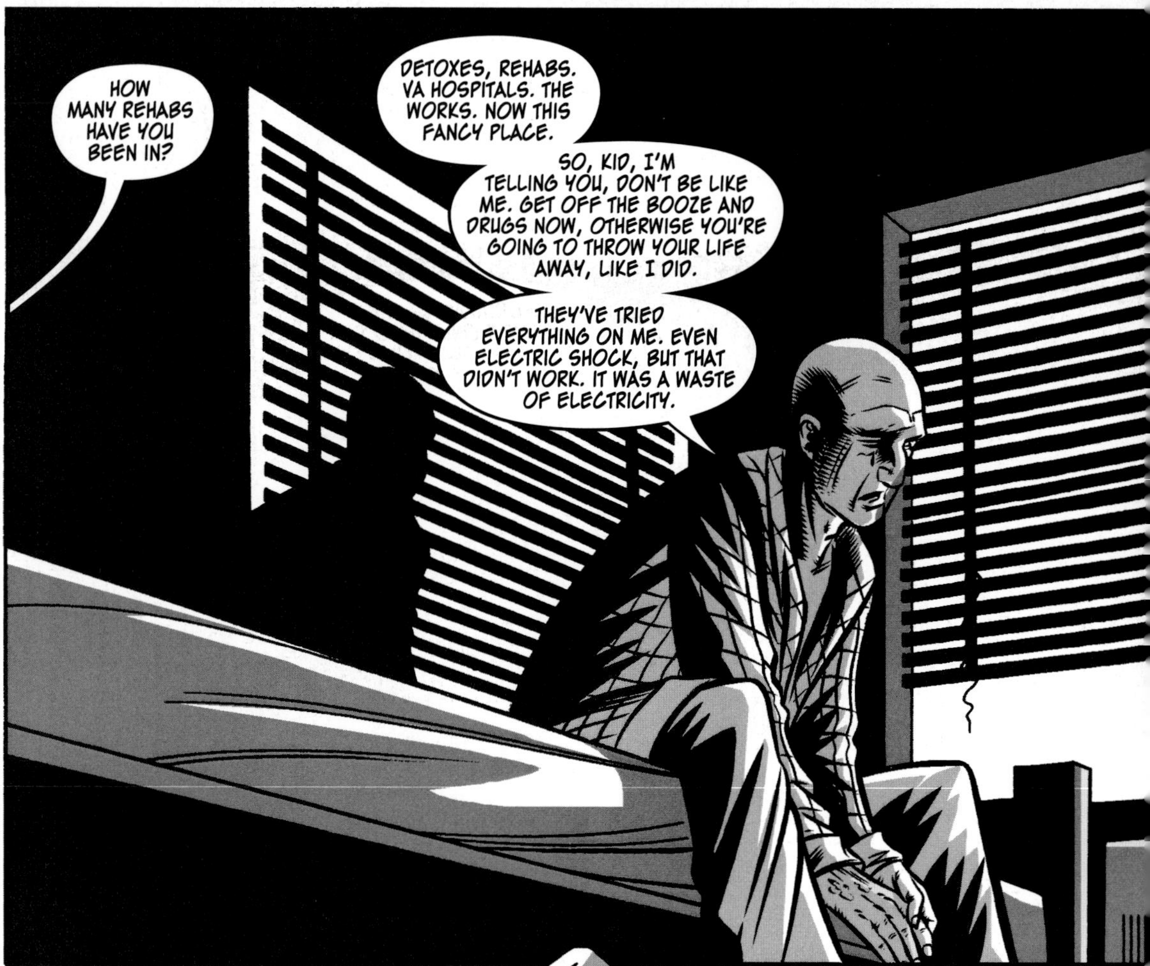
HOW MANY REHABS HAVE YOU BEEN IN?
DETOXES, REHABS. VA HOSPITALS. THE WORKS. NOW THIS FANCY PLACE.
SO, KID, I'M TELLING YOU, DON'T BE LIKE ME. GET OFF THE BOOZE AND DRUGS NOW, OTHERWISE YOU'RE GOING TO THROW YOUR LIFE AWAY, LIKE I DID.
THEY'VE TRIED EVERYTHING ON ME. EVEN ELECTRIC SHOCK, BUT THAT DIDN'T WORK. IT WAS A WASTE OF ELECTRICITY.

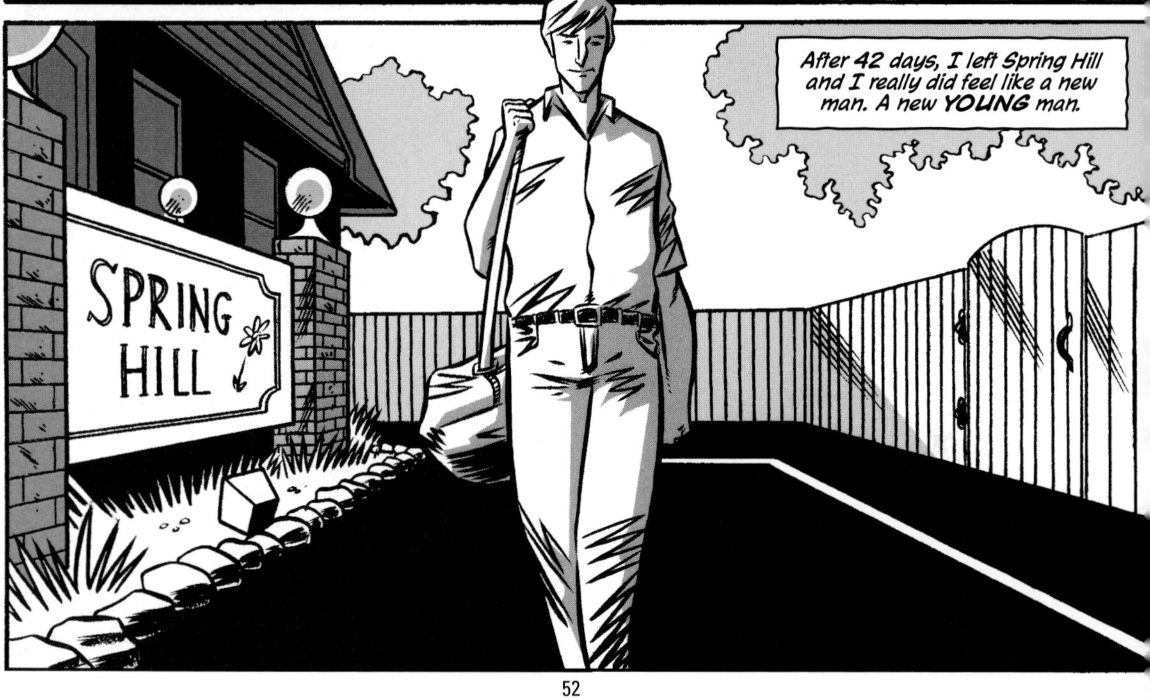
After 42 days, I left Spring Hill and I really did feel like a new man. A new YOUNG man.
SPRING HILL

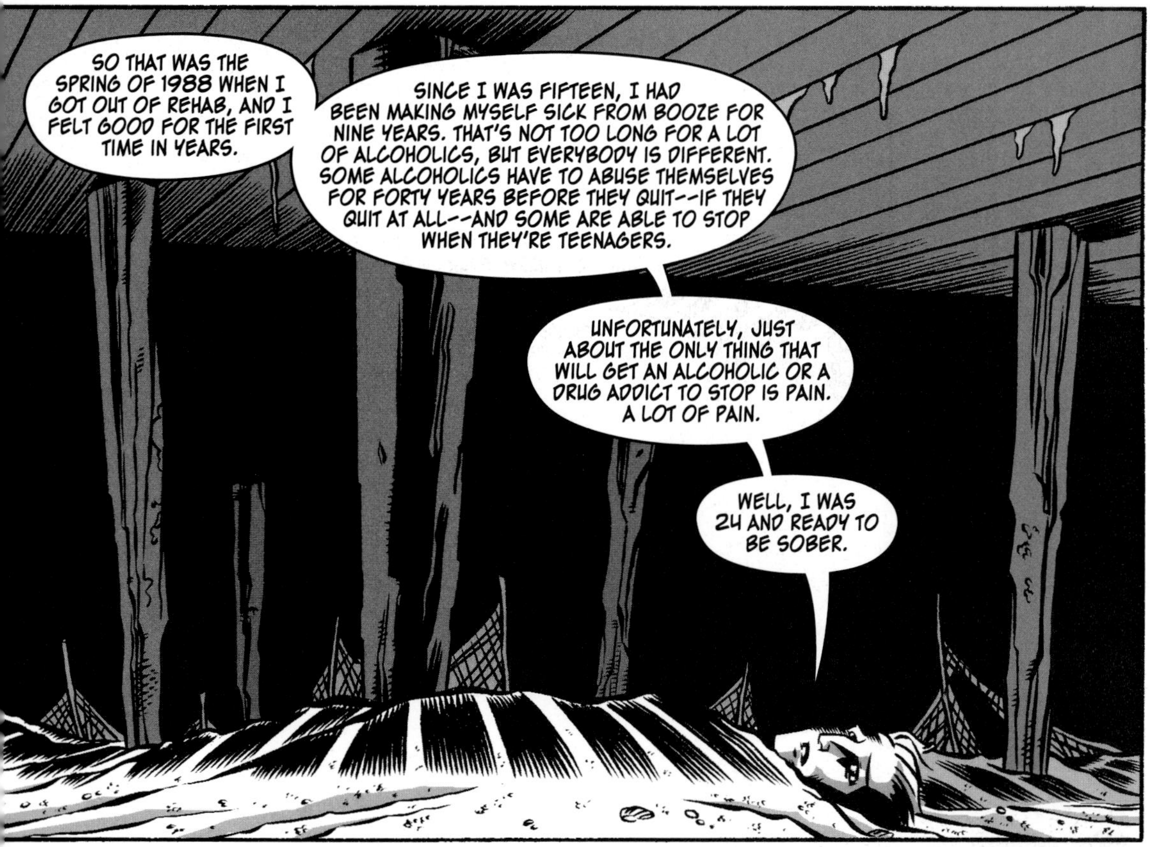
SO THAT WAS THE SPRING OF 1988 WHEN I GOT OUT OF REHAB, AND I FELT GOOD FOR THE FIRST TIME IN YEARS.
SINCE I WAS FIFTEEN, I HAD BEEN MAKING MYSELF SICK FROM BOOZE FOR NINE YEARS. THAT'S NOT TOO LONG FOR A LOT OF ALCOHOLICS, BUT EVERYBODY IS DIFFERENT. SOME ALCOHOLICS HAVE TO ABUSE THEMSELVES FOR FORTY YEARS BEFORE THEY QUIT--IF THEY QUIT AT ALL--AND SOME ARE ABLE TO STOP WHEN THEY'RE TEENAGERS.
UNFORTUNATELY, JUST ABOUT THE ONLY THING THAT WILL GET AN ALCOHOLIC OR A DRUG ADDICT TO STOP IS PAIN. A LOT OF PAIN.
WELL, I WAS 24 AND READY TO BE SOBER.

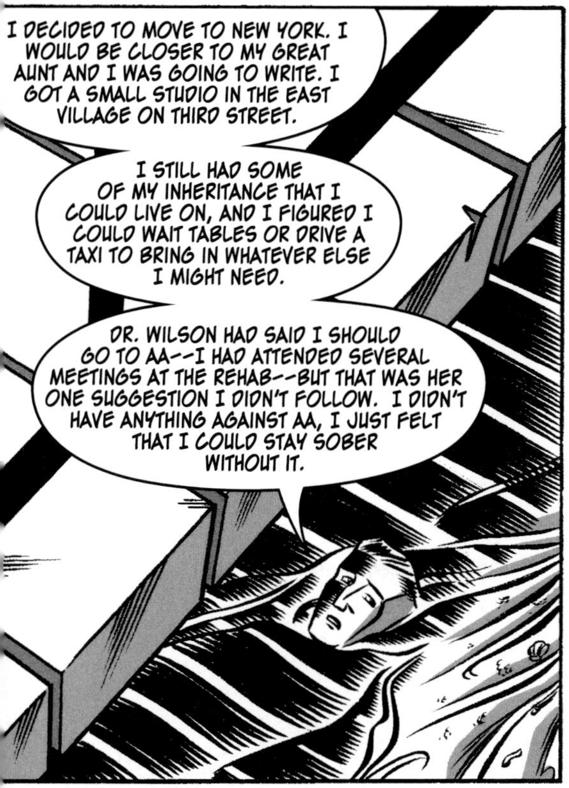
I DECIDED TO MOVE TO NEW YORK. I WOULD BE CLOSER TO MY GREAT AUNT AND I WAS GOING TO WRITE. I GOT A SMALL STUDIO IN THE EAST VILLAGE ON THIRD STREET.
I STILL HAD SOME OF MY INHERITANCE THAT I COULD LIVE ON, AND I FIGURED I COULD WAIT TABLES OR DRIVE A TAXI TO BRING IN WHATEVER ELSE I MIGHT NEED.
DR. WILSON HAD SAID I SHOULD GO TO AA--I HAD ATTENDED SEVERAL MEETINGS AT THE REHAB--BUT THAT WAS HER ONE SUGGESTION I DIDN'T FOLLOW. I DIDN'T HAVE ANYTHING AGAINST AA, I JUST FELT THAT I COULD STAY SOBER WITHOUT IT.

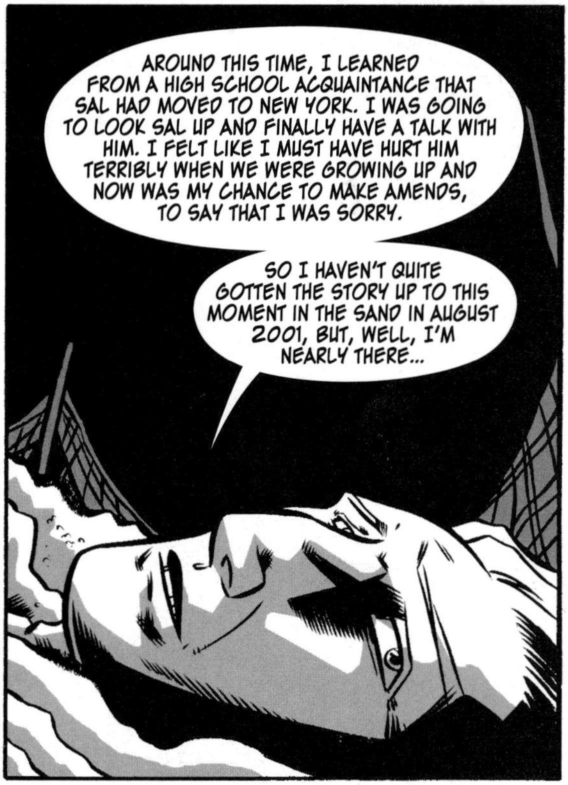
AROUND THIS TIME, I LEARNED FROM A HIGH SCHOOL ACQUAINTANCE THAT SAL HAD MOVED TO NEW YORK. I WAS GOING TO LOOK SAL UP AND FINALLY HAVE A TALK WITH HIM. I FELT LIKE I MUST HAVE HURT HIM TERRIBLY WHEN WE WERE GROWING UP AND NOW WAS MY CHANCE TO MAKE AMENDS, TO SAY THAT I WAS SORRY.
SO I HAVEN'T QUITE GOTTEN THE STORY UP TO THIS MOMENT IN THE SAND IN AUGUST 2001, BUT, WELL, I'M NEARLY THERE...

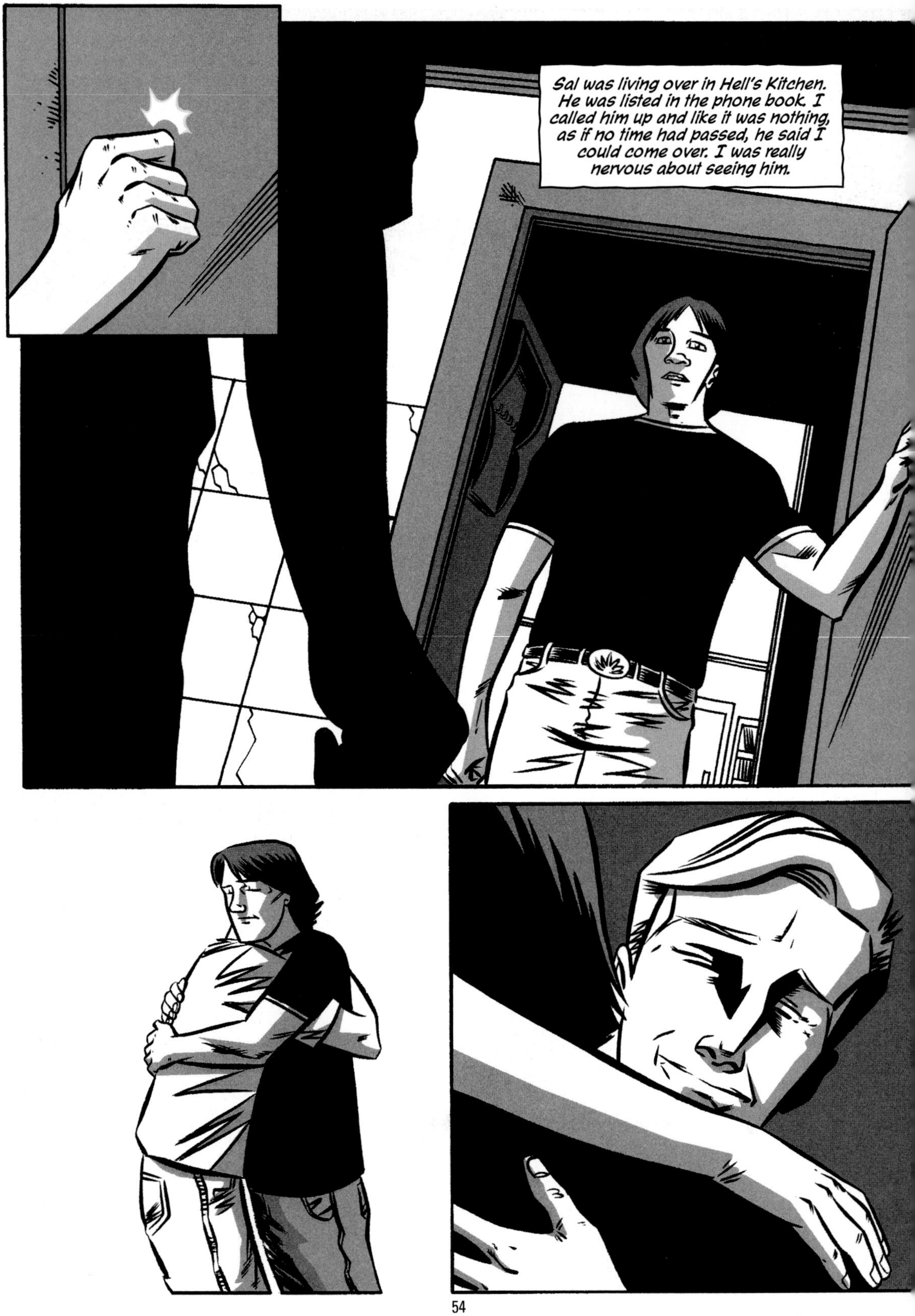
Sal was living over in Hell's Kitchen. He was listed in the phone book. I called him up and like it was nothing, as if no time had passed, he said I could come over. I was really nervous about seeing him.

...IT WAS A BAD CAR ACCIDENT, JUST A FEW MONTHS AFTER I GRADUATED.

I'M SORRY.

I told him about my parents and he was kind and sympathetic.

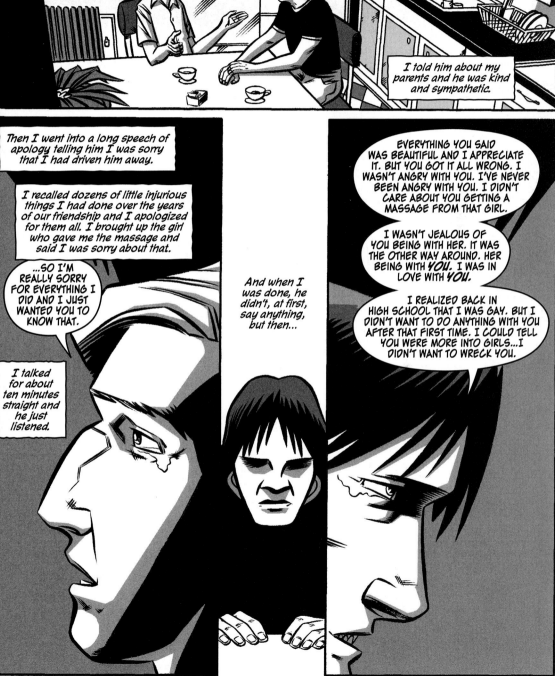

Then I went into a long speech of apology telling him I was sorry that I had driven him away.

I recalled dozens of little injurious things I had done over the years of our friendship and I apologized for them all. I brought up the girl who gave me the massage and said I was sorry about that.

...SO I'M REALLY SORRY FOR EVERYTHING I DID AND I JUST WANTED YOU TO KNOW THAT.

And when I was done, he didn't, at first, say anything, but then...

I talked for about ten minutes straight and he just listened.

EVERYTHING YOU SAID WAS BEAUTIFUL AND I APPRECIATE IT. BUT YOU GOT IT ALL WRONG. I WASN'T ANGRY WITH YOU. I'VE NEVER BEEN ANGRY WITH YOU. I DIDN'T CARE ABOUT YOU GETTING A MASSAGE FROM THAT GIRL.

I WASN'T JEALOUS OF YOU BEING WITH HER. IT WAS THE OTHER WAY AROUND. HER BEING WITH *YOU*. I WAS IN LOVE WITH *YOU*.

I REALIZED BACK IN HIGH SCHOOL THAT I WAS GAY. BUT I DIDN'T WANT TO DO ANYTHING WITH YOU AFTER THAT FIRST TIME. I COULD TELL YOU WERE MORE INTO GIRLS...I DIDN'T WANT TO WRECK YOU.

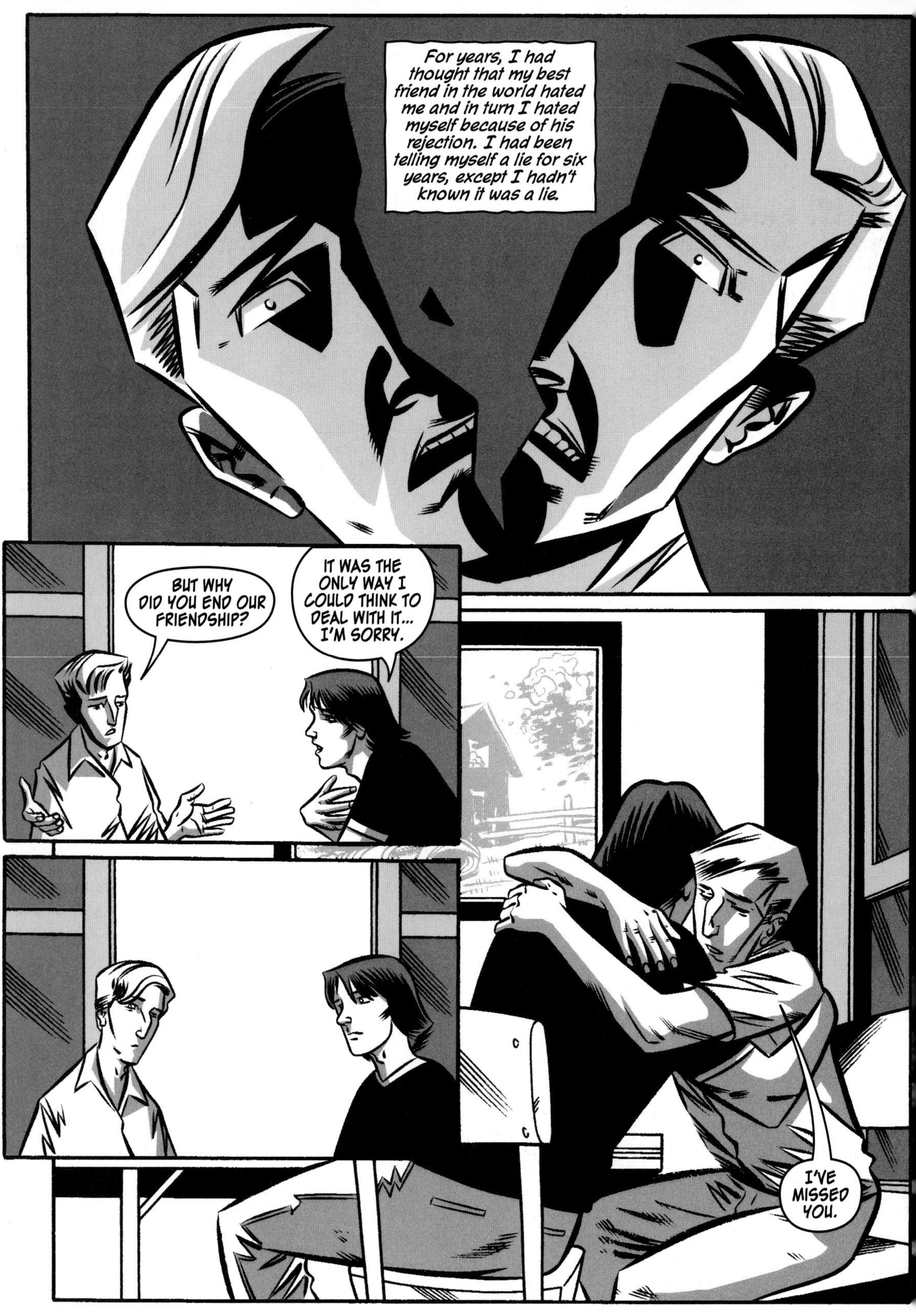
For years, I had thought that my best friend in the world hated me and in turn I hated myself because of his rejection. I had been telling myself a lie for six years, except I hadn't known it was a lie.
BUT WHY DID YOU END OUR FRIENDSHIP?
IT WAS THE ONLY WAY I COULD THINK TO DEAL WITH IT... I'M SORRY.
I'VE MISSED YOU.

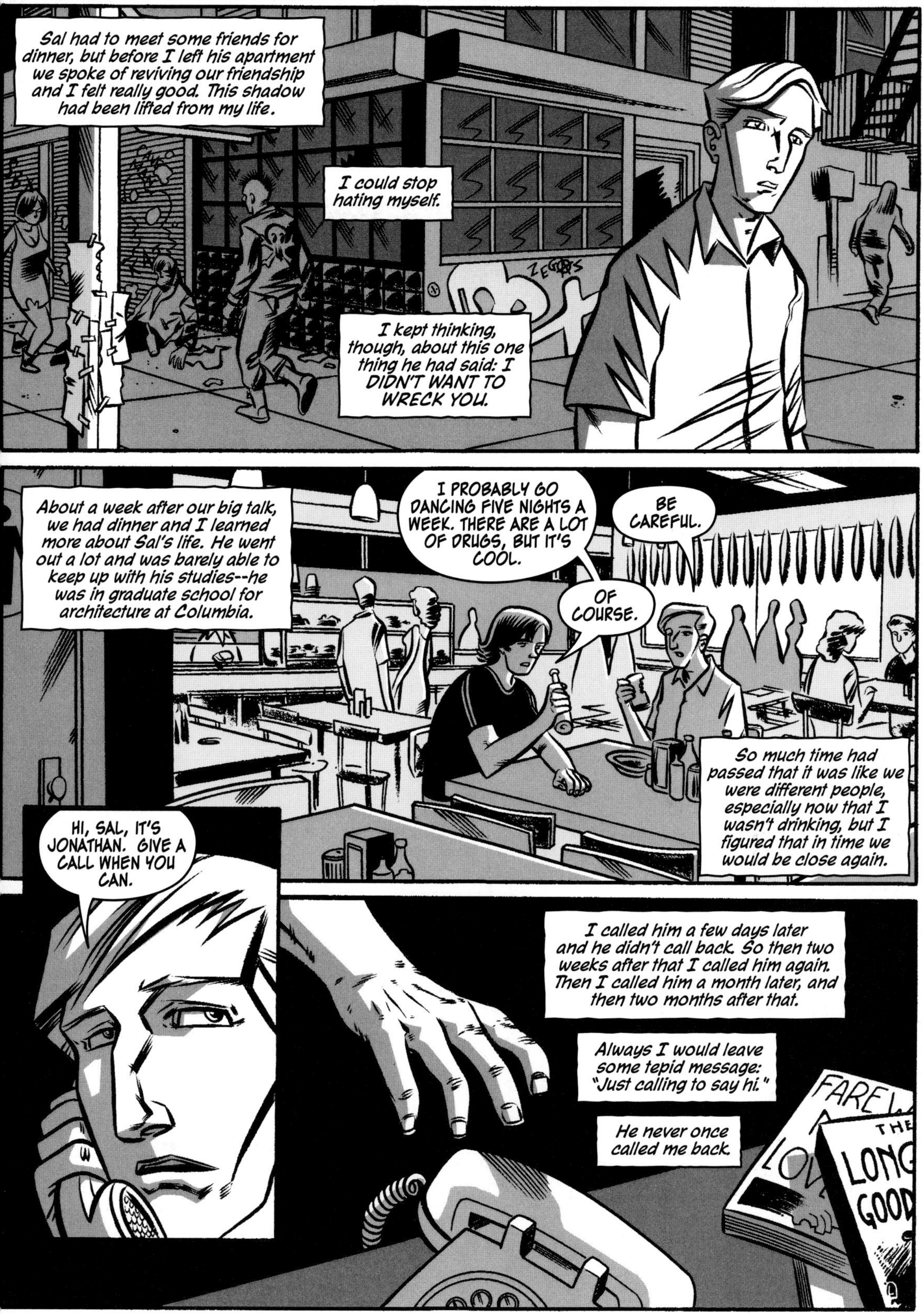
Sal had to meet some friends for dinner, but before I left his apartment we spoke of reviving our friendship and I felt really good. This shadow had been lifted from my life.
I could stop hating myself.
I kept thinking, though, about this one thing he had said: I DIDN'T WANT TO WRECK YOU.
About a week after our big talk, we had dinner and I learned more about Sal's life. He went out a lot and was barely able to keep up with his studies--he was in graduate school for architecture at Columbia.
I PROBABLY GO DANCING FIVE NIGHTS A WEEK. THERE ARE A LOT OF DRUGS, BUT IT'S COOL.
BE CAREFUL.
OF COURSE.
So much time had passed that it was like we were different people, especially now that I wasn't drinking, but I figured that in time we would be close again.
HI, SAL, IT'S JONATHAN. GIVE A CALL WHEN YOU CAN.
I called him a few days later and he didn't call back. So then two weeks after that I called him again. Then I called him a month later, and then two months after that.
Always I would leave some tepid message: "Just calling to say hi."
He never once called me back.

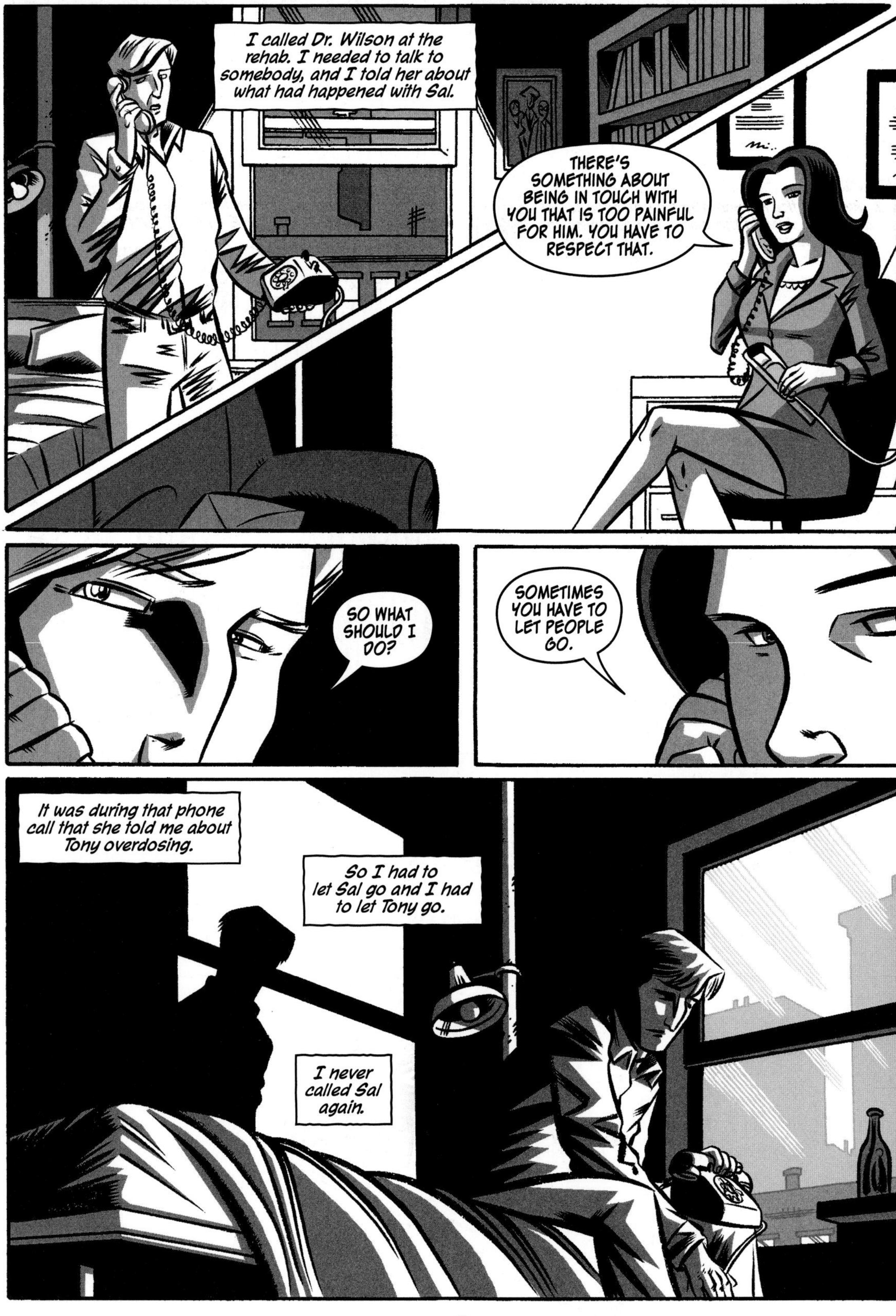
I called Dr. Wilson at the rehab. I needed to talk to somebody, and I told her about what had happened with Sal.
THERE'S SOMETHING ABOUT BEING IN TOUCH WITH YOU THAT IS TOO PAINFUL FOR HIM. YOU HAVE TO RESPECT THAT.
SO WHAT SHOULD I DO?
SOMETIMES YOU HAVE TO LET PEOPLE GO.
It was during that phone call that she told me about Tony overdosing.
So I had to let Sal go and I had to let Tony go.
I never called Sal again.

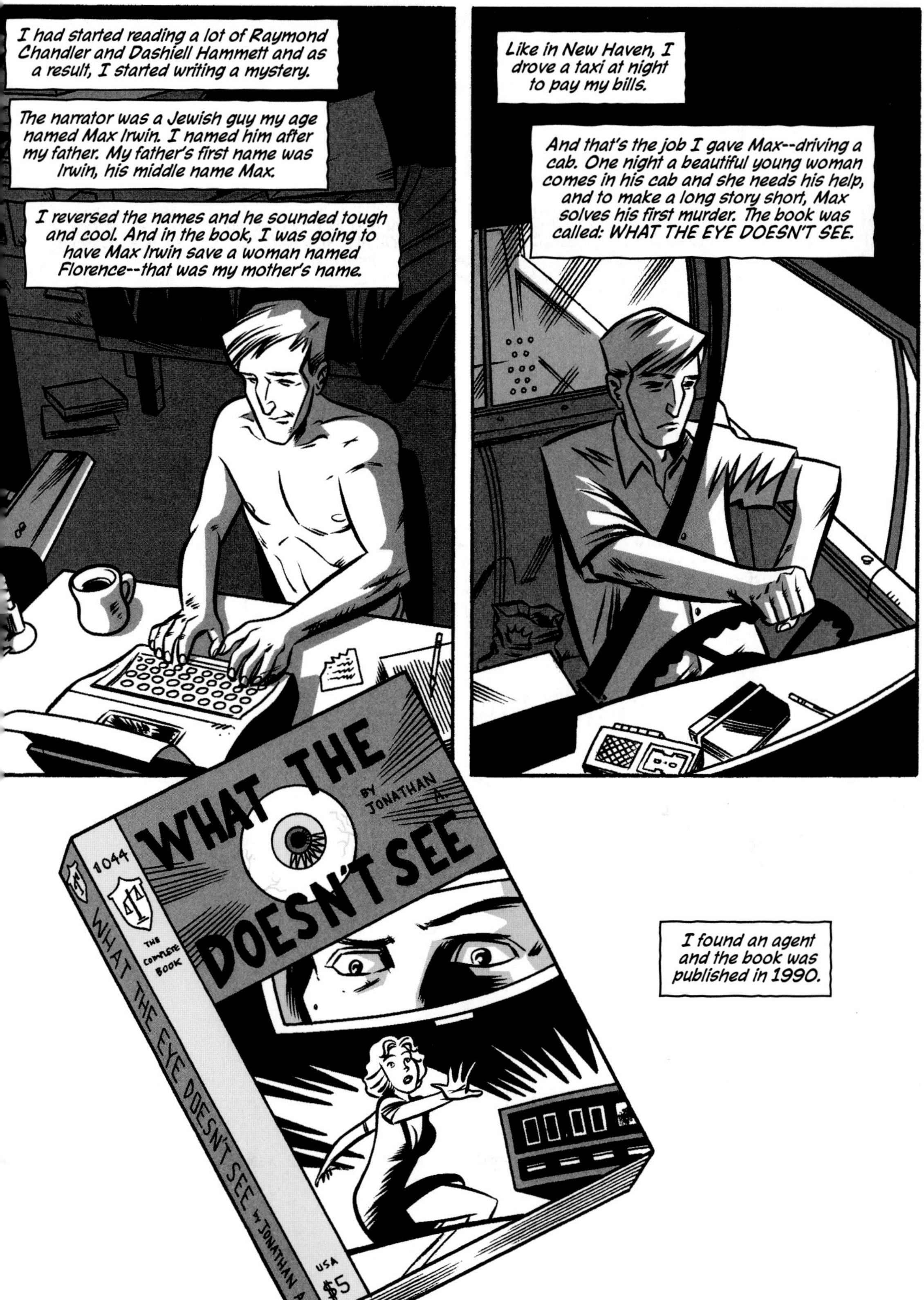
I had started reading a lot of Raymond Chandler and Dashiell Hammett and as a result, I started writing a mystery.
The narrator was a Jewish guy my age named Max Irwin. I named him after my father. My father's first name was Irwin, his middle name Max.
I reversed the names and he sounded tough and cool. And in the book, I was going to have Max Irwin save a woman named Florence--that was my mother's name.
Like in New Haven, I drove a taxi at night to pay my bills.
And that's the job I gave Max--driving a cab. One night a beautiful young woman comes in his cab and she needs his help, and to make a long story short, Max solves his first murder. The book was called: WHAT THE EYE DOESN'T SEE.
WHAT THE
DOESN'T SEE
BY JONATHAN A.
1044
THE COMPLETE BOOK
WHAT THE EYE DOESN'T SEE by JONATHAN A.
USA
$5
00.00
I found an agent and the book was published in 1990.

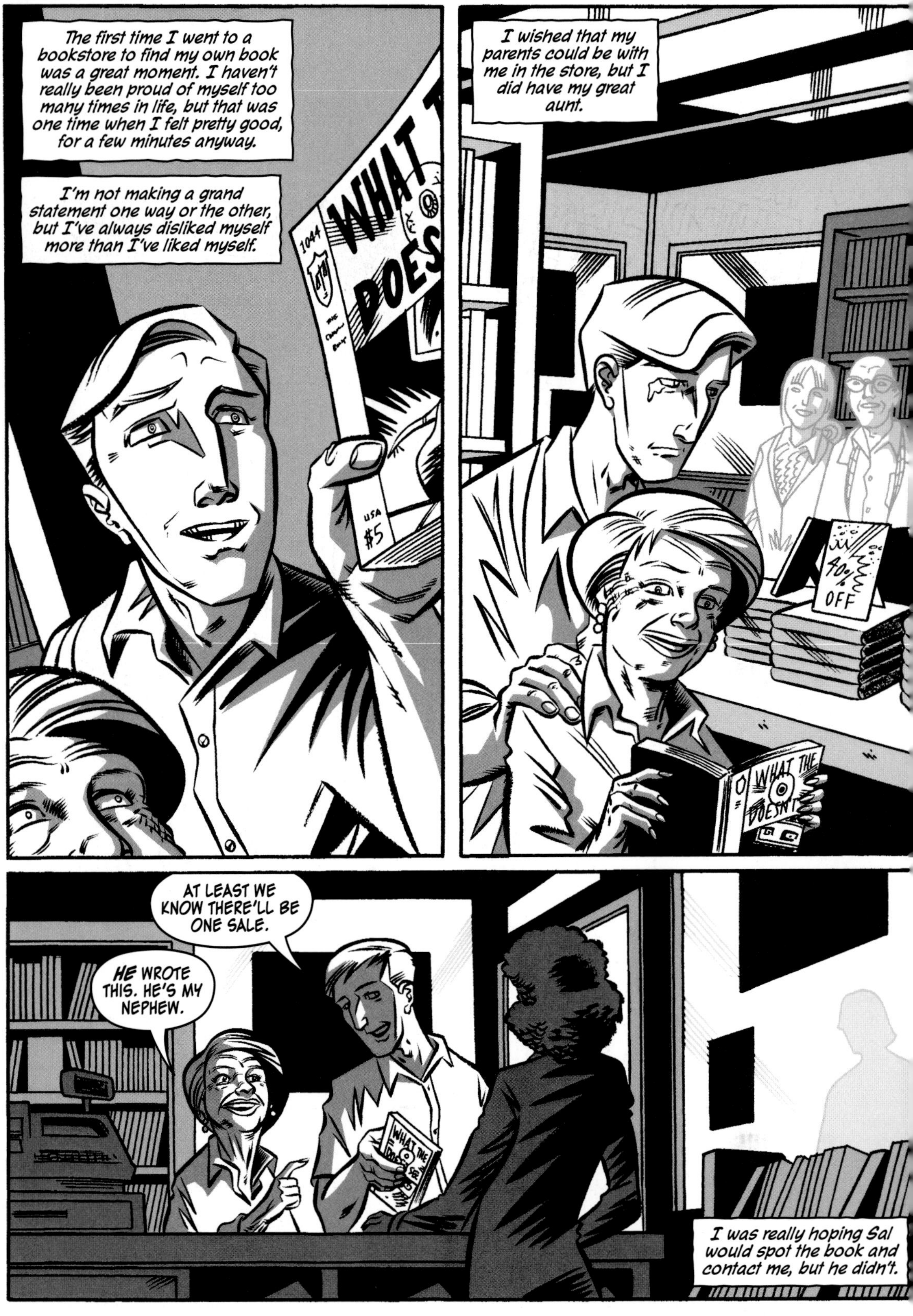
The first time I went to a bookstore to find my own book was a great moment. I haven't really been proud of myself too many times in life, but that was one time when I felt pretty good, for a few minutes anyway.
I'm not making a grand statement one way or the other, but I've always disliked myself more than I've liked myself.
USA $5
I wished that my parents could be with me in the store, but I did have my great aunt.
40% OFF
AT LEAST WE KNOW THERE'LL BE ONE SALE.
HE WROTE THIS. HE'S MY NEPHEW.
I was really hoping Sal would spot the book and contact me, but he didn't.

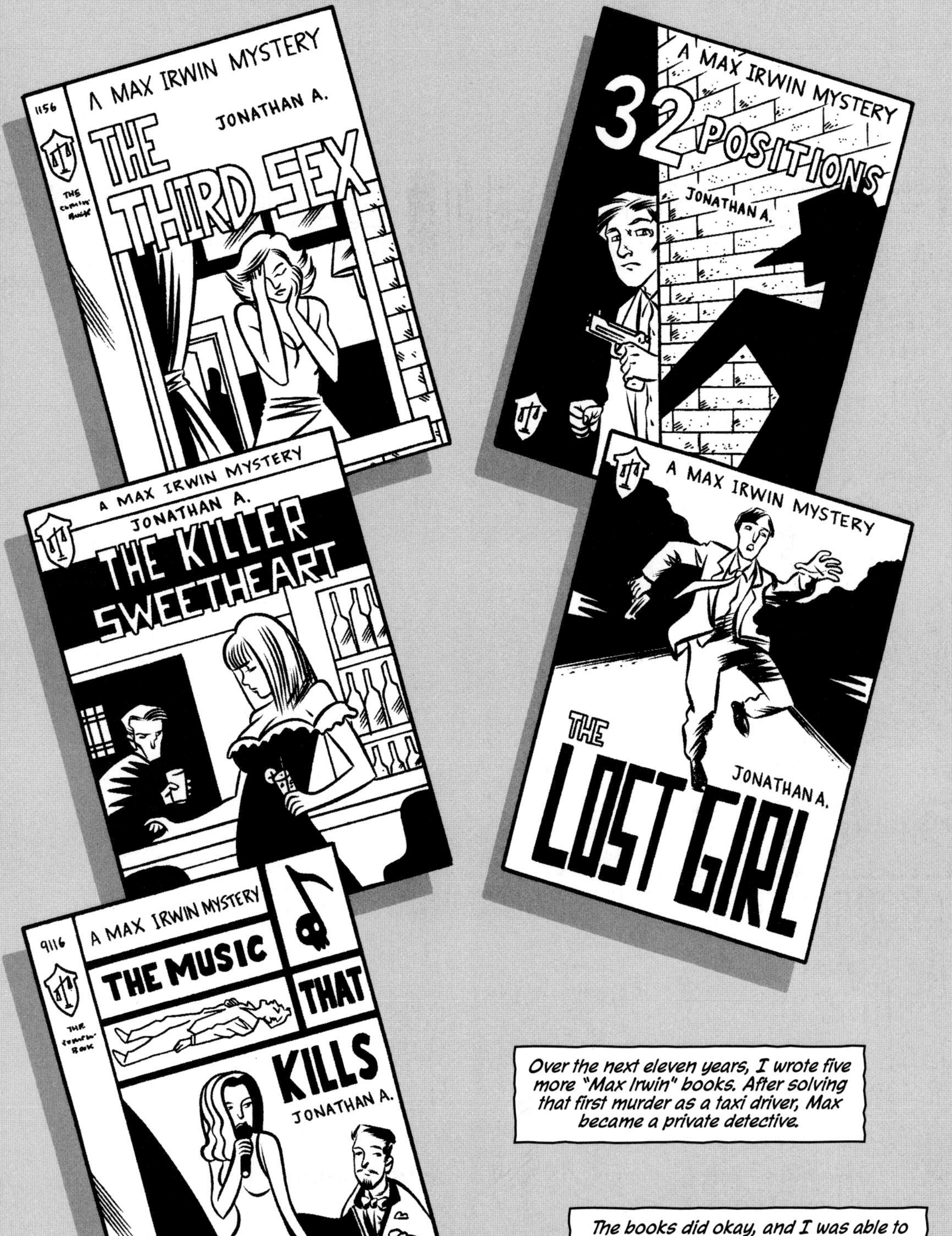
A MAX IRWIN MYSTERY
1156
JONATHAN A.
THE THIRD SEX
A MAX IRWIN MYSTERY
32 POSITIONS
JONATHAN A.
A MAX IRWIN MYSTERY
JONATHAN A.
THE KILLER SWEETHEART
A MAX IRWIN MYSTERY
THE LOST GIRL
JONATHAN A.
A MAX IRWIN MYSTERY
9116
THE MUSIC THAT KILLS
JONATHAN A.
USA
$5
Over the next eleven years, I wrote five more "Max Irwin" books. After solving that first murder as a taxi driver, Max became a private detective.
The books did okay, and I was able to make a living. I also did some freelance journalism, and once in a while I taught a writing class at the New School.

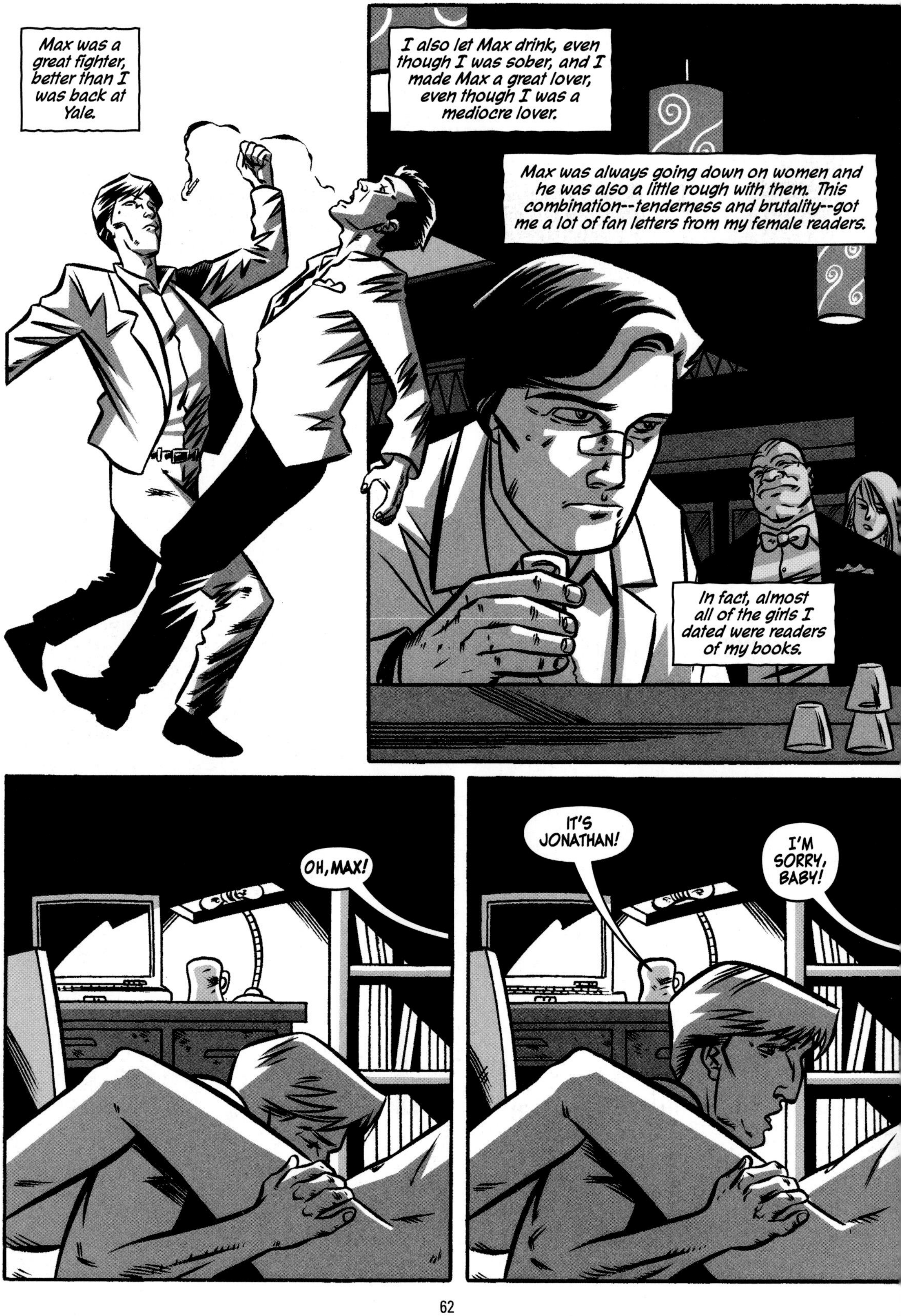
Max was a great fighter, better than I was back at Yale.
I also let Max drink, even though I was sober, and I made Max a great lover, even though I was a mediocre lover.
Max was always going down on women and he was also a little rough with them. This combination--tenderness and brutality--got me a lot of fan letters from my female readers.
In fact, almost all of the girls I dated were readers of my books.
OH, MAX!
IT'S JONATHAN!
I'M SORRY, BABY!

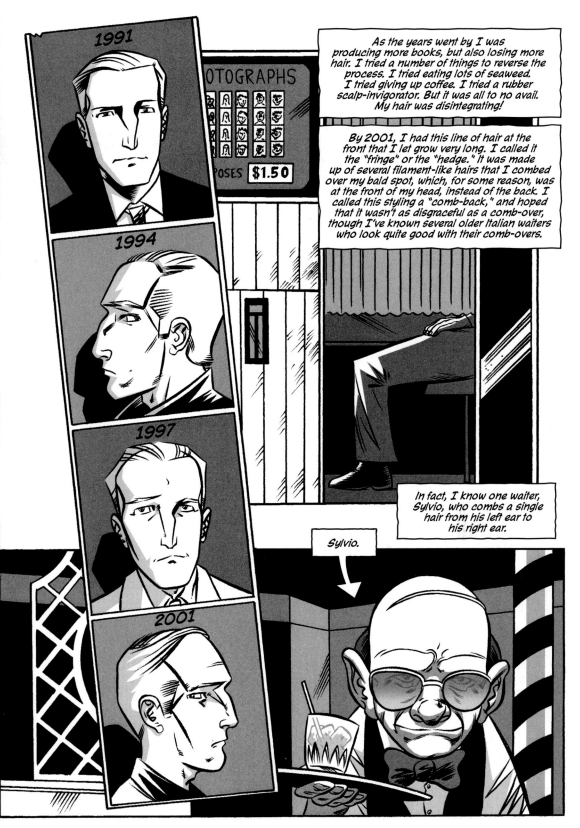

1991

1994

1997

2001

OTOGRAPHS
POSES $1.50

As the years went by I was producing more books, but also losing more hair. I tried a number of things to reverse the process. I tried eating lots of seaweed. I tried giving up coffee. I tried a rubber scalp-invigorator. But it was all to no avail. My hair was disintegrating!

By 2001, I had this line of hair at the front that I let grow very long. I called it the "fringe" or the "hedge." It was made up of several filament-like hairs that I combed over my bald spot, which, for some reason, was at the front of my head, instead of the back. I called this styling a "comb-back," and hoped that it wasn't as disgraceful as a comb-over, though I've known several older Italian waiters who look quite good with their comb-overs.

In fact, I know one waiter, Sylvio, who combs a single hair from his left ear to his right ear.

Sylvio.

As the years went by there were four constants in my life--writing, not drinking, worrying about my hair, and visiting my Great Aunt Sadie on Sundays. We'd have lunch and play cards. We did this for years.

In 1989, when I was working on my first novel, WHAT THE EYE DOESN'T SEE, she was 79 and she had one of her breasts removed.

DO YOU WANT TO SEE THE SCAR?

OKAY...

I'm not sure why I wanted to see it--morbid curiosity, I guess.

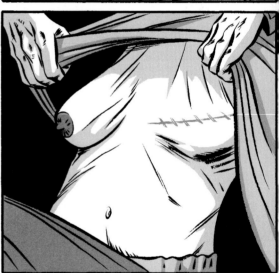

THIS IS LIFE. YOU CAN'T BE SQUEAMISH.

She was trying to make me tough, but it didn't work.

My Great Aunt and I were very close, but sometimes we were too close.

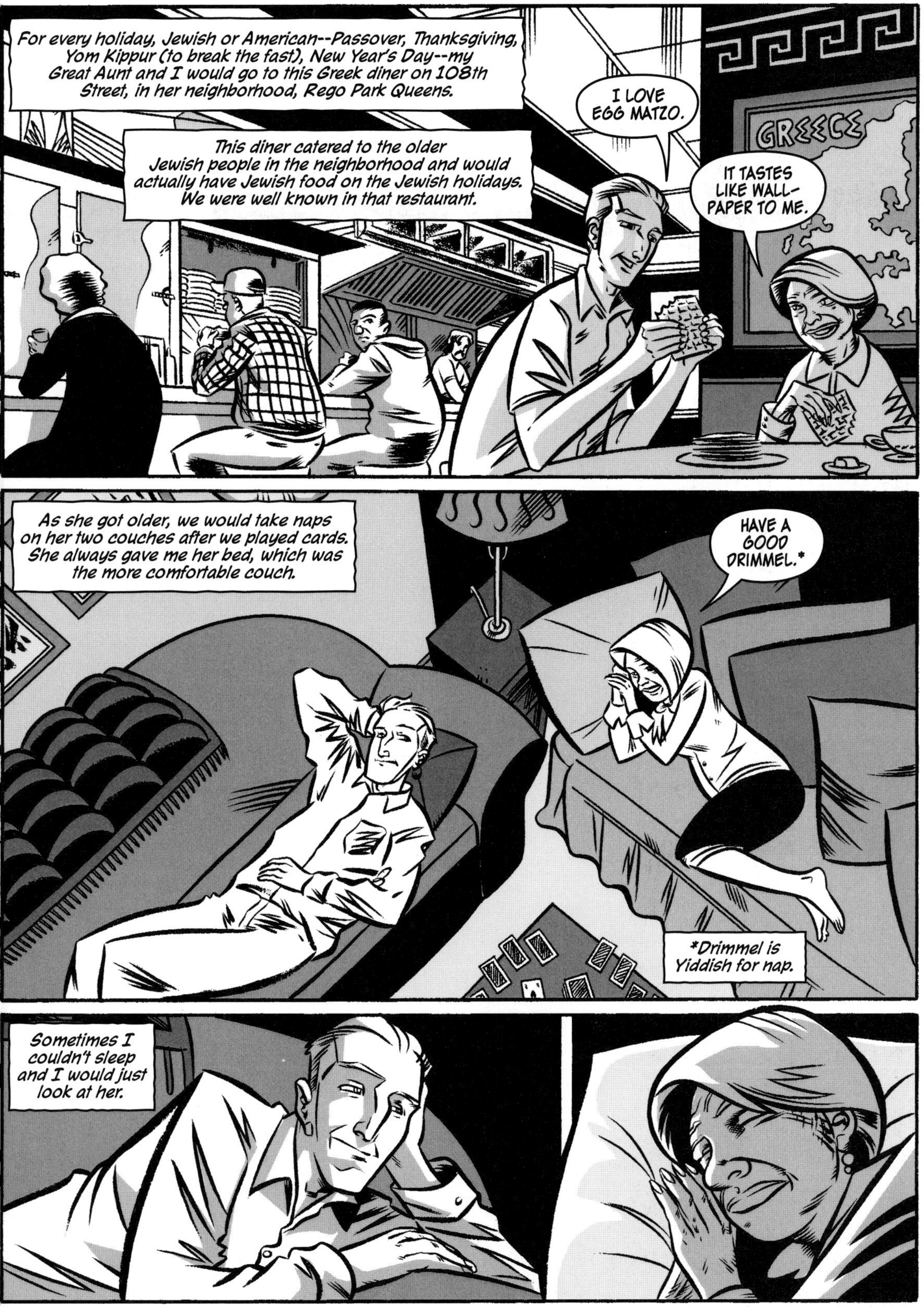
For every holiday, Jewish or American--Passover, Thanksgiving, Yom Kippur (to break the fast), New Year's Day--my Great Aunt and I would go to this Greek diner on 108th Street, in her neighborhood, Rego Park Queens.
This diner catered to the older Jewish people in the neighborhood and would actually have Jewish food on the Jewish holidays. We were well known in that restaurant.
I LOVE EGG MATZO.
GREECE
IT TASTES LIKE WALL-PAPER TO ME.
As she got older, we would take naps on her two couches after we played cards. She always gave me her bed, which was the more comfortable couch.
HAVE A GOOD DRIMMEL.*
*Drimmel is Yiddish for nap.
Sometimes I couldn't sleep and I would just look at her.

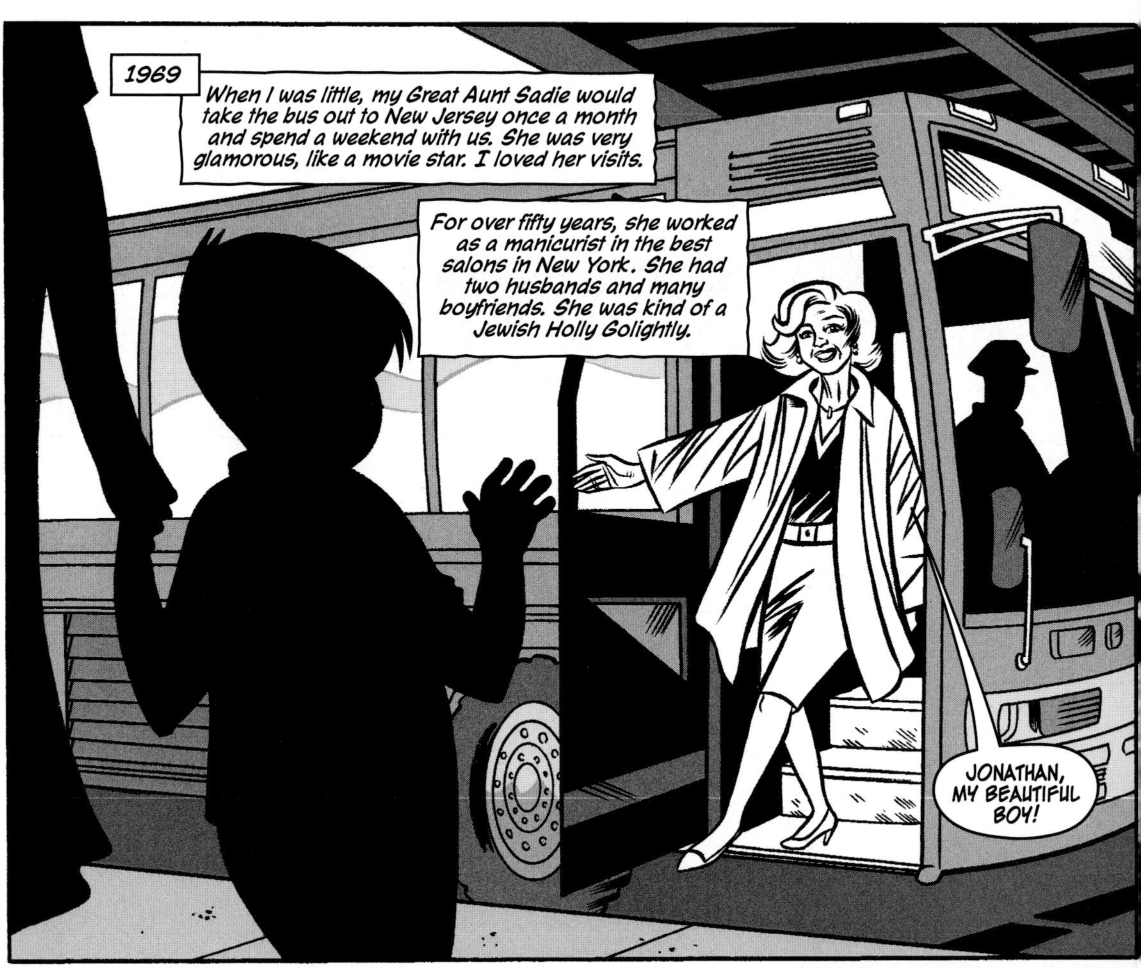
1969
When I was little, my Great Aunt Sadie would take the bus out to New Jersey once a month and spend a weekend with us. She was very glamorous, like a movie star. I loved her visits.
For over fifty years, she worked as a manicurist in the best salons in New York. She had two husbands and many boyfriends. She was kind of a Jewish Holly Golightly.
JONATHAN, MY BEAUTIFUL BOY!

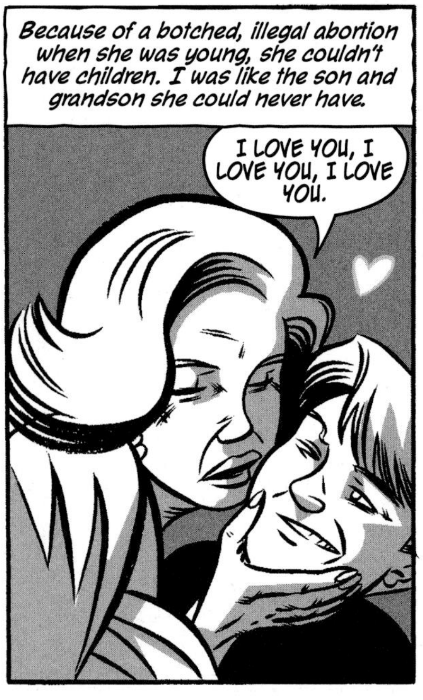
Because of a botched, illegal abortion when she was young, she couldn't have children. I was like the son and grandson she could never have.
I LOVE YOU, I LOVE YOU, I LOVE YOU.

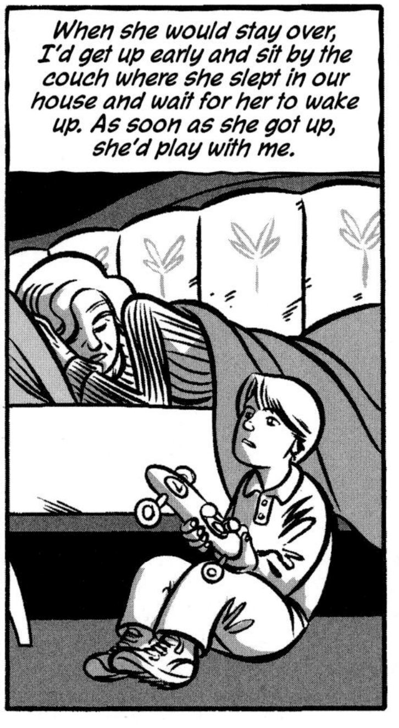
When she would stay over, I'd get up early and sit by the couch where she slept in our house and wait for her to wake up. As soon as she got up, she'd play with me.

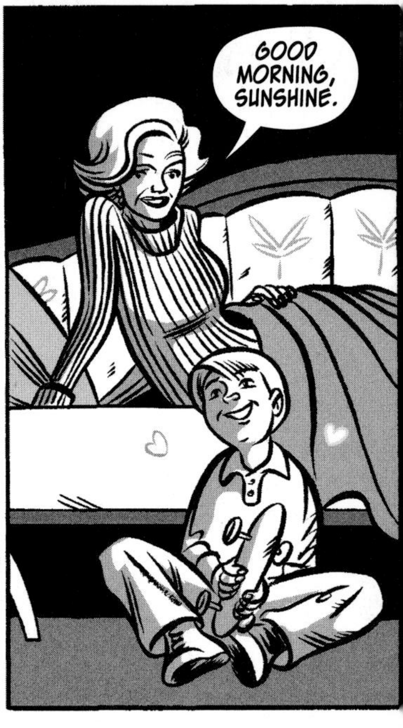
GOOD MORNING, SUNSHINE.

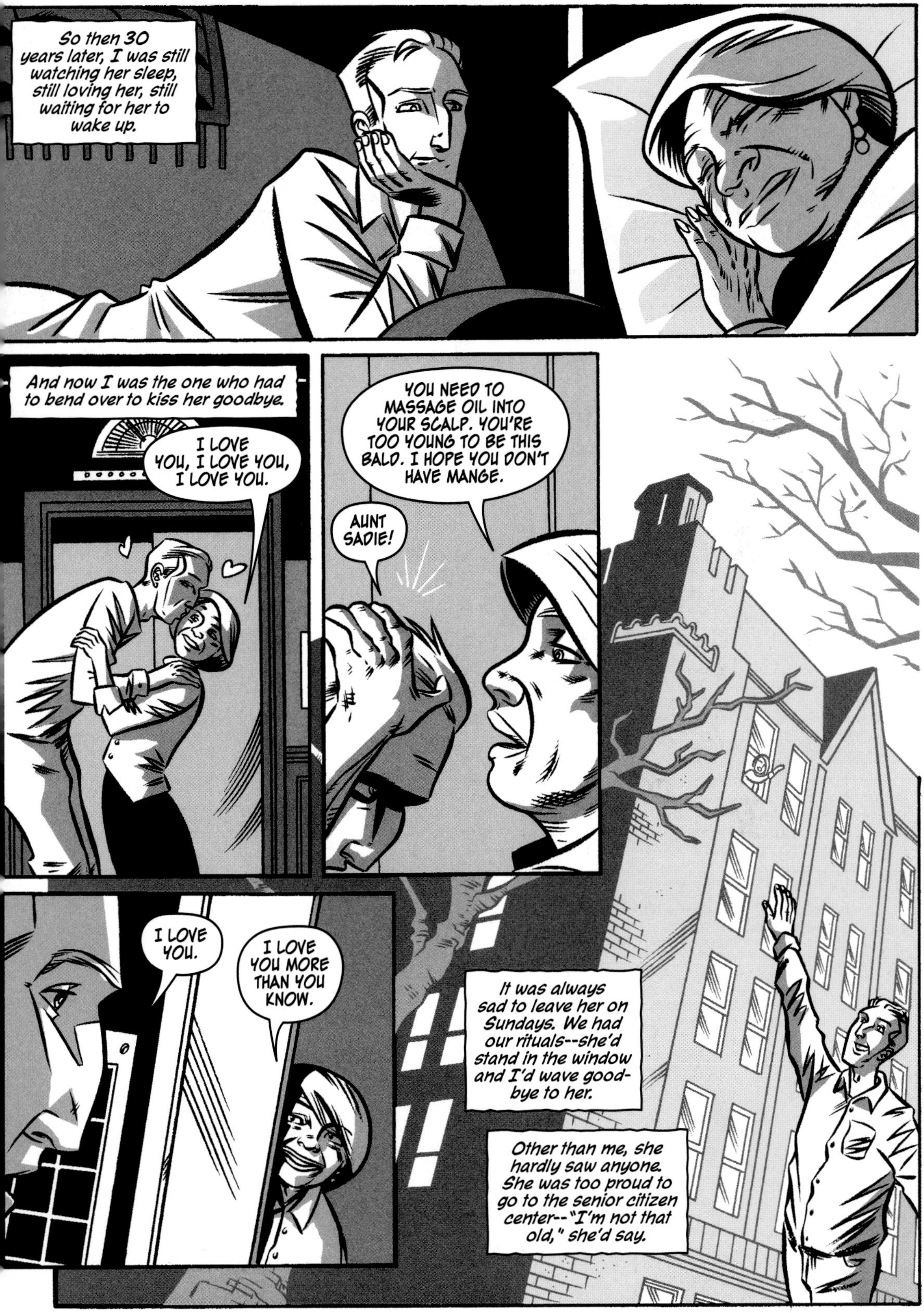
So then 30 years later, I was still watching her sleep, still loving her, still waiting for her to wake up.
And now I was the one who had to bend over to kiss her goodbye.
I LOVE YOU, I LOVE YOU, I LOVE YOU.
YOU NEED TO MASSAGE OIL INTO YOUR SCALP. YOU'RE TOO YOUNG TO BE THIS BALD. I HOPE YOU DON'T HAVE MANGE.
AUNT SADIE!
I LOVE YOU.
I LOVE YOU MORE THAN YOU KNOW.
It was always sad to leave her on Sundays. We had our rituals--she'd stand in the window and I'd wave goodbye to her.
Other than me, she hardly saw anyone. She was too proud to go to the senior citizen center--"I'm not that old," she'd say.

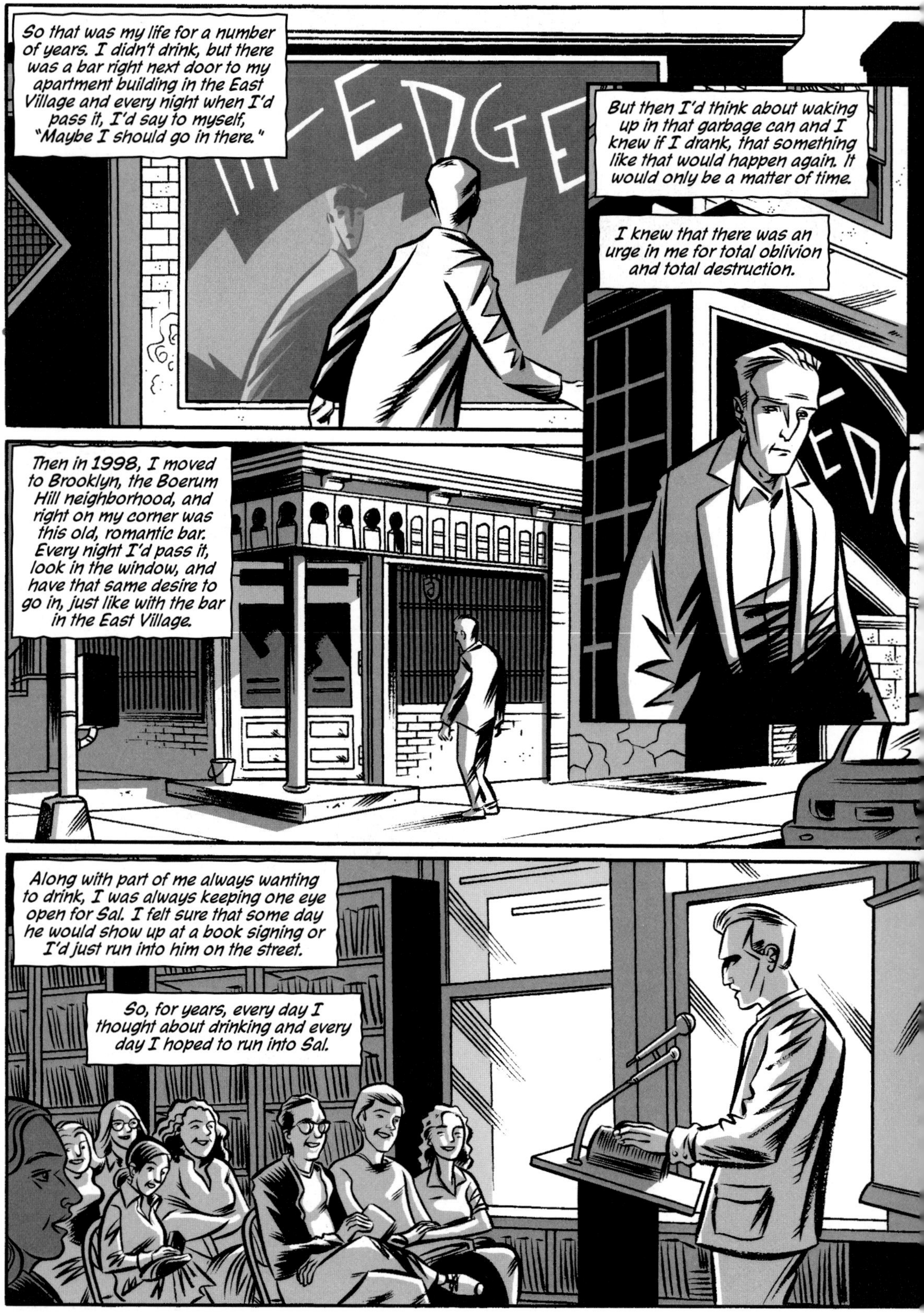
So that was my life for a number of years. I didn't drink, but there was a bar right next door to my apartment building in the East Village and every night when I'd pass it, I'd say to myself, "Maybe I should go in there."
But then I'd think about waking up in that garbage can and I knew if I drank, that something like that would happen again. It would only be a matter of time.
I knew that there was an urge in me for total oblivion and total destruction.
Then in 1998, I moved to Brooklyn, the Boerum Hill neighborhood, and right on my corner was this old, romantic bar. Every night I'd pass it, look in the window, and have that same desire to go in, just like with the bar in the East Village.
Along with part of me always wanting to drink, I was always keeping one eye open for Sal. I felt sure that some day he would show up at a book signing or I'd just run into him on the street.
So, for years, every day I thought about drinking and every day I hoped to run into Sal.

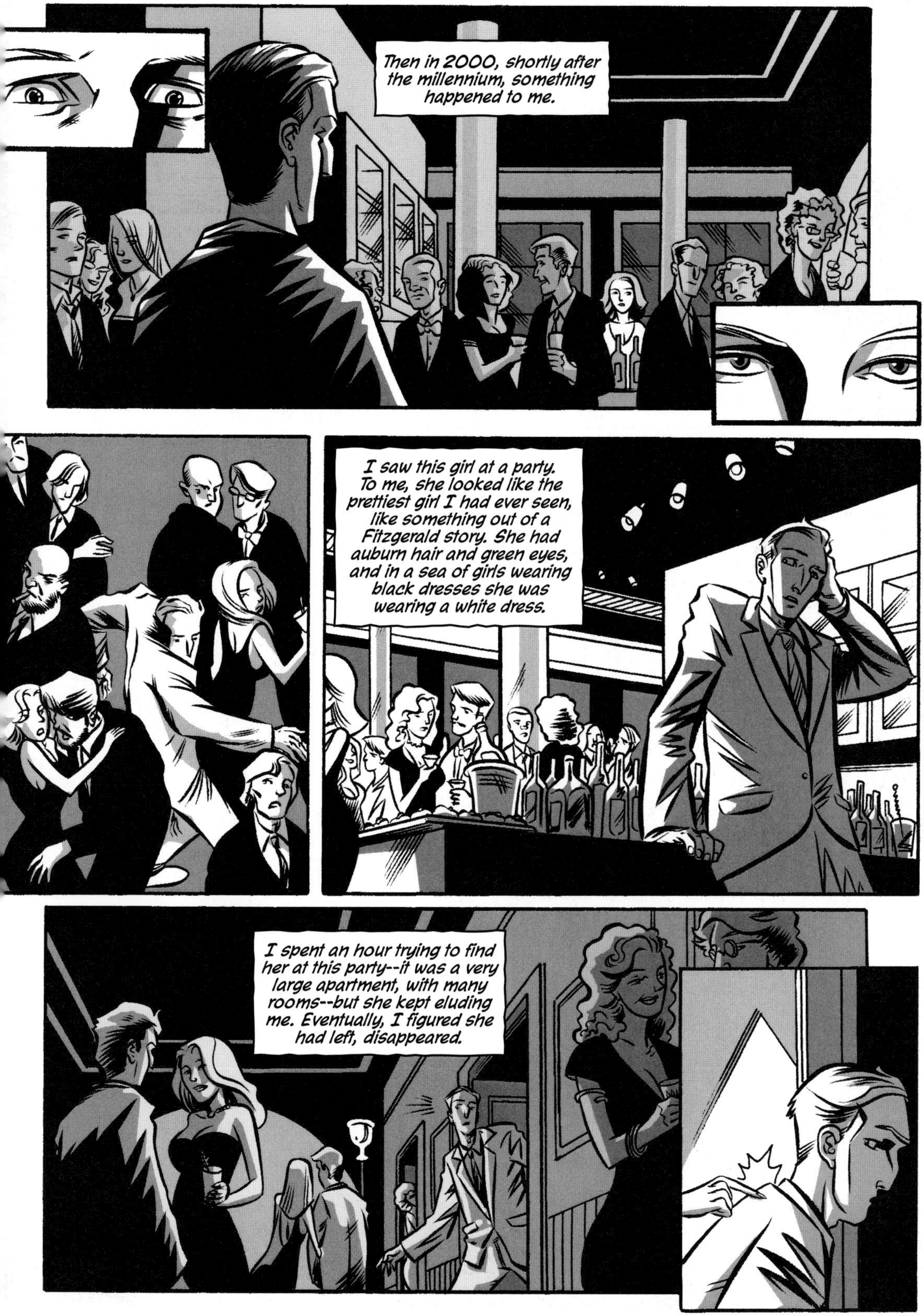
Then in 2000, shortly after the millennium, something happened to me.
I saw this girl at a party. To me, she looked like the prettiest girl I had ever seen, like something out of a Fitzgerald story. She had auburn hair and green eyes, and in a sea of girls wearing black dresses she was wearing a white dress.
I spent an hour trying to find her at this party--it was a very large apartment, with many rooms--but she kept eluding me. Eventually, I figured she had left, disappeared.

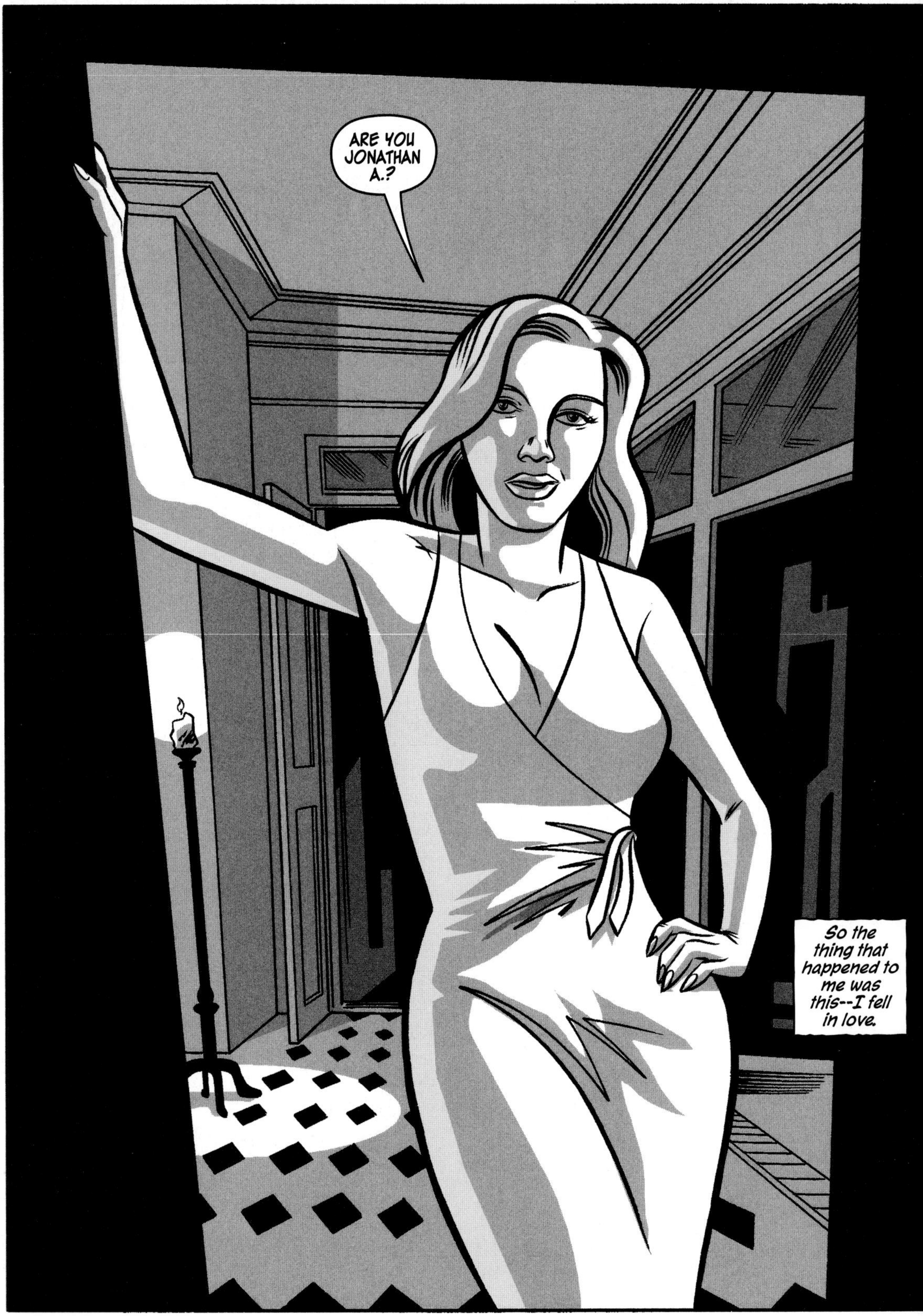
ARE YOU JONATHAN A.?
So the thing that happened to me was this--I fell in love.

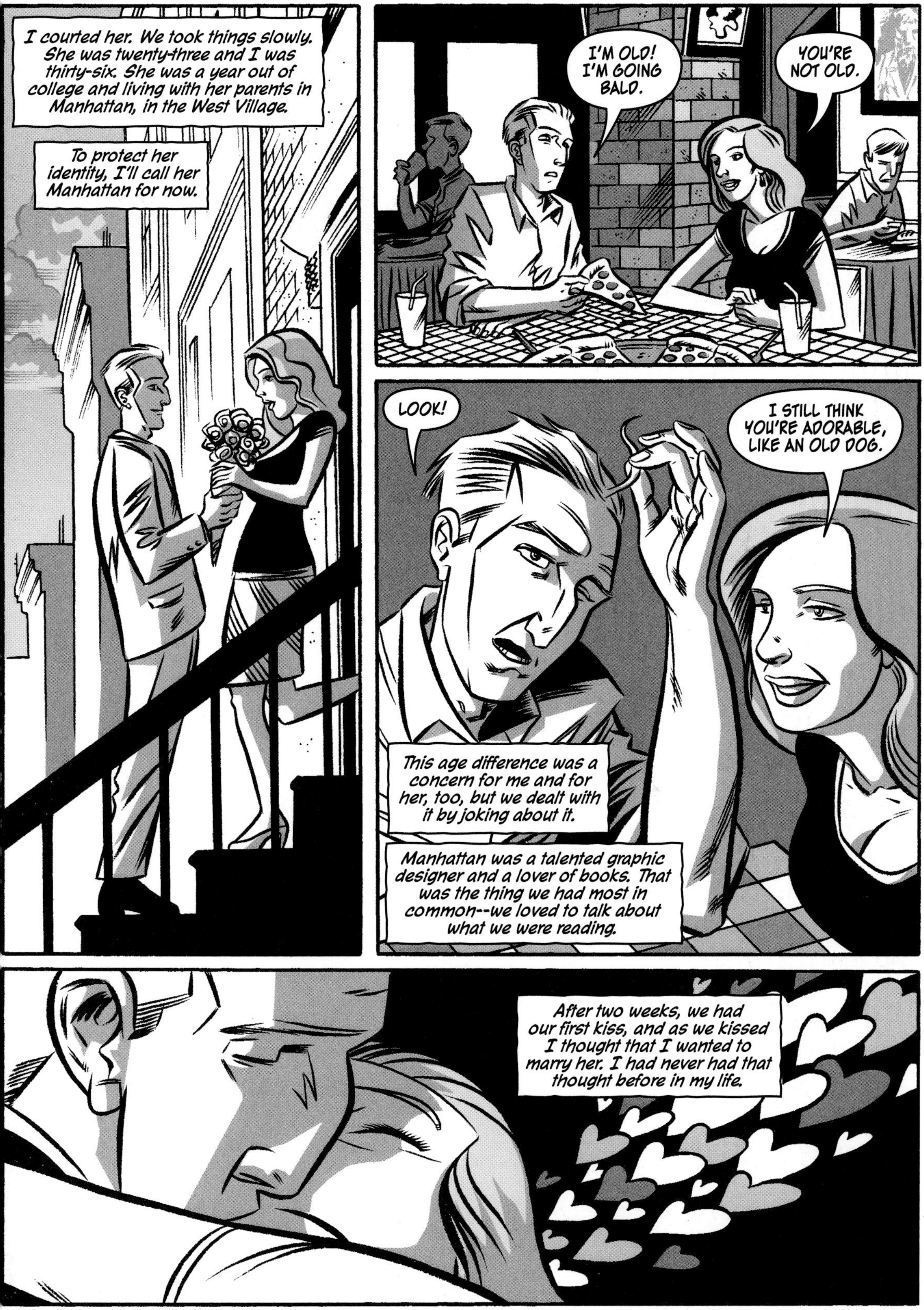
I courted her. We took things slowly. She was twenty-three and I was thirty-six. She was a year out of college and living with her parents in Manhattan, in the West Village.
To protect her identity, I'll call her Manhattan for now.
I'M OLD! I'M GOING BALD.
YOU'RE NOT OLD.
LOOK!
I STILL THINK YOU'RE ADORABLE, LIKE AN OLD DOG.
This age difference was a concern for me and for her, too, but we dealt with it by joking about it.
Manhattan was a talented graphic designer and a lover of books. That was the thing we had most in common--we loved to talk about what we were reading.
After two weeks, we had our first kiss, and as we kissed I thought that I wanted to marry her. I had never had that thought before in my life.

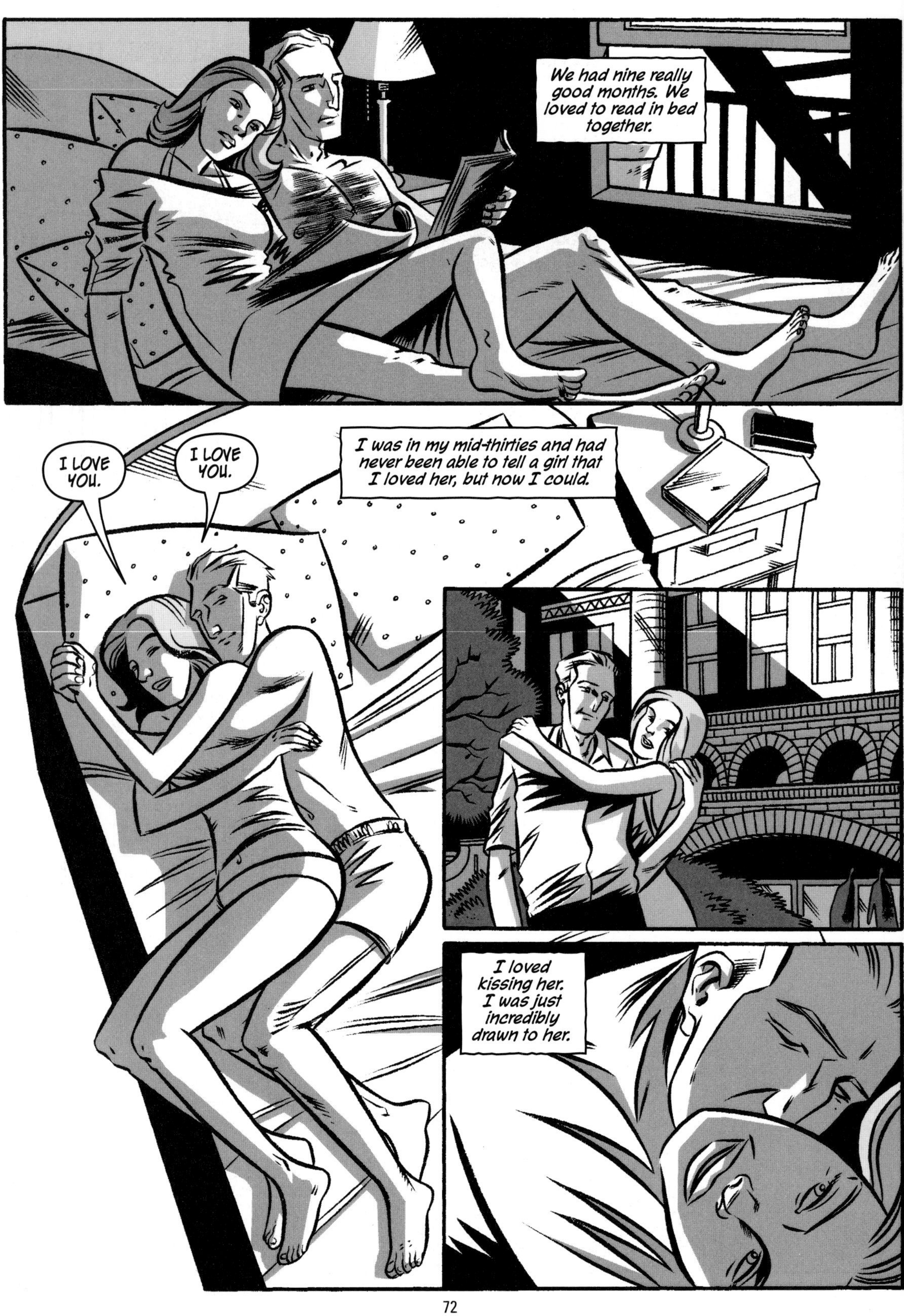
We had nine really good months. We loved to read in bed together.
I was in my mid-thirties and had never been able to tell a girl that I loved her, but now I could.
I LOVE YOU.
I LOVE YOU.
I loved kissing her. I was just incredibly drawn to her.

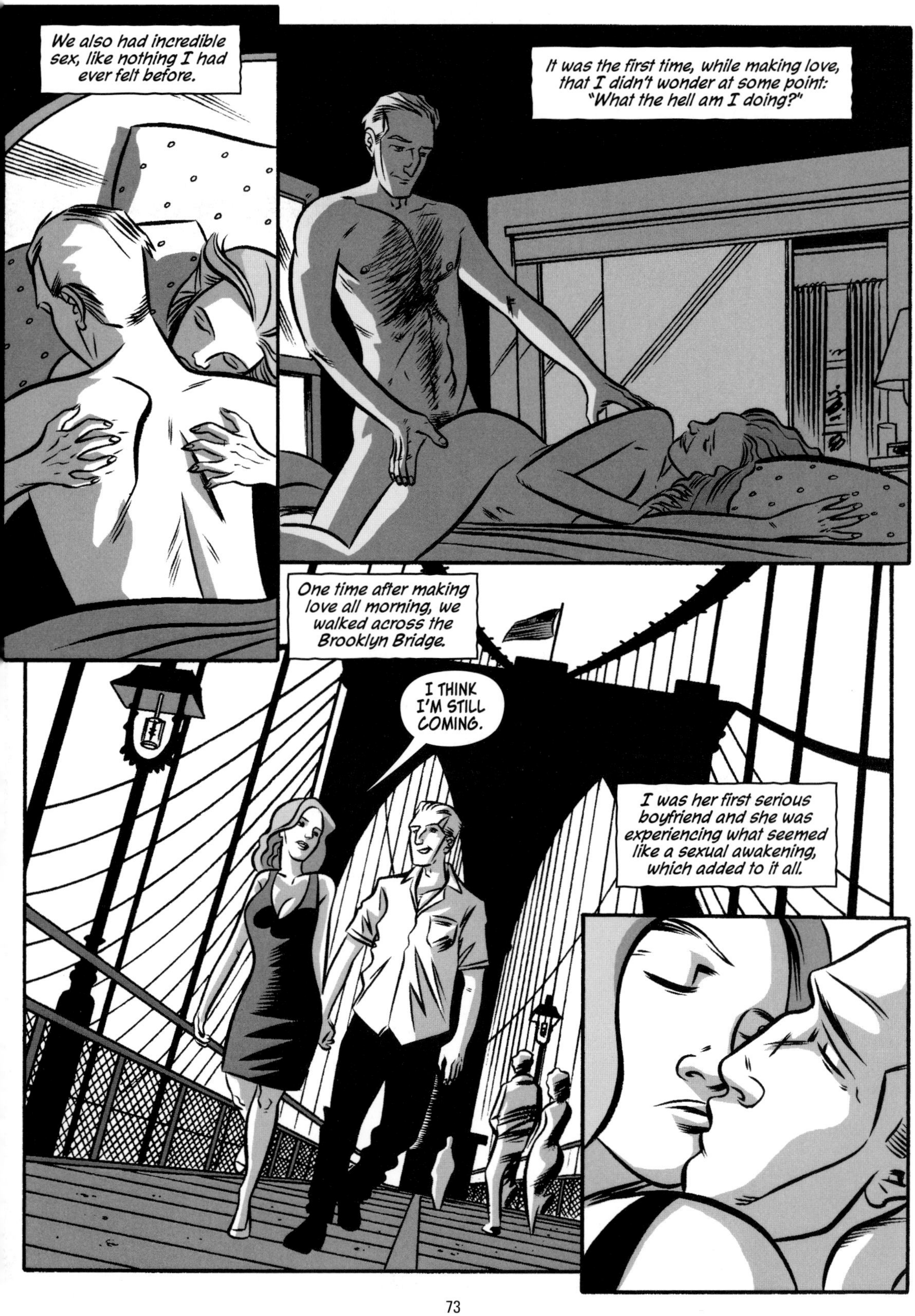
We also had incredible sex, like nothing I had ever felt before.
It was the first time, while making love, that I didn't wonder at some point: "What the hell am I doing?"
One time after making love all morning, we walked across the Brooklyn Bridge.
I THINK I'M STILL COMING.
I was her first serious boyfriend and she was experiencing what seemed like a sexual awakening, which added to it all.

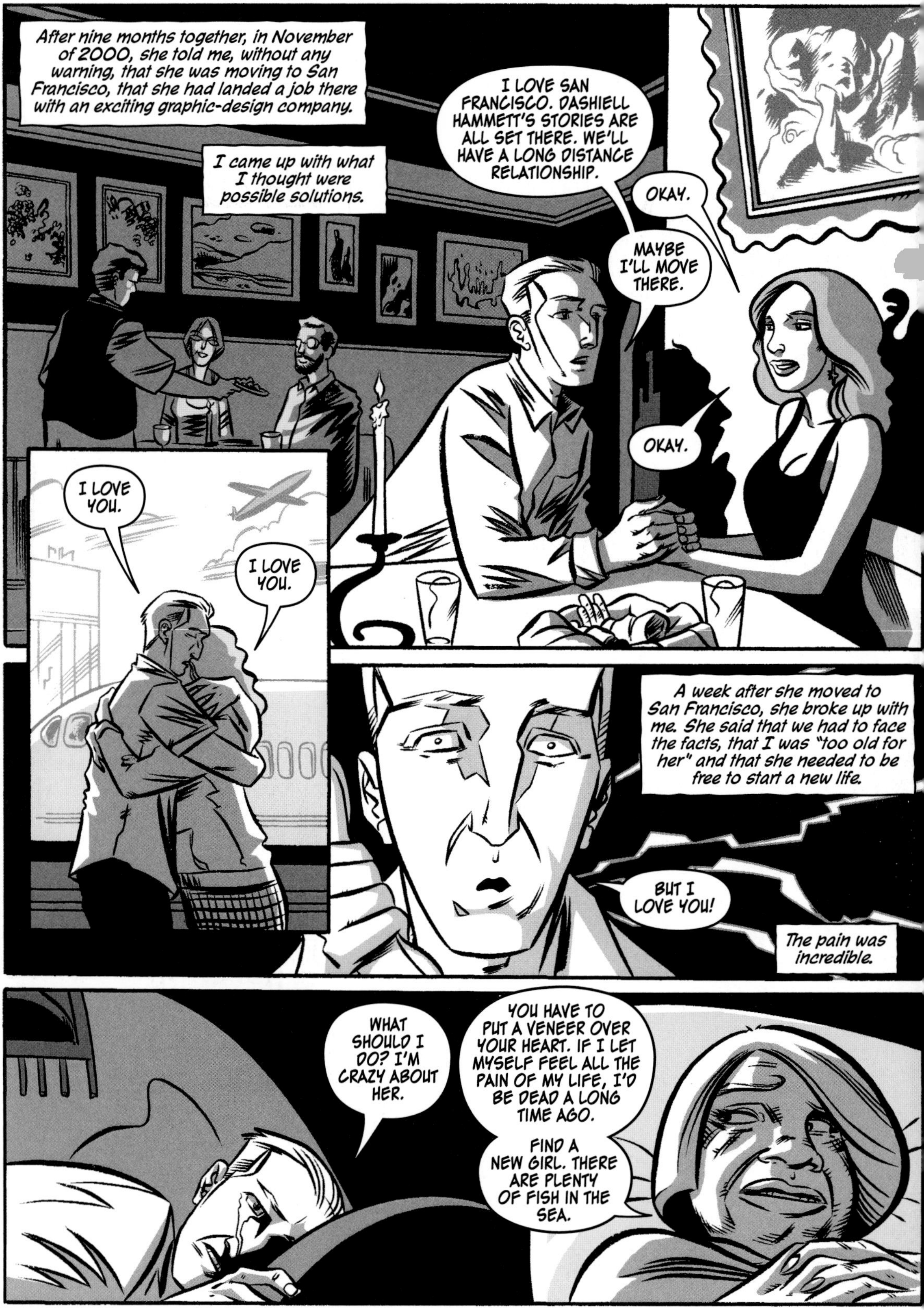
After nine months together, in November of 2000, she told me, without any warning, that she was moving to San Francisco, that she had landed a job there with an exciting graphic-design company.
I came up with what I thought were possible solutions.
I LOVE SAN FRANCISCO. DASHIELL HAMMETT'S STORIES ARE ALL SET THERE. WE'LL HAVE A LONG DISTANCE RELATIONSHIP.
OKAY.
MAYBE I'LL MOVE THERE.
OKAY.
I LOVE YOU.
I LOVE YOU.
A week after she moved to San Francisco, she broke up with me. She said that we had to face the facts, that I was "too old for her" and that she needed to be free to start a new life.
BUT I LOVE YOU!
The pain was incredible.
WHAT SHOULD I DO? I'M CRAZY ABOUT HER.
YOU HAVE TO PUT A VENEER OVER YOUR HEART. IF I LET MYSELF FEEL ALL THE PAIN OF MY LIFE, I'D BE DEAD A LONG TIME AGO.
FIND A NEW GIRL. THERE ARE PLENTY OF FISH IN THE SEA.

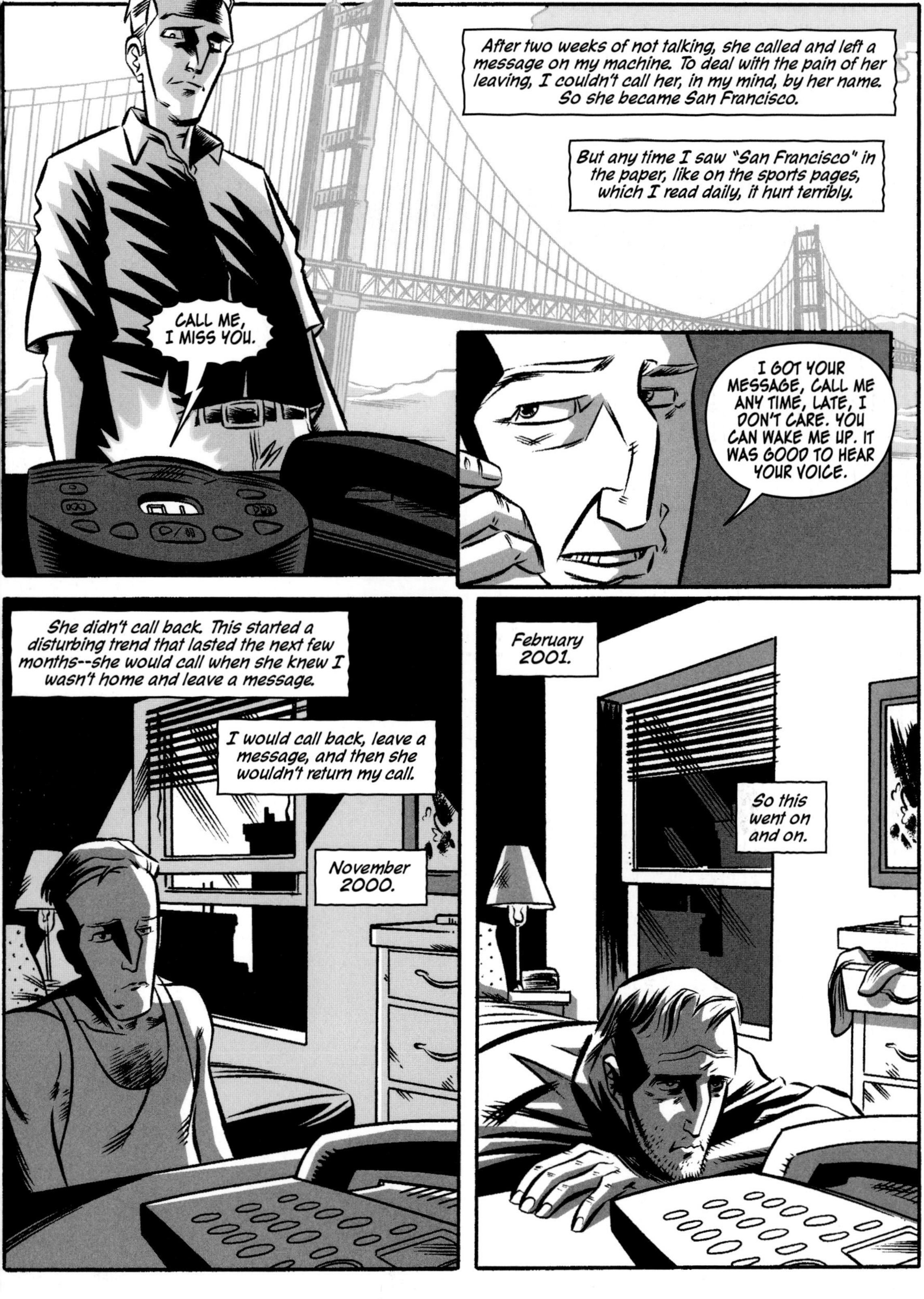
After two weeks of not talking, she called and left a message on my machine. To deal with the pain of her leaving, I couldn't call her, in my mind, by her name. So she became San Francisco.
But any time I saw "San Francisco" in the paper, like on the sports pages, which I read daily, it hurt terribly.
CALL ME, I MISS YOU.
I GOT YOUR MESSAGE, CALL ME ANY TIME, LATE, I DON'T CARE. YOU CAN WAKE ME UP. IT WAS GOOD TO HEAR YOUR VOICE.
She didn't call back. This started a disturbing trend that lasted the next few months--she would call when she knew I wasn't home and leave a message.
I would call back, leave a message, and then she wouldn't return my call.
November 2000.
February 2001.
So this went on and on.

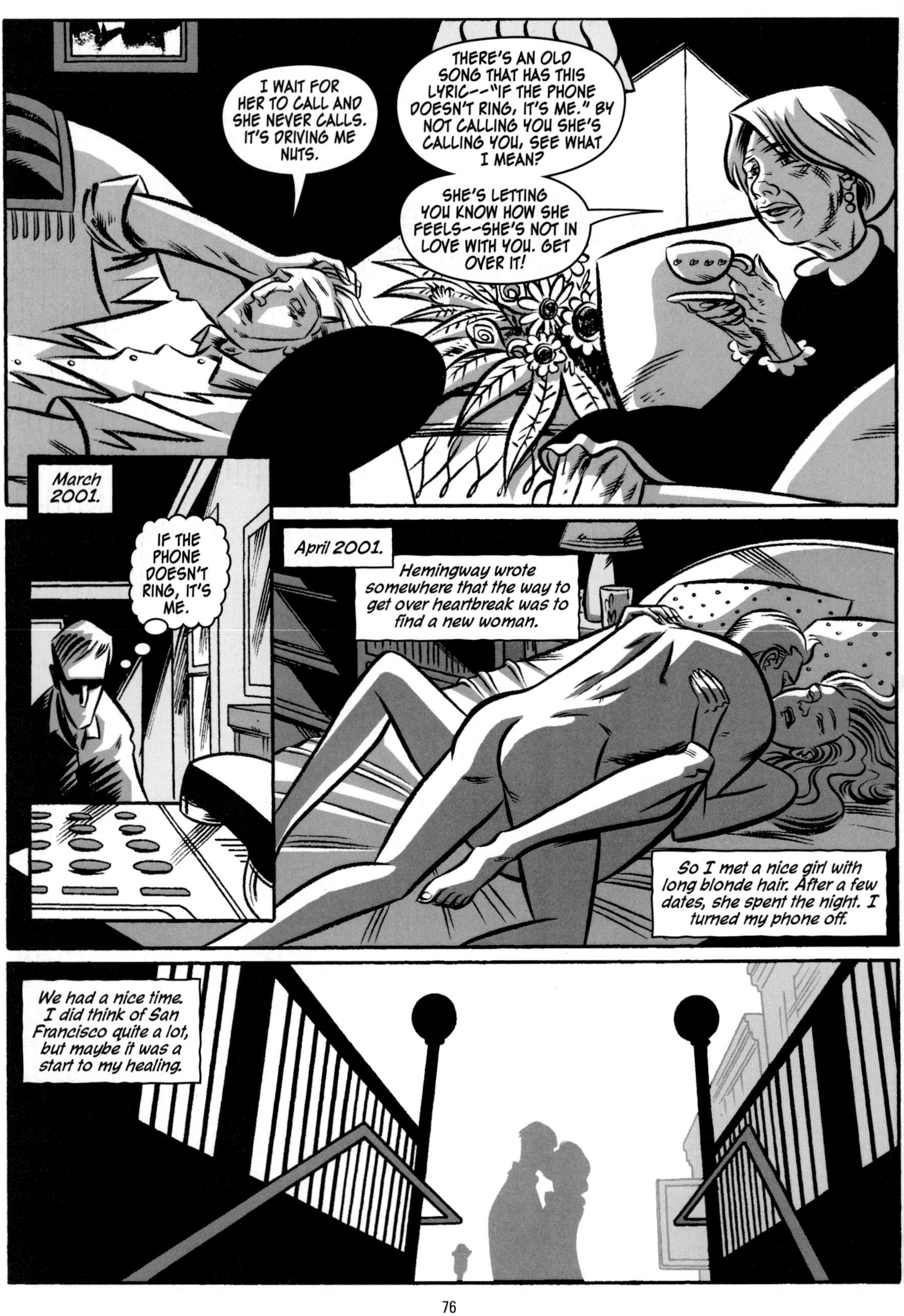
I WAIT FOR HER TO CALL AND SHE NEVER CALLS. IT'S DRIVING ME NUTS.
THERE'S AN OLD SONG THAT HAS THIS LYRIC--"IF THE PHONE DOESN'T RING, IT'S ME." BY NOT CALLING YOU SHE'S CALLING YOU, SEE WHAT I MEAN?
SHE'S LETTING YOU KNOW HOW SHE FEELS--SHE'S NOT IN LOVE WITH YOU. GET OVER IT!
March 2001.
IF THE PHONE DOESN'T RING, IT'S ME.
April 2001.
Hemingway wrote somewhere that the way to get over heartbreak was to find a new woman.
So I met a nice girl with long blonde hair. After a few dates, she spent the night. I turned my phone off.
We had a nice time. I did think of San Francisco quite a lot, but maybe it was a start to my healing.

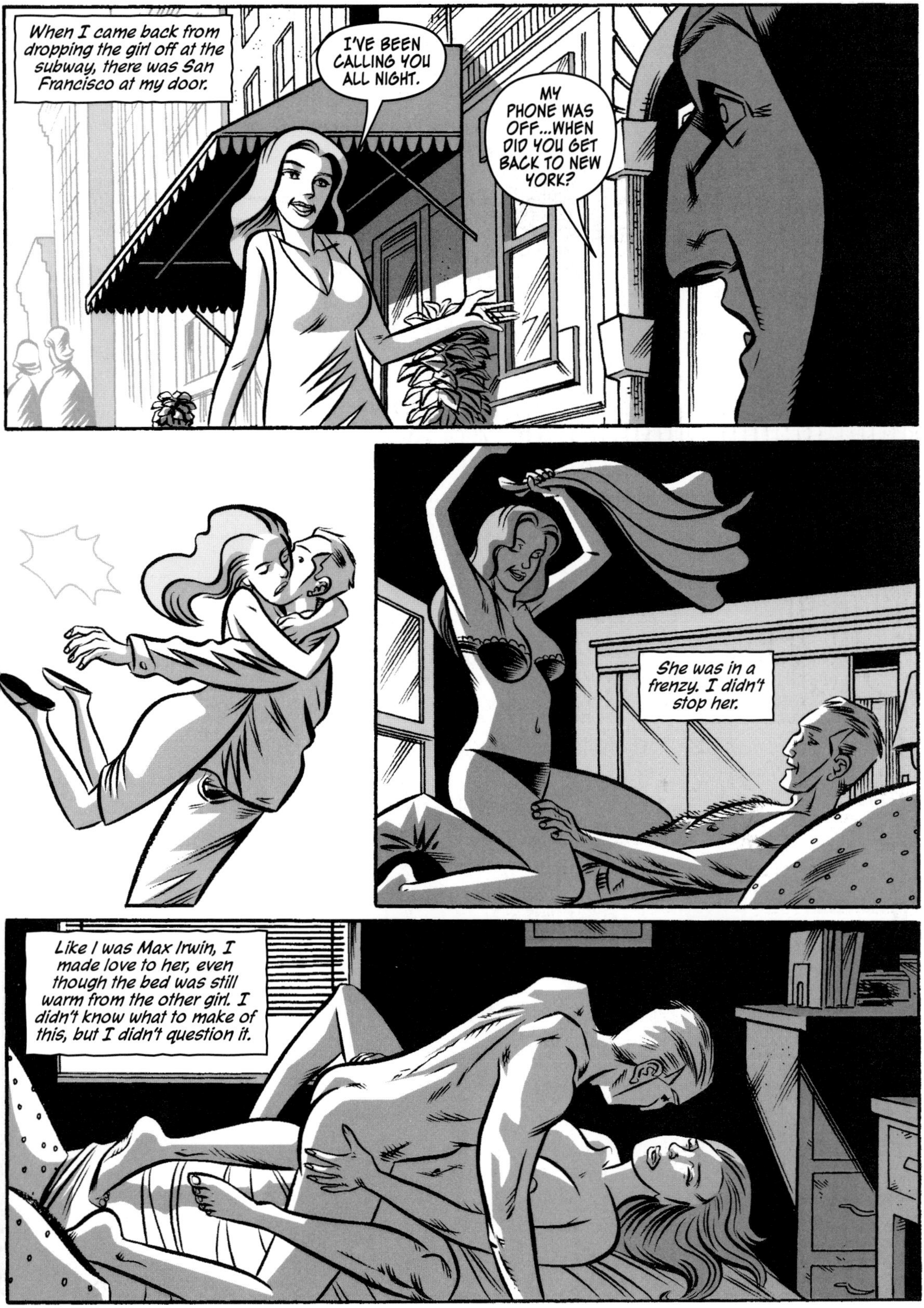

When I came back from dropping the girl off at the subway, there was San Francisco at my door.
I'VE BEEN CALLING YOU ALL NIGHT.
MY PHONE WAS OFF...WHEN DID YOU GET BACK TO NEW YORK?
She was in a frenzy. I didn't stop her.
Like I was Max Irwin, I made love to her, even though the bed was still warm from the other girl. I didn't know what to make of this, but I didn't question it.

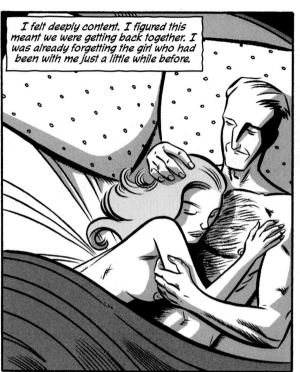

I felt deeply content. I figured this meant we were getting back together. I was already forgetting the girl who had been with me just a little while before.

Then she found, on her pillow, a very long blonde hair, which was many shades lighter than her shoulder-length auburn locks.

WHAT'S THIS????

IT'S MINE.

The color was right...

OH, MY GOD!!! THAT'S WHY YOU DIDN'T ANSWER YOUR PHONE--YOU HAD SOMEONE UP HERE!

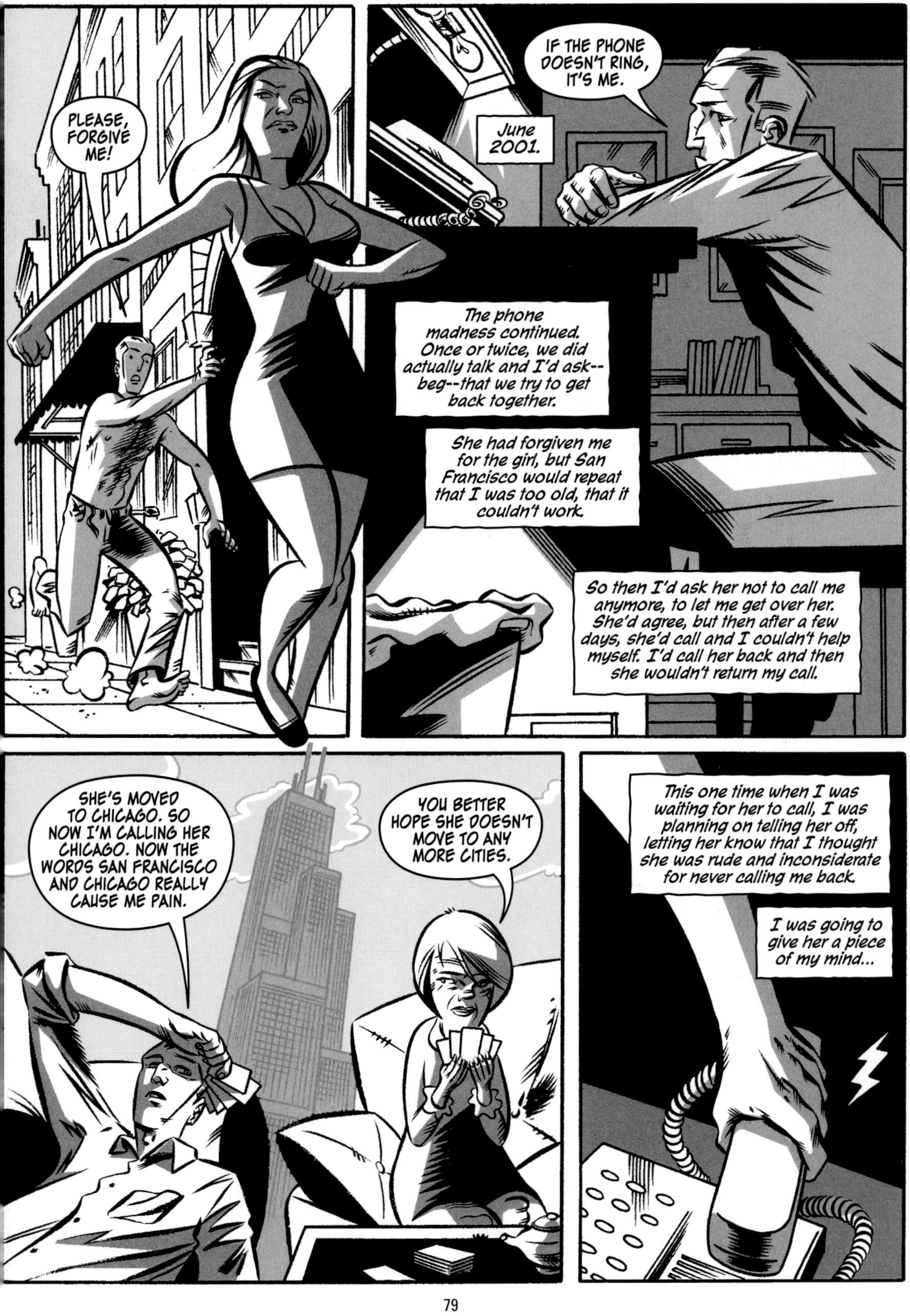
PLEASE, FORGIVE ME!
IF THE PHONE DOESN'T RING, IT'S ME.
June 2001.
The phone madness continued. Once or twice, we did actually talk and I'd ask--beg--that we try to get back together.
She had forgiven me for the girl, but San Francisco would repeat that I was too old, that it couldn't work.
So then I'd ask her not to call me anymore, to let me get over her. She'd agree, but then after a few days, she'd call and I couldn't help myself. I'd call her back and then she wouldn't return my call.
SHE'S MOVED TO CHICAGO. SO NOW I'M CALLING HER CHICAGO. NOW THE WORDS SAN FRANCISCO AND CHICAGO REALLY CAUSE ME PAIN.
YOU BETTER HOPE SHE DOESN'T MOVE TO ANY MORE CITIES.
This one time when I was waiting for her to call, I was planning on telling her off, letting her know that I thought she was rude and inconsiderate for never calling me back.
I was going to give her a piece of my mind...

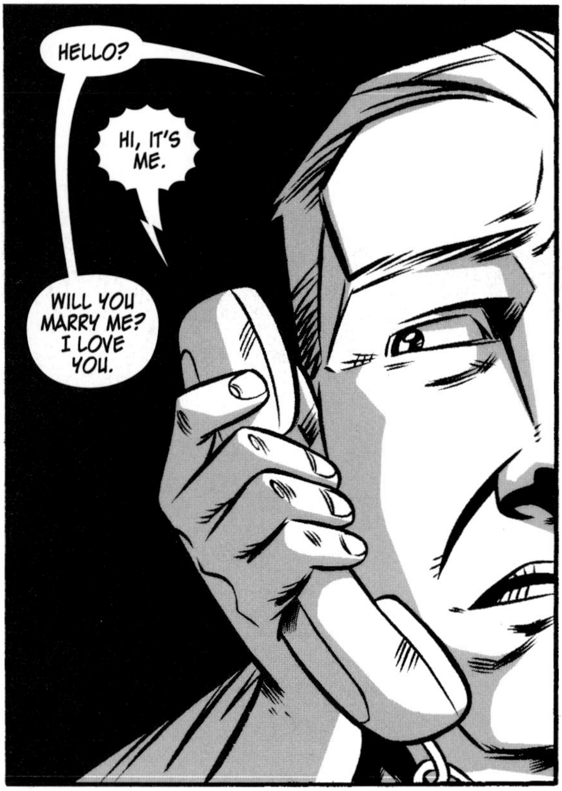
HELLO?
HI, IT'S ME.
WILL YOU MARRY ME? I LOVE YOU.

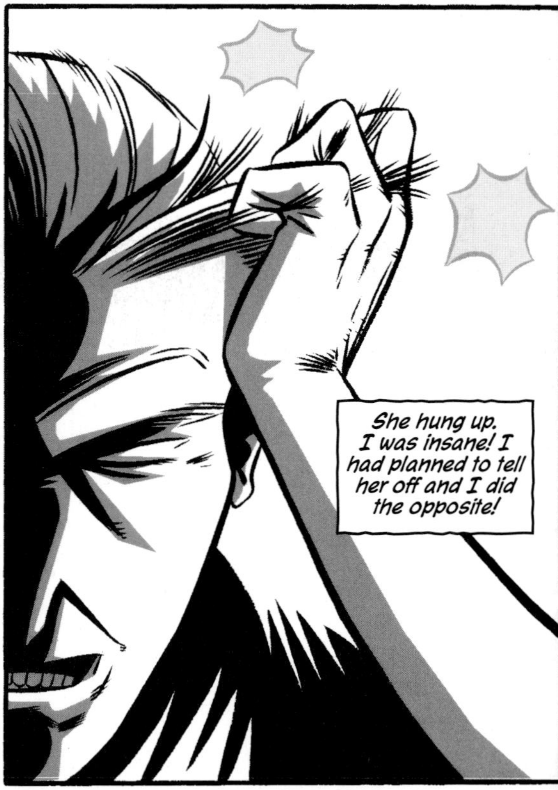
She hung up. I was insane! I had planned to tell her off and I did the opposite!

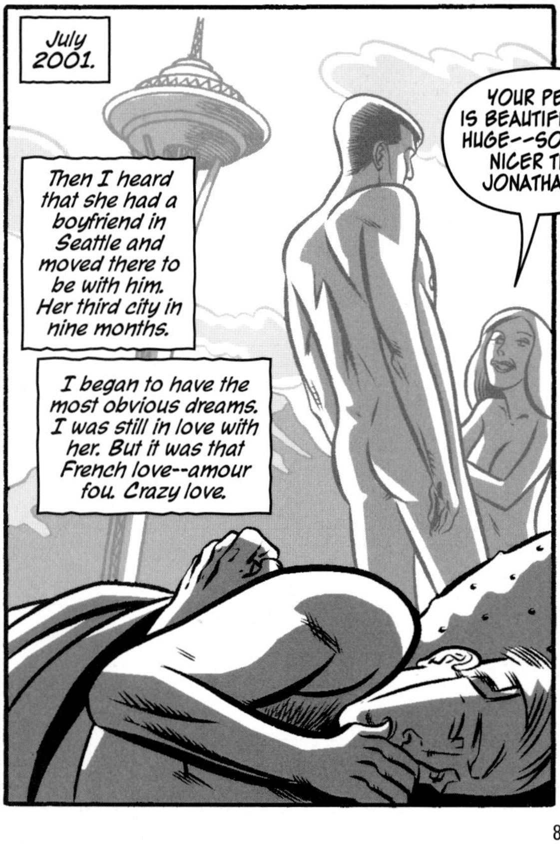
July 2001.
Then I heard that she had a boyfriend in Seattle and moved there to be with him. Her third city in nine months.
YOUR PENIS IS BEAUTIFUL AND HUGE--SO MUCH NICER THAN JONATHAN'S.
I began to have the most obvious dreams. I was still in love with her. But it was that French love--amour fou. Crazy love.

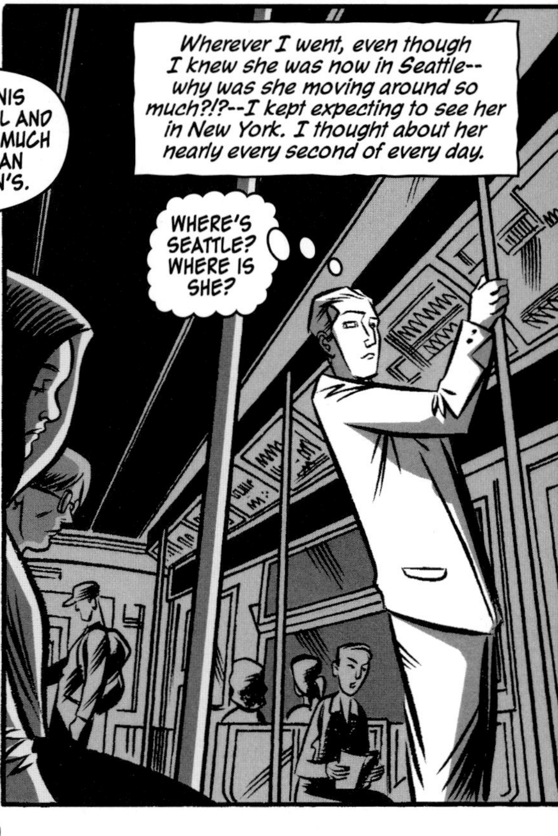
Wherever I went, even though I knew she was now in Seattle--why was she moving around so much?!?--I kept expecting to see her in New York. I thought about her nearly every second of every day.
WHERE'S SEATTLE? WHERE IS SHE?

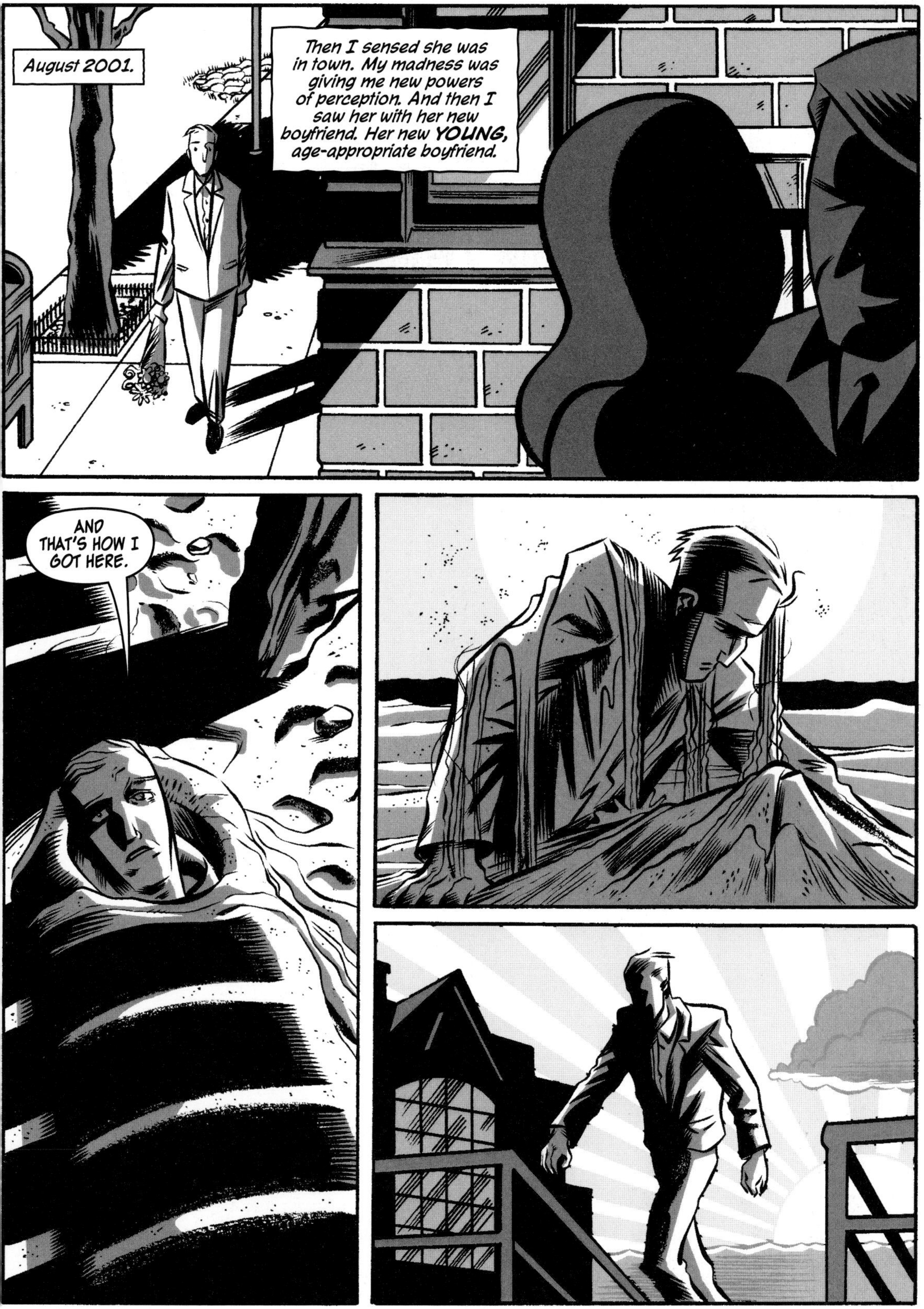
August 2001.
Then I sensed she was in town. My madness was giving me new powers of perception. And then I saw her with her new boyfriend. Her new YOUNG, age-appropriate boyfriend.
AND THAT'S HOW I GOT HERE.

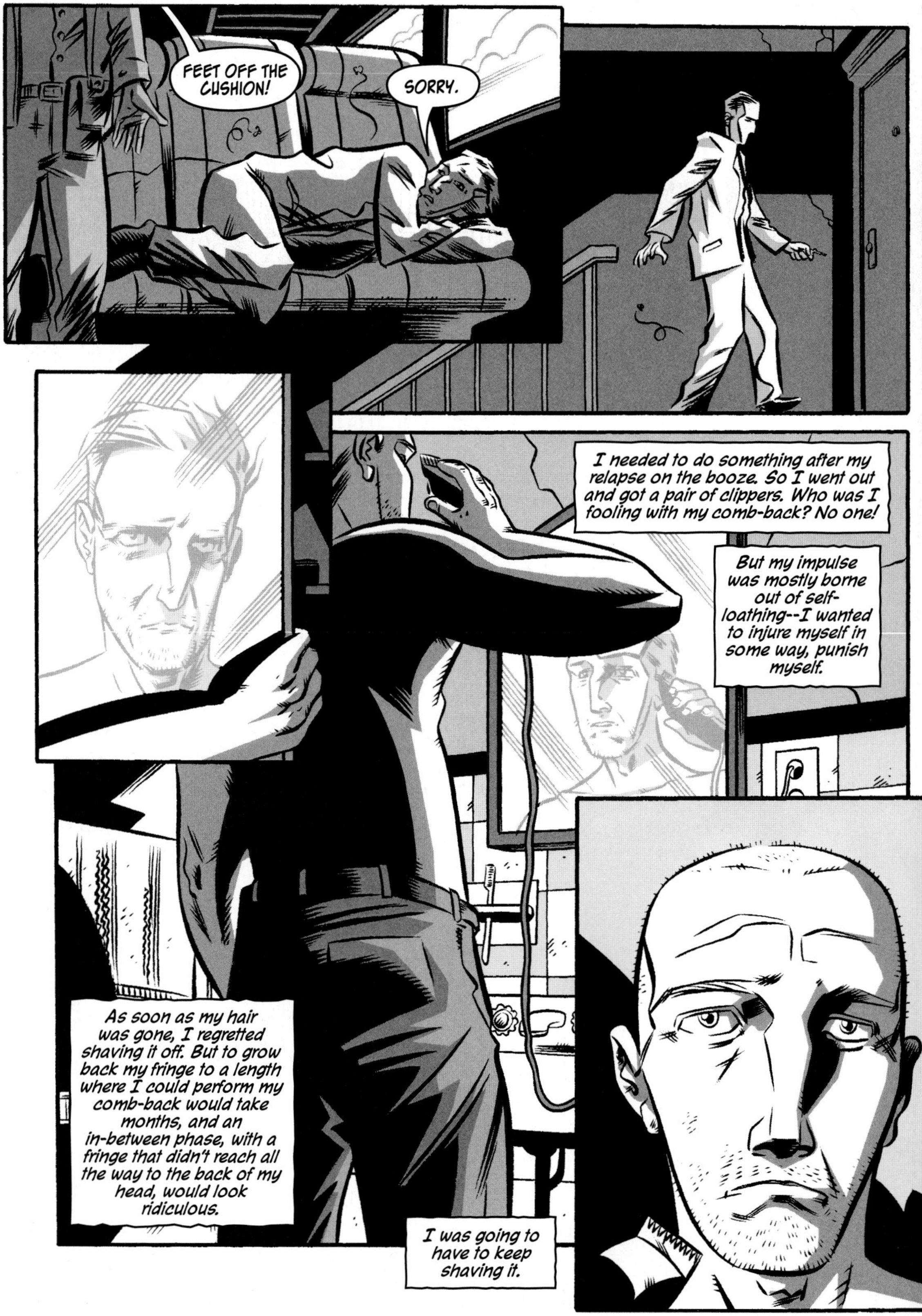
FEET OFF THE CUSHION!
SORRY.
I needed to do something after my relapse on the booze. So I went out and got a pair of clippers. Who was I fooling with my comb-back? No one!
But my impulse was mostly borne out of self-loathing--I wanted to injure myself in some way, punish myself.
As soon as my hair was gone, I regretted shaving it off. But to grow back my fringe to a length where I could perform my comb-back would take months, and an in-between phase, with a fringe that didn't reach all the way to the back of my head, would look ridiculous.
I was going to have to keep shaving it.

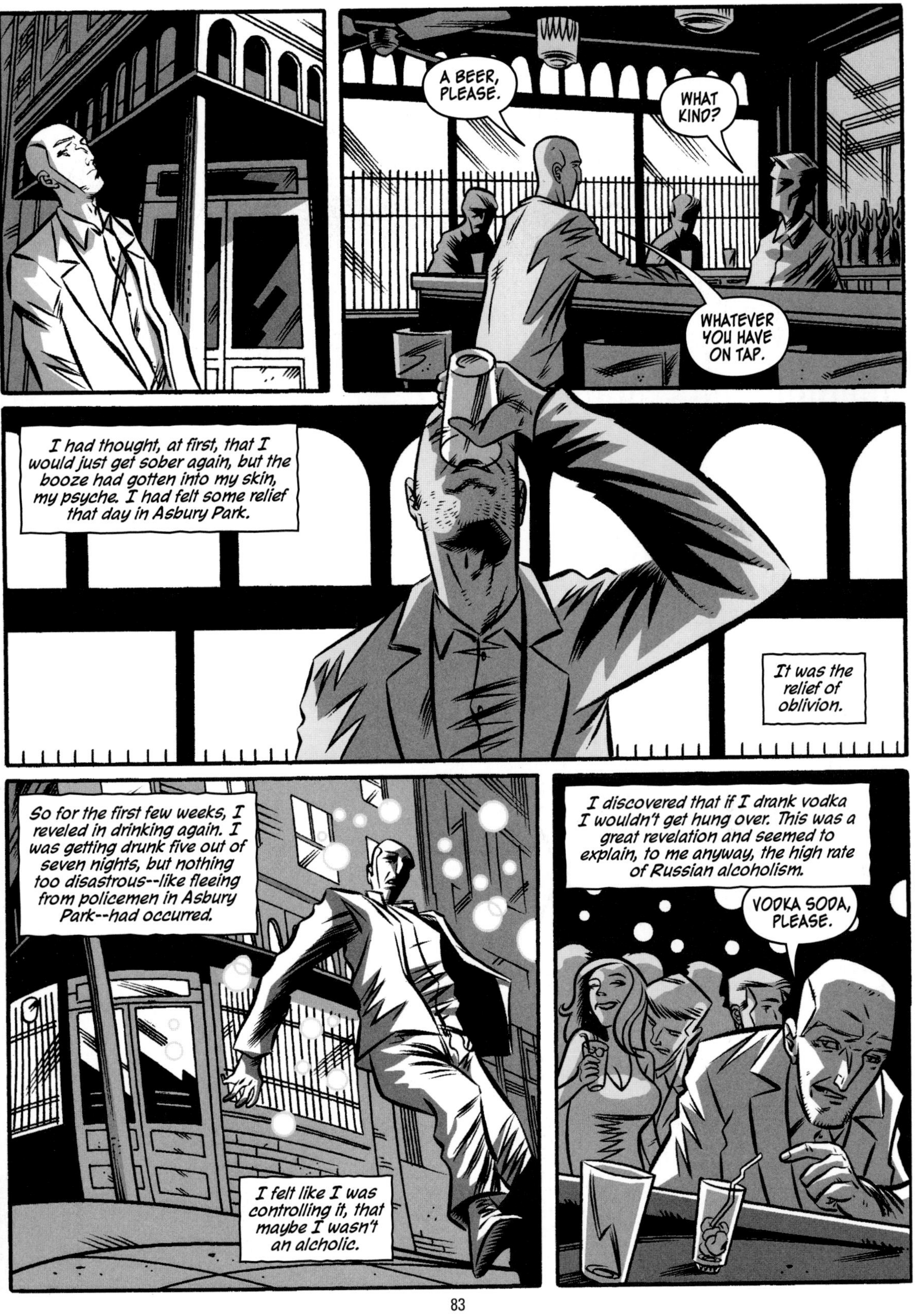

A BEER, PLEASE.
WHAT KIND?
WHATEVER YOU HAVE ON TAP.
I had thought, at first, that I would just get sober again, but the booze had gotten into my skin, my psyche. I had felt some relief that day in Asbury Park.
It was the relief of oblivion.
So for the first few weeks, I reveled in drinking again. I was getting drunk five out of seven nights, but nothing too disastrous--like fleeing from policemen in Asbury Park--had occurred.
I felt like I was controlling it, that maybe I wasn't an alcholic.
I discovered that if I drank vodka I wouldn't get hung over. This was a great revelation and seemed to explain, to me anyway, the high rate of Russian alcoholism.
VODKA SODA, PLEASE.

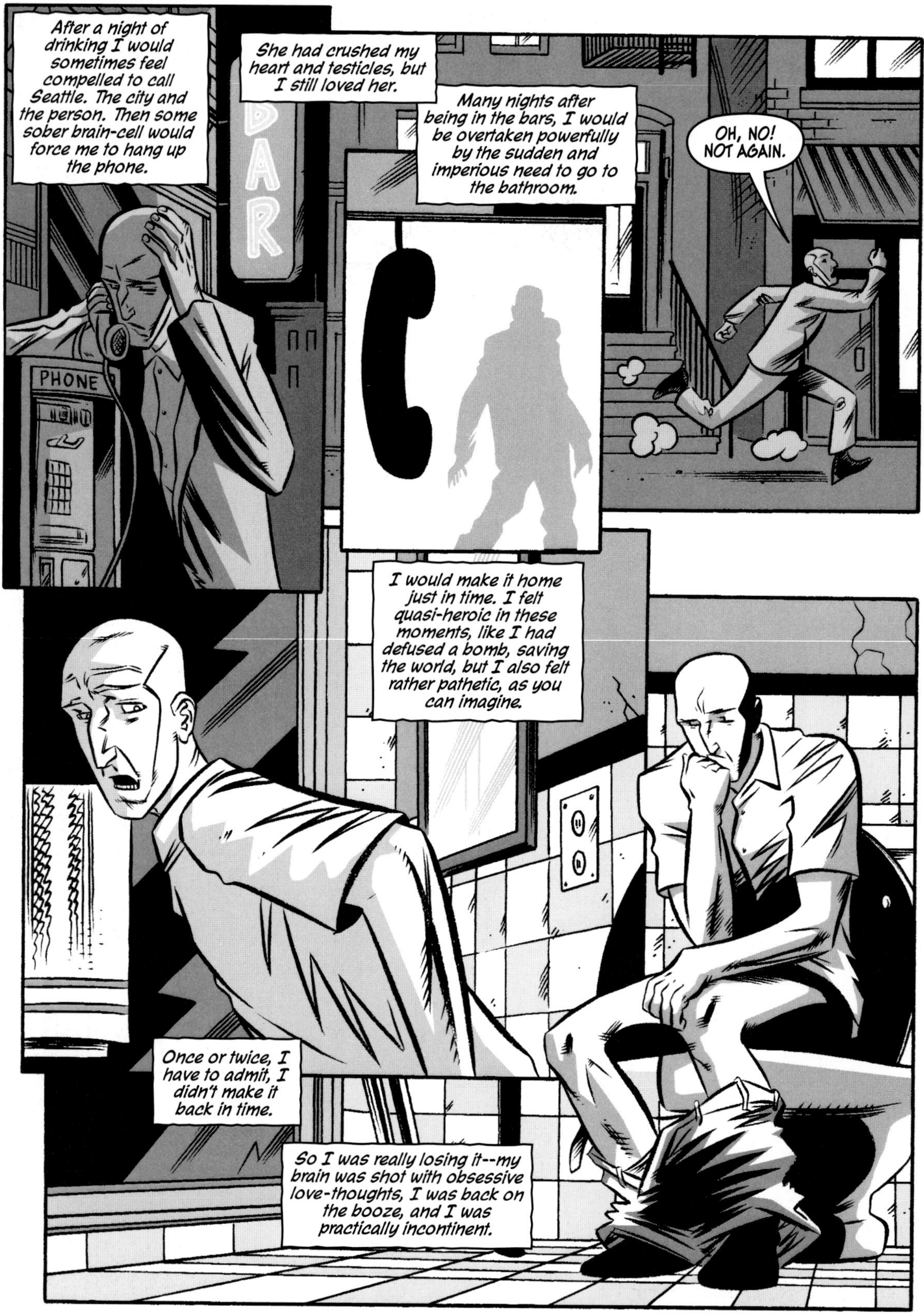
After a night of drinking I would sometimes feel compelled to call Seattle. The city and the person. Then some sober brain-cell would force me to hang up the phone.
PHONE
BAR
She had crushed my heart and testicles, but I still loved her.
Many nights after being in the bars, I would be overtaken powerfully by the sudden and imperious need to go to the bathroom.
OH, NO! NOT AGAIN.
I would make it home just in time. I felt quasi-heroic in these moments, like I had defused a bomb, saving the world, but I also felt rather pathetic, as you can imagine.
Once or twice, I have to admit, I didn't make it back in time.
So I was really losing it--my brain was shot with obsessive love-thoughts, I was back on the booze, and I was practically incontinent.

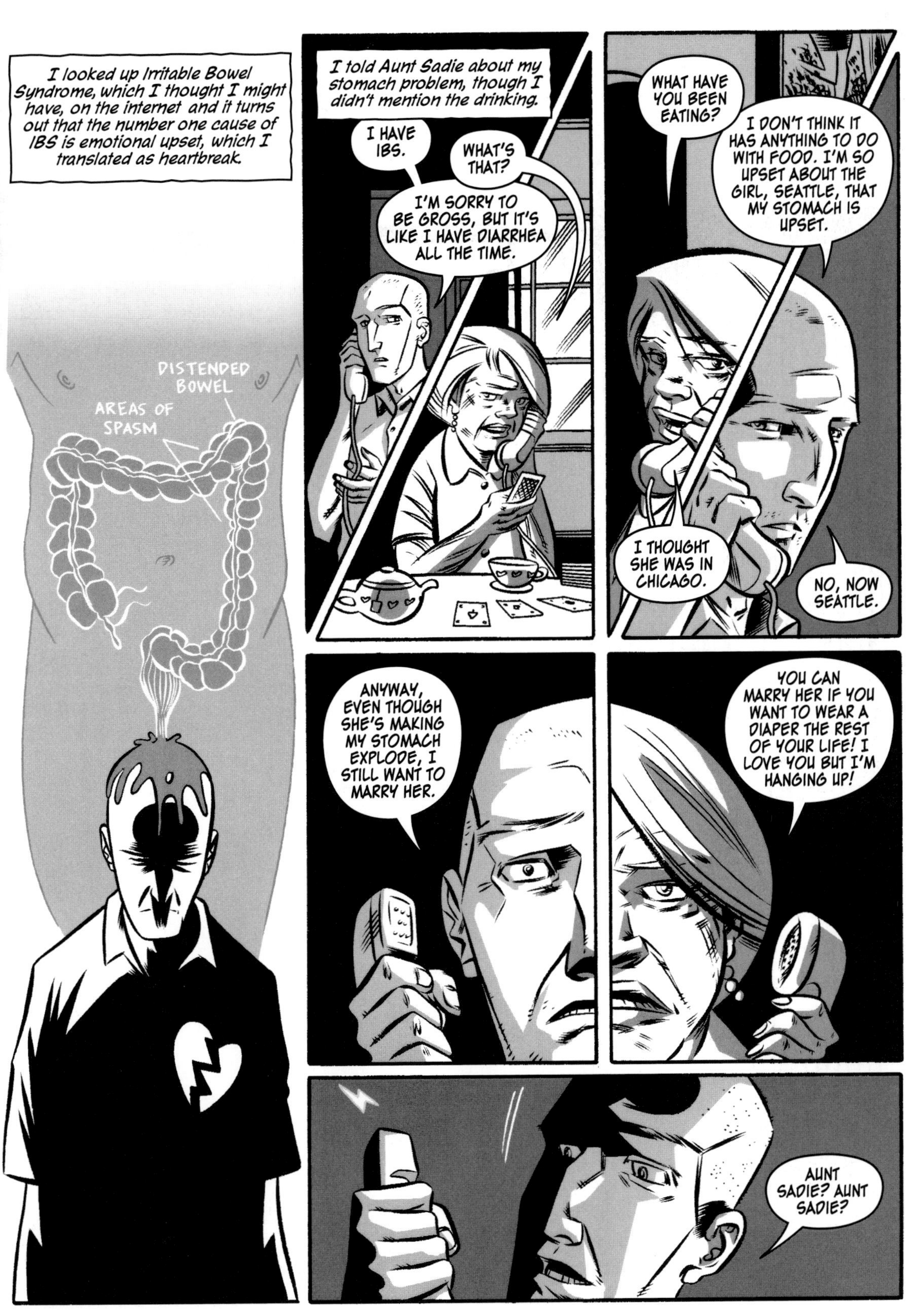

I looked up Irritable Bowel Syndrome, which I thought I might have, on the internet and it turns out that the number one cause of IBS is emotional upset, which I translated as heartbreak.
DISTENDED BOWEL
AREAS OF SPASM
I told Aunt Sadie about my stomach problem, though I didn't mention the drinking.
I HAVE IBS.
WHAT'S THAT?
I'M SORRY TO BE GROSS, BUT IT'S LIKE I HAVE DIARRHEA ALL THE TIME.
WHAT HAVE YOU BEEN EATING?
I DON'T THINK IT HAS ANYTHING TO DO WITH FOOD. I'M SO UPSET ABOUT THE GIRL, SEATTLE, THAT MY STOMACH IS UPSET.
I THOUGHT SHE WAS IN CHICAGO.
NO, NOW SEATTLE.
ANYWAY, EVEN THOUGH SHE'S MAKING MY STOMACH EXPLODE, I STILL WANT TO MARRY HER.
YOU CAN MARRY HER IF YOU WANT TO WEAR A DIAPER THE REST OF YOUR LIFE! I LOVE YOU BUT I'M HANGING UP!
AUNT SADIE? AUNT SADIE?

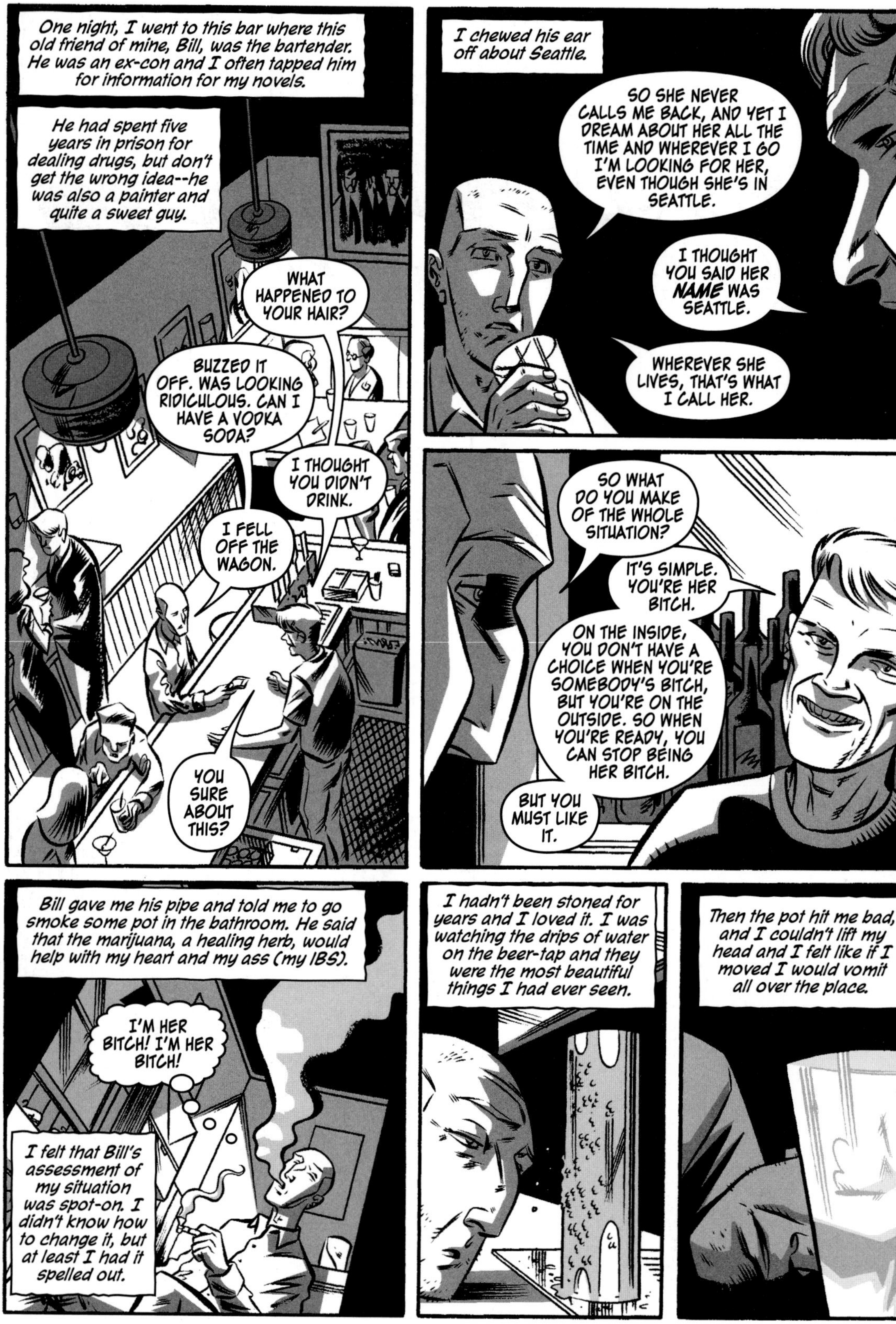
One night, I went to this bar where this old friend of mine, Bill, was the bartender. He was an ex-con and I often tapped him for information for my novels.
He had spent five years in prison for dealing drugs, but don't get the wrong idea--he was also a painter and quite a sweet guy.
WHAT HAPPENED TO YOUR HAIR?
BUZZED IT OFF. WAS LOOKING RIDICULOUS. CAN I HAVE A VODKA SODA?
I THOUGHT YOU DIDN'T DRINK.
I FELL OFF THE WAGON.
YOU SURE ABOUT THIS?
I chewed his ear off about Seattle.
SO SHE NEVER CALLS ME BACK, AND YET I DREAM ABOUT HER ALL THE TIME AND WHEREVER I GO I'M LOOKING FOR HER, EVEN THOUGH SHE'S IN SEATTLE.
I THOUGHT YOU SAID HER NAME WAS SEATTLE.
WHEREVER SHE LIVES, THAT'S WHAT I CALL HER.
SO WHAT DO YOU MAKE OF THE WHOLE SITUATION?
IT'S SIMPLE. YOU'RE HER BITCH.
ON THE INSIDE, YOU DON'T HAVE A CHOICE WHEN YOU'RE SOMEBODY'S BITCH, BUT YOU'RE ON THE OUTSIDE. SO WHEN YOU'RE READY, YOU CAN STOP BEING HER BITCH.
BUT YOU MUST LIKE IT.
Bill gave me his pipe and told me to go smoke some pot in the bathroom. He said that the marijuana, a healing herb, would help with my heart and my ass (my IBS).
I'M HER BITCH! I'M HER BITCH!
I felt that Bill's assessment of my situation was spot-on. I didn't know how to change it, but at least I had it spelled out.
I hadn't been stoned for years and I loved it. I was watching the drips of water on the beer-tap and they were the most beautiful things I had ever seen.
Then the pot hit me bad, and I couldn't lift my head and I felt like if I moved I would vomit all over the place.

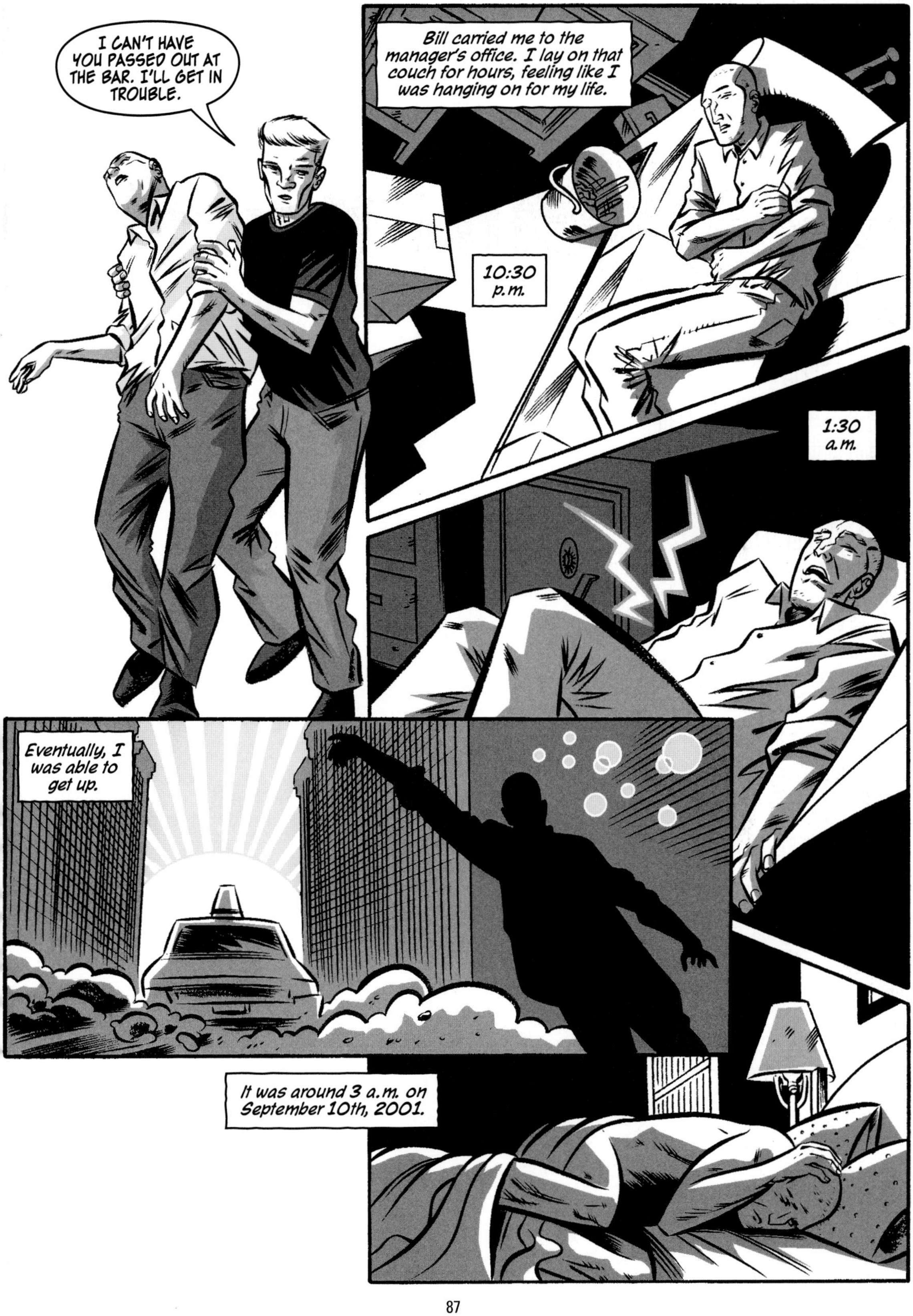

I CAN'T HAVE YOU PASSED OUT AT THE BAR. I'LL GET IN TROUBLE.
Bill carried me to the manager's office. I lay on that couch for hours, feeling like I was hanging on for my life.
10:30 p.m.
1:30 a.m.
Eventually, I was able to get up.
It was around 3 a.m. on September 10th, 2001.

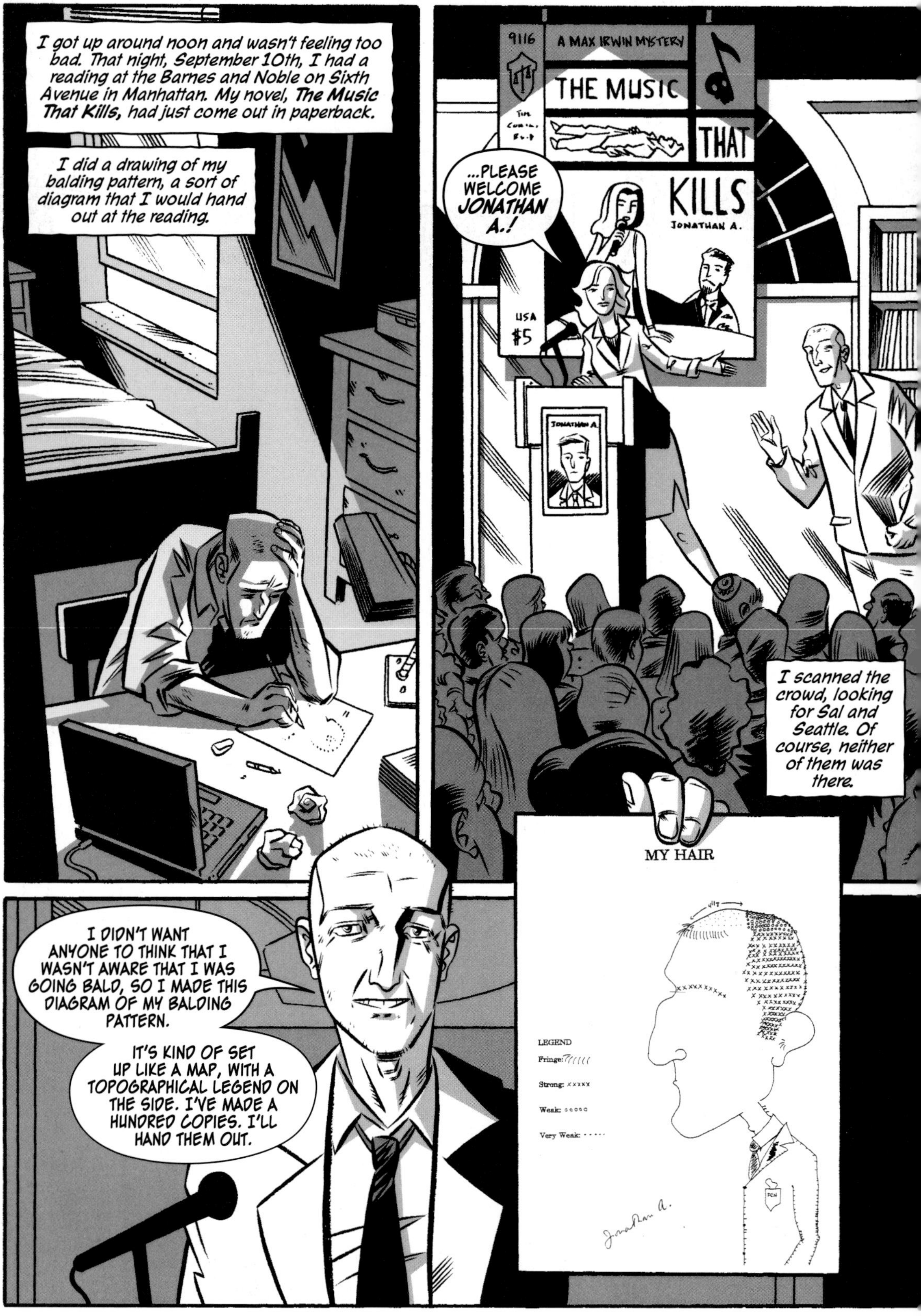
I got up around noon and wasn't feeling too bad. That night, September 10th, I had a reading at the Barnes and Noble on Sixth Avenue in Manhattan. My novel, The Music That Kills, had just come out in paperback.
I did a drawing of my balding pattern, a sort of diagram that I would hand out at the reading.
A MAX IRWIN MYSTERY
THE MUSIC THAT KILLS
JONATHAN A.
USA $5
...PLEASE WELCOME JONATHAN A.!
JONATHAN A.
I scanned the crowd, looking for Sal and Seattle. Of course, neither of them was there.
I DIDN'T WANT ANYONE TO THINK THAT I WASN'T AWARE THAT I WAS GOING BALD, SO I MADE THIS DIAGRAM OF MY BALDING PATTERN.
IT'S KIND OF SET UP LIKE A MAP, WITH A TOPOGRAPHICAL LEGEND ON THE SIDE. I'VE MADE A HUNDRED COPIES. I'LL HAND THEM OUT.
MY HAIR
LEGEND
Fringe:
Strong:
Weak:
Very Weak:
Jonathan A.

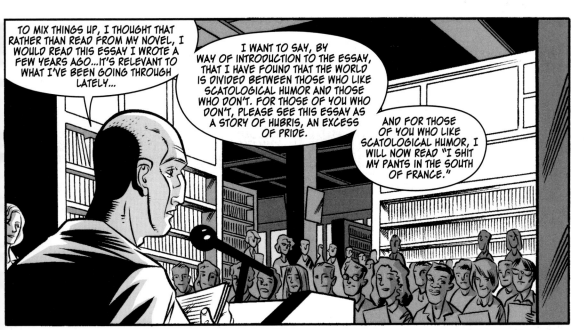

TO MIX THINGS UP, I THOUGHT THAT RATHER THAN READ FROM MY NOVEL, I WOULD READ THIS ESSAY I WROTE A FEW YEARS AGO...IT'S RELEVANT TO WHAT I'VE BEEN GOING THROUGH LATELY...

I WANT TO SAY, BY WAY OF INTRODUCTION TO THE ESSAY, THAT I HAVE FOUND THAT THE WORLD IS DIVIDED BETWEEN THOSE WHO LIKE SCATOLOGICAL HUMOR AND THOSE WHO DON'T. FOR THOSE OF YOU WHO DON'T, PLEASE SEE THIS ESSAY AS A STORY OF HUBRIS, AN EXCESS OF PRIDE.

AND FOR THOSE OF YOU WHO LIKE SCATOLOGICAL HUMOR, I WILL NOW READ "I SHIT MY PANTS IN THE SOUTH OF FRANCE."

I read them this story of how when I was nineteen I went to the south of France with a friend from Yale. We were there to take a French course.

One night I was very drunk and bought a tuna fish sandwich from a **CLOCHARD**, which is French for bum. I bought it right off his hand, where it was resting **SANS** napkin.

Le Pub

It was late at night. All the cafés were closed.

After five minutes in my system that sandwich exploded. We were racing back into town, where we hoped one café was still open.

I'M NOT GOING TO MAKE IT!

89

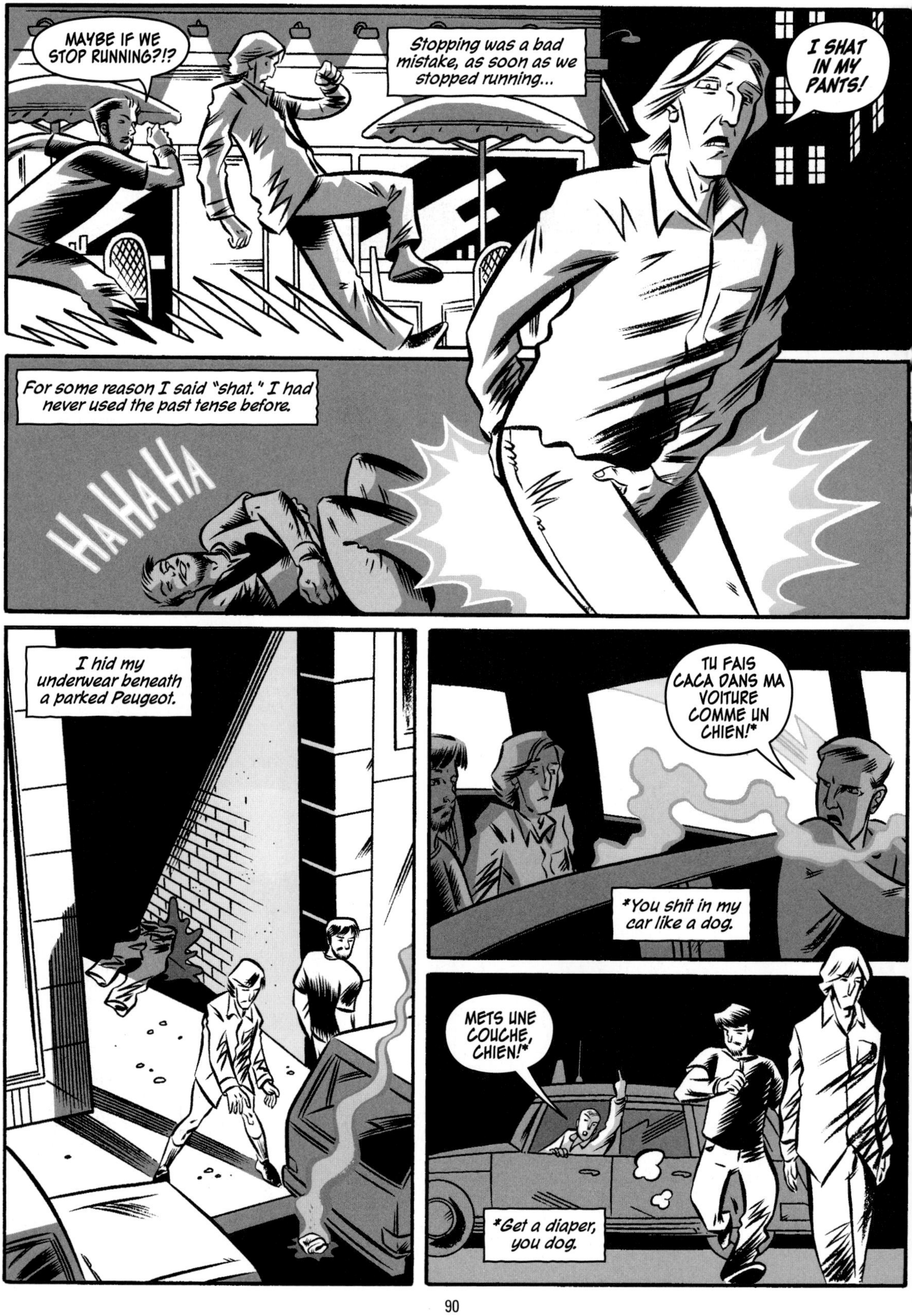
MAYBE IF WE STOP RUNNING?!?
Stopping was a bad mistake, as soon as we stopped running...
I SHAT IN MY PANTS!
For some reason I said "shat." I had never used the past tense before.
HaHaHaHa
I hid my underwear beneath a parked Peugeot.
TU FAIS CACA DANS MA VOITURE COMME UN CHIEN!*
*You shit in my car like a dog.
METS UNE COUCHE, CHIEN!*
*Get a diaper, you dog.

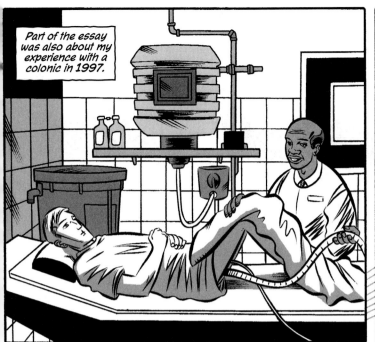

Part of the essay was also about my experience with a colonic in 1997.

After the colonic, which I enjoyed, something went wrong.

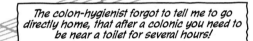

The colon-hygienist forgot to tell me to go directly home, that after a colonic you need to be near a toilet for several hours!

There was a big wet spot on the seat of my pants, looking like a Rorschach blot, and I deciphered its simple psychological message: You're a loser!

OH, GOD!

The essay went over very well. I didn't tell them about my current state of near-daily incontinence, but by regaling them with these two earlier embarrassing incidents was sort of a way to confess.

HAHAHA

After the reading some fans took me out drinking. I got really drunk and played the maudlin fool. It's embarrassing to think about.

I'M IN LOVE WITH THIS GIRL. I CALL HER SEATTLE. I'M HER BITCH.

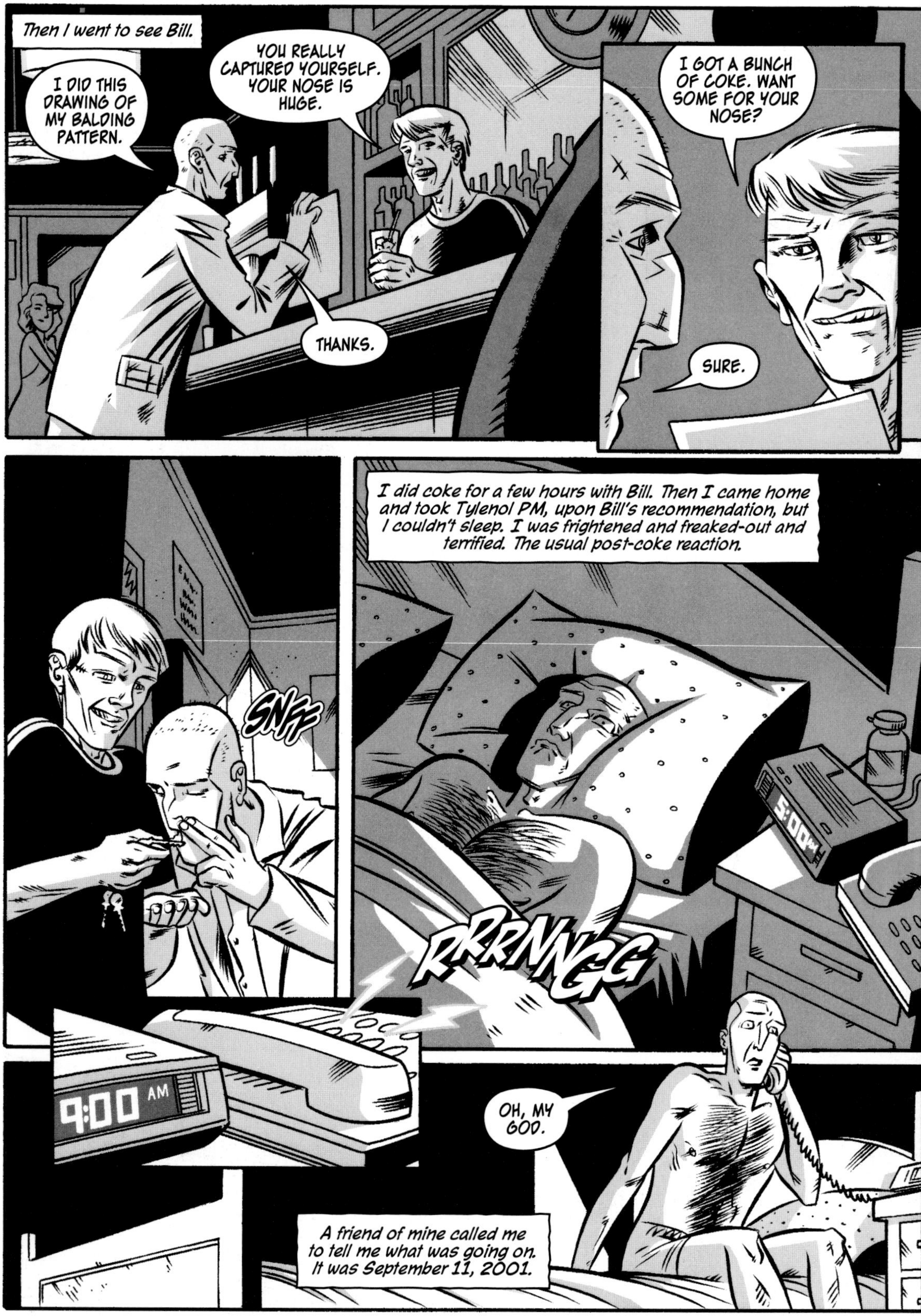
Then I went to see Bill.
I DID THIS DRAWING OF MY BALDING PATTERN.
YOU REALLY CAPTURED YOURSELF. YOUR NOSE IS HUGE.
THANKS.
I GOT A BUNCH OF COKE. WANT SOME FOR YOUR NOSE?
SURE.
SNFF
I did coke for a few hours with Bill. Then I came home and took Tylenol PM, upon Bill's recommendation, but I couldn't sleep. I was frightened and freaked-out and terrified. The usual post-coke reaction.
5:00
RRRNNGG
9:00 AM
OH, MY GOD.
A friend of mine called me to tell me what was going on. It was September 11, 2001.

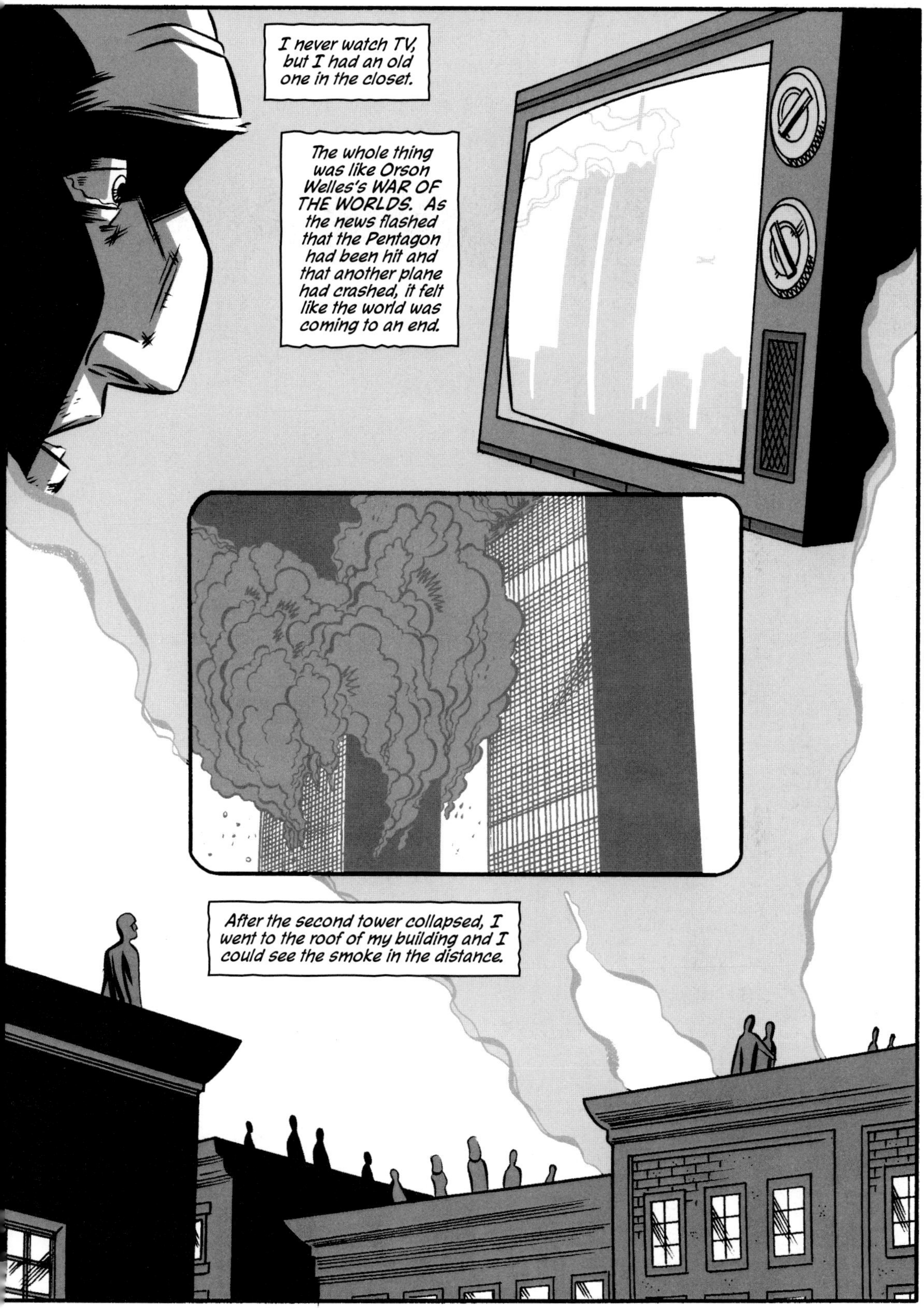
I never watch TV, but I had an old one in the closet.
The whole thing was like Orson Welles's WAR OF THE WORLDS. As the news flashed that the Pentagon had been hit and that another plane had crashed, it felt like the world was coming to an end.
After the second tower collapsed, I went to the roof of my building and I could see the smoke in the distance.

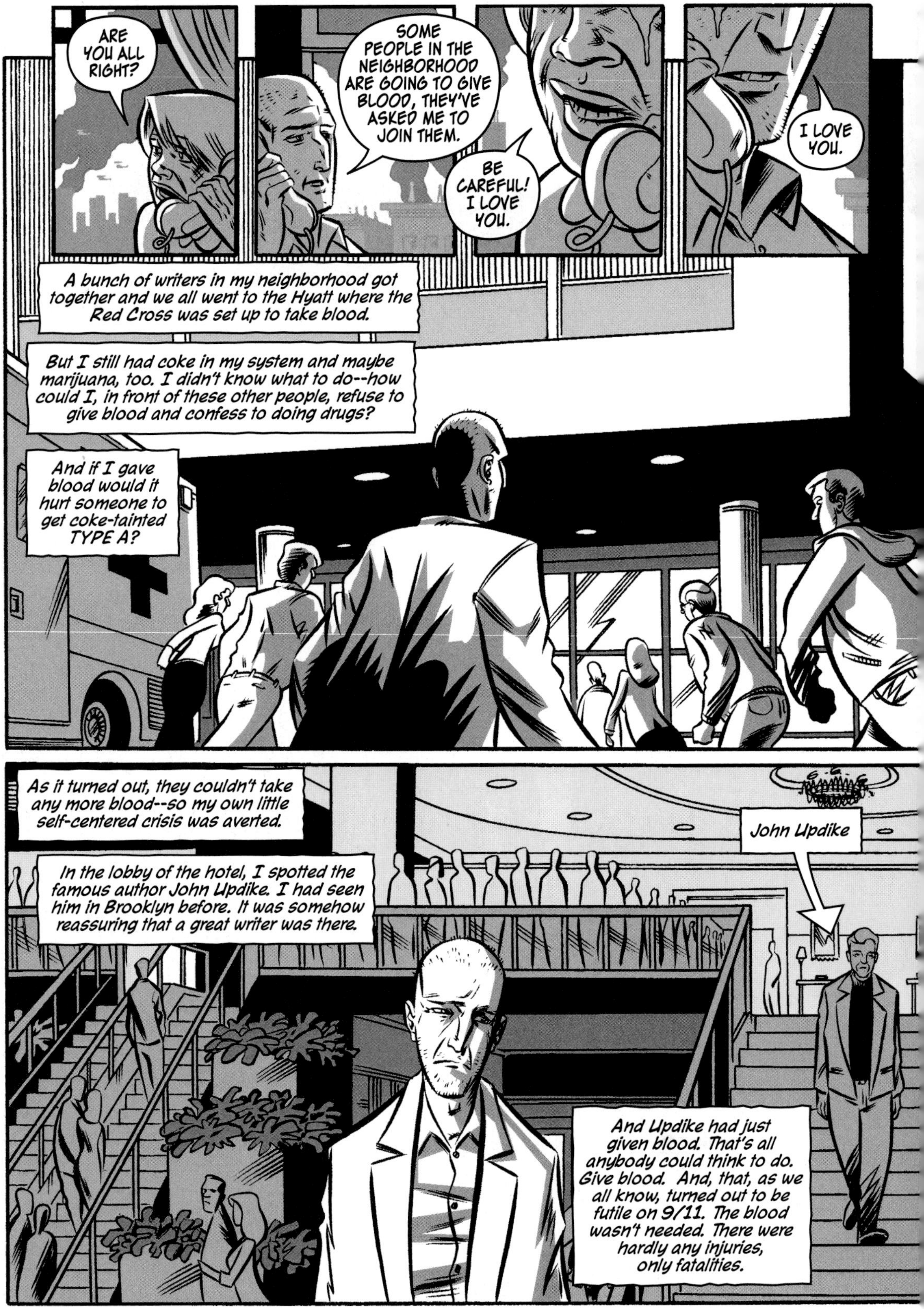
ARE YOU ALL RIGHT?
SOME PEOPLE IN THE NEIGHBORHOOD ARE GOING TO GIVE BLOOD, THEY'VE ASKED ME TO JOIN THEM.
BE CAREFUL! I LOVE YOU.
I LOVE YOU.
A bunch of writers in my neighborhood got together and we all went to the Hyatt where the Red Cross was set up to take blood.
But I still had coke in my system and maybe marijuana, too. I didn't know what to do--how could I, in front of these other people, refuse to give blood and confess to doing drugs?
And if I gave blood would it hurt someone to get coke-tainted TYPE A?
As it turned out, they couldn't take any more blood--so my own little self-centered crisis was averted.
John Updike
In the lobby of the hotel, I spotted the famous author John Updike. I had seen him in Brooklyn before. It was somehow reassuring that a great writer was there.
And Updike had just given blood. That's all anybody could think to do. Give blood. And, that, as we all know, turned out to be futile on 9/11. The blood wasn't needed. There were hardly any injuries, only fatalities.

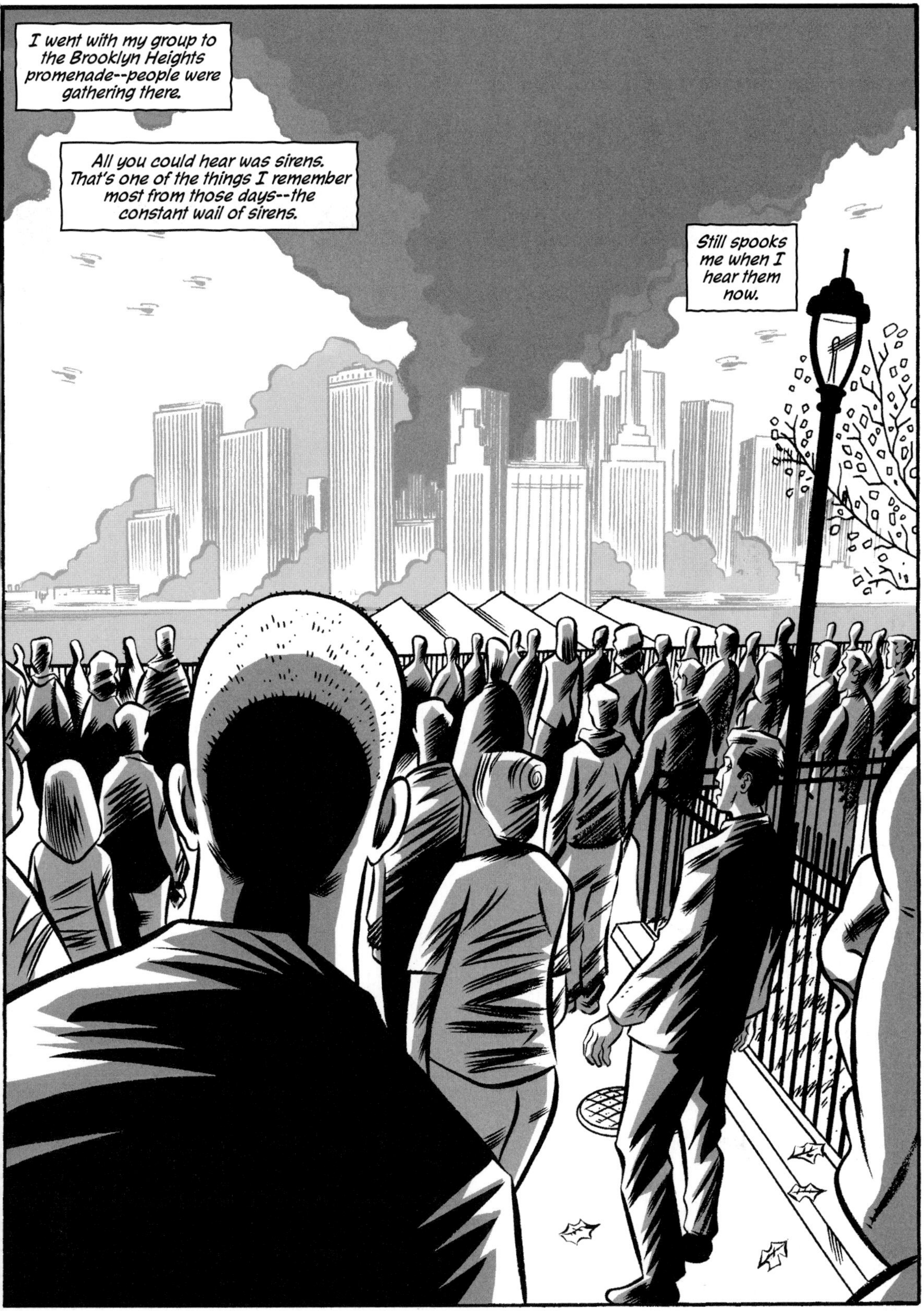
I went with my group to the Brooklyn Heights promenade--people were gathering there.
All you could hear was sirens. That's one of the things I remember most from those days--the constant wail of sirens.
Still spooks me when I hear them now.

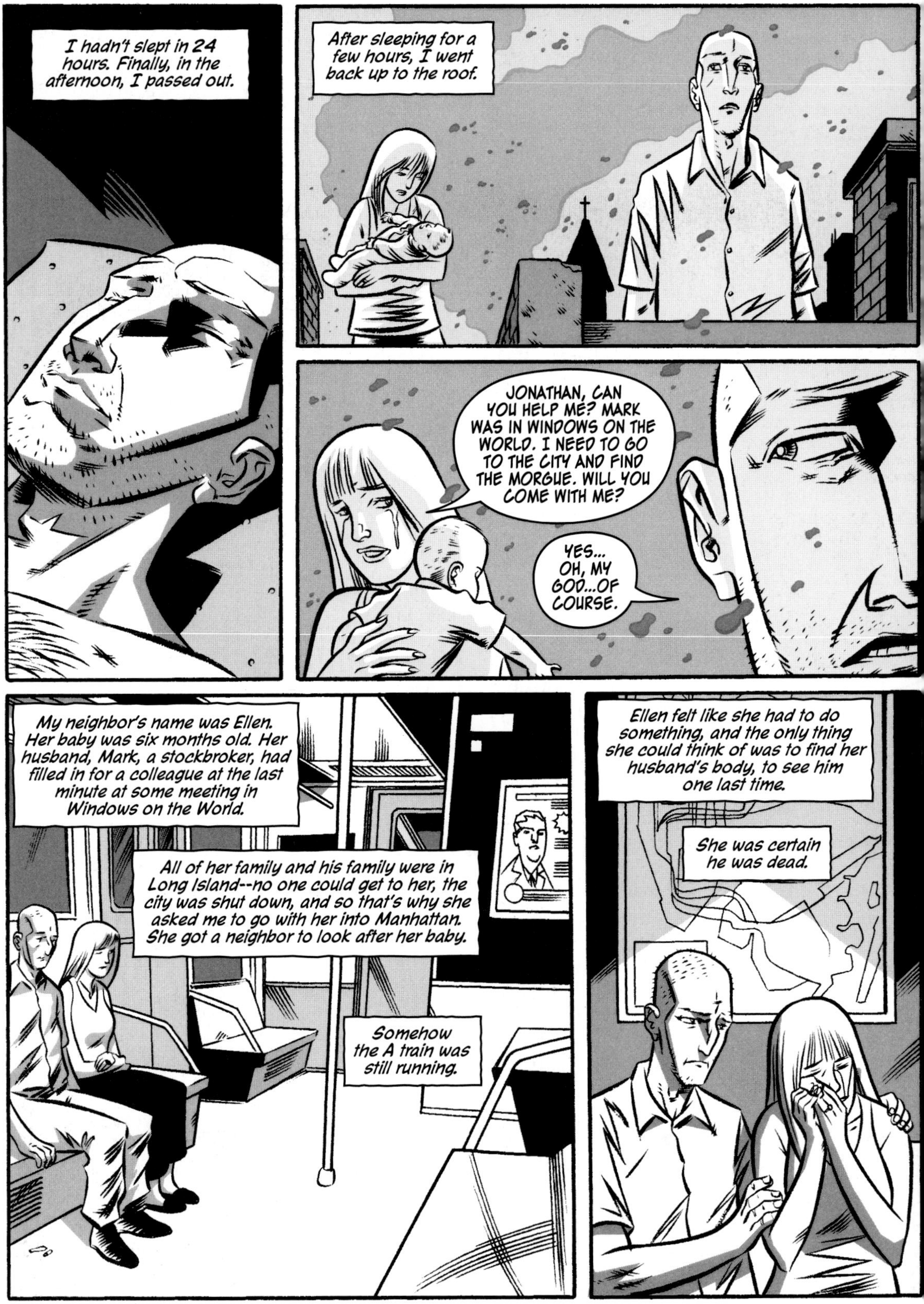
I hadn't slept in 24 hours. Finally, in the afternoon, I passed out.
After sleeping for a few hours, I went back up to the roof.
JONATHAN, CAN YOU HELP ME? MARK WAS IN WINDOWS ON THE WORLD. I NEED TO GO TO THE CITY AND FIND THE MORGUE. WILL YOU COME WITH ME?
YES... OH, MY GOD...OF COURSE.
My neighbor's name was Ellen. Her baby was six months old. Her husband, Mark, a stockbroker, had filled in for a colleague at the last minute at some meeting in Windows on the World.
All of her family and his family were in Long Island--no one could get to her, the city was shut down, and so that's why she asked me to go with her into Manhattan. She got a neighbor to look after her baby.
Somehow the A train was still running.
Ellen felt like she had to do something, and the only thing she could think of was to find her husband's body, to see him one last time.
She was certain he was dead.

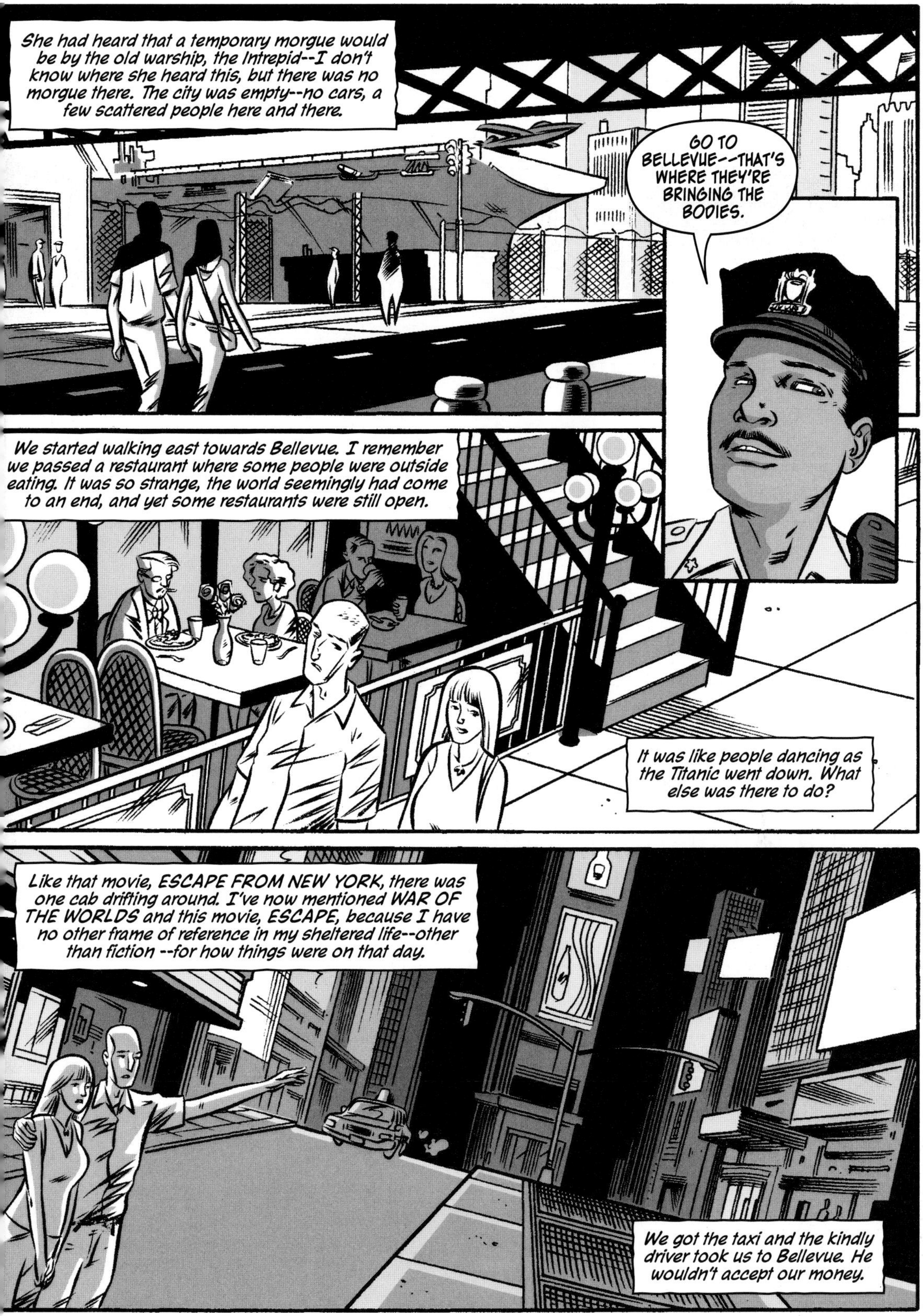
She had heard that a temporary morgue would be by the old warship, the Intrepid--I don't know where she heard this, but there was no morgue there. The city was empty--no cars, a few scattered people here and there.
GO TO BELLEVUE--THAT'S WHERE THEY'RE BRINGING THE BODIES.
We started walking east towards Bellevue. I remember we passed a restaurant where some people were outside eating. It was so strange, the world seemingly had come to an end, and yet some restaurants were still open.
It was like people dancing as the Titanic went down. What else was there to do?
Like that movie, ESCAPE FROM NEW YORK, there was one cab drifting around. I've now mentioned WAR OF THE WORLDS and this movie, ESCAPE, because I have no other frame of reference in my sheltered life--other than fiction --for how things were on that day.
We got the taxi and the kindly driver took us to Bellevue. He wouldn't accept our money.

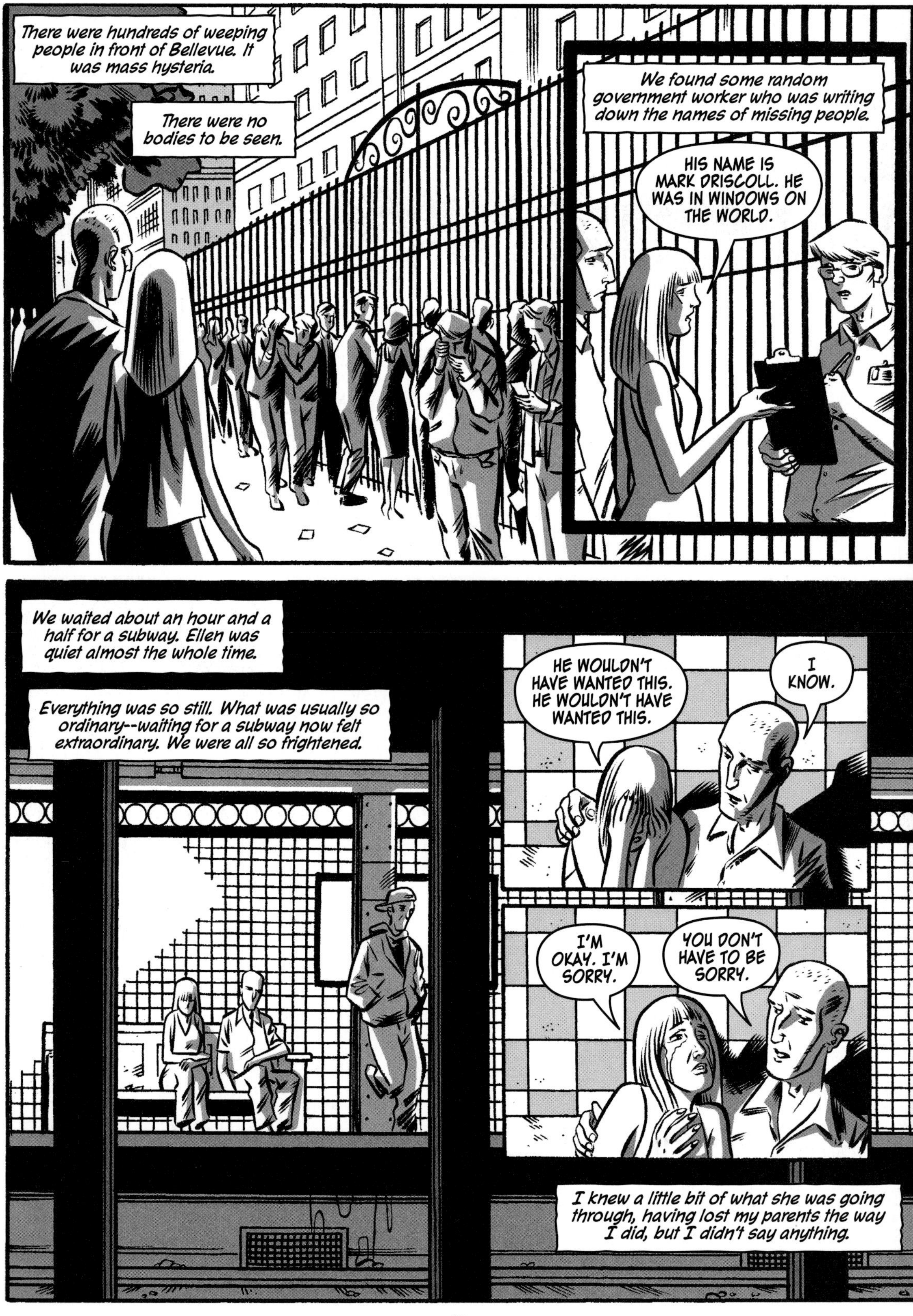
There were hundreds of weeping people in front of Bellevue. It was mass hysteria.
There were no bodies to be seen.
We found some random government worker who was writing down the names of missing people.
HIS NAME IS MARK DRISCOLL. HE WAS IN WINDOWS ON THE WORLD.
We waited about an hour and a half for a subway. Ellen was quiet almost the whole time.
Everything was so still. What was usually so ordinary--waiting for a subway now felt extraordinary. We were all so frightened.
HE WOULDN'T HAVE WANTED THIS. HE WOULDN'T HAVE WANTED THIS.
I KNOW.
I'M OKAY. I'M SORRY.
YOU DON'T HAVE TO BE SORRY.
I knew a little bit of what she was going through, having lost my parents the way I did, but I didn't say anything.

Mary, our sweet neighbor, had dutifully been baby-sitting.

We had been neighbors for four years, but I had never been in Ellen's apartment before. I looked around--this is where Mark had lived. He would never return.

THANK YOU, JONATHAN.

I CAN STAY ON YOUR COUCH, IF YOU LIKE.

THAT'S ALL RIGHT. I'LL BE OKAY. MARY IS GOING TO STAY WITH ME.

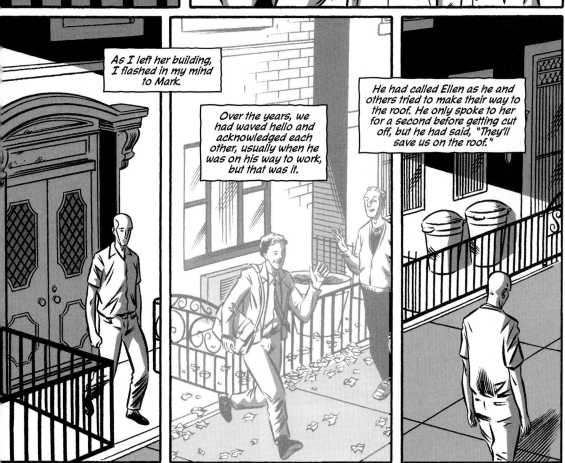

As I left her building, I flashed in my mind to Mark.

Over the years, we had waved hello and acknowledged each other, usually when he was on his way to work, but that was it.

He had called Ellen as he and others tried to make their way to the roof. He only spoke to her for a second before getting cut off, but he had said, "They'll save us on the roof."

On September 12th, like the rest of the country, I spent most of the day watching the news.

HELLO?

YES, I'M OKAY...

It was Seattle.

I WISH I HAD DIED...

It was kind of her to call. She said she had tried the day before but all the circuits had been busy. We didn't speak long. There wasn't much to say.

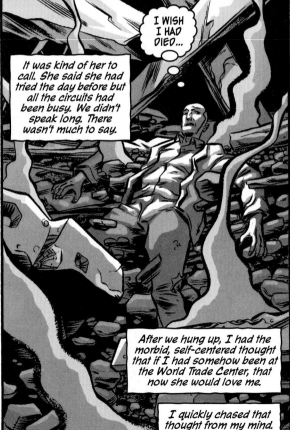

After we hung up, I had the morbid, self-centered thought that if I had somehow been at the World Trade Center, that now she would love me.

I quickly chased that thought from my mind.

On September 10th, I was reading an essay about incontinence and passing around a diagram of my balding pattern--my life, I felt, couldn't be more frivolous and ridiculous and meaningless.

And as the world came apart at the seams, I didn't even have the fortitude not to drink.

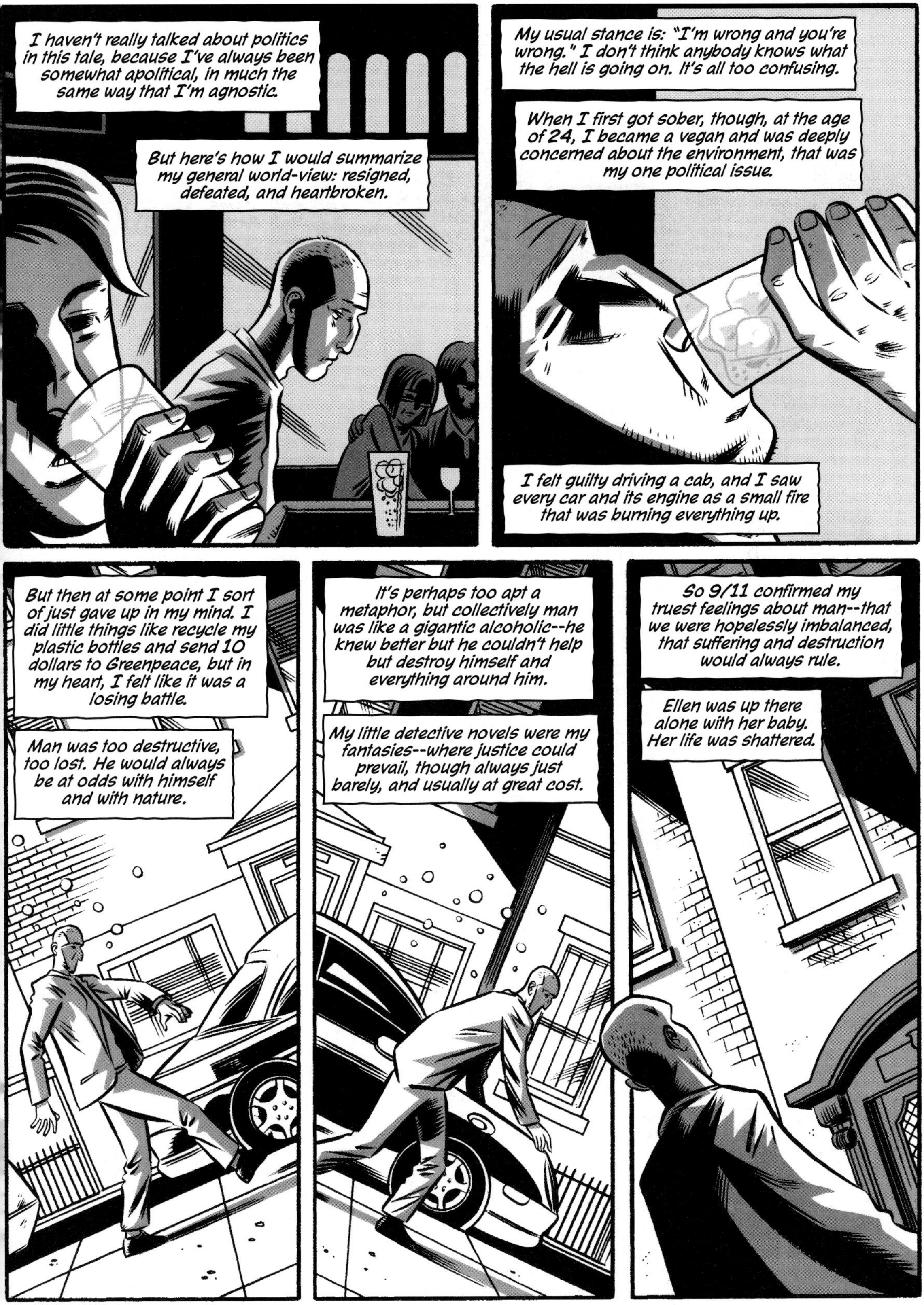
I haven't really talked about politics in this tale, because I've always been somewhat apolitical, in much the same way that I'm agnostic.
But here's how I would summarize my general world-view: resigned, defeated, and heartbroken.
My usual stance is: "I'm wrong and you're wrong." I don't think anybody knows what the hell is going on. It's all too confusing.
When I first got sober, though, at the age of 24, I became a vegan and was deeply concerned about the environment, that was my one political issue.
I felt guilty driving a cab, and I saw every car and its engine as a small fire that was burning everything up.
But then at some point I sort of just gave up in my mind. I did little things like recycle my plastic bottles and send 10 dollars to Greenpeace, but in my heart, I felt like it was a losing battle.
Man was too destructive, too lost. He would always be at odds with himself and with nature.
It's perhaps too apt a metaphor, but collectively man was like a gigantic alcoholic--he knew better but he couldn't help but destroy himself and everything around him.
My little detective novels were my fantasies--where justice could prevail, though always just barely, and usually at great cost.
So 9/11 confirmed my truest feelings about man--that we were hopelessly imbalanced, that suffering and destruction would always rule.
Ellen was up there alone with her baby. Her life was shattered.

I had no hope for the world, but that doesn't mean I didn't somewhere inside still have hope for my own little life, except all that hope was centered insanely on one person.

THANKS FOR CALLING ME TODAY... I APPRECIATE IT...BYE...YOU DON'T HAVE TO CALL ME BACK...I HOPE YOU'RE ALL RIGHT...I ADORE YOU ...BYE...

As always, I left a message. I tried not to slur my words.

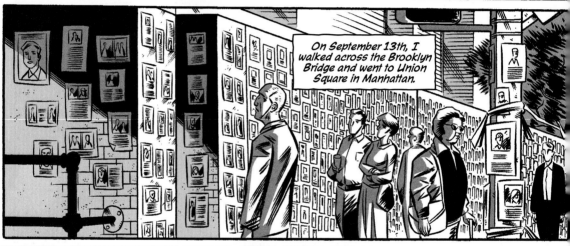

On September 13th, I walked across the Brooklyn Bridge and went to Union Square in Manhattan.

There were no cars south of 14th Street, the city was under martial law. I walked down University Place and saw a huge crowd up ahead.

EXCUSE ME, DO YOU KNOW WHAT'S HAPPENING?

CLINTON IS HERE, HE'S GOING AROUND HUGGING PEOPLE.

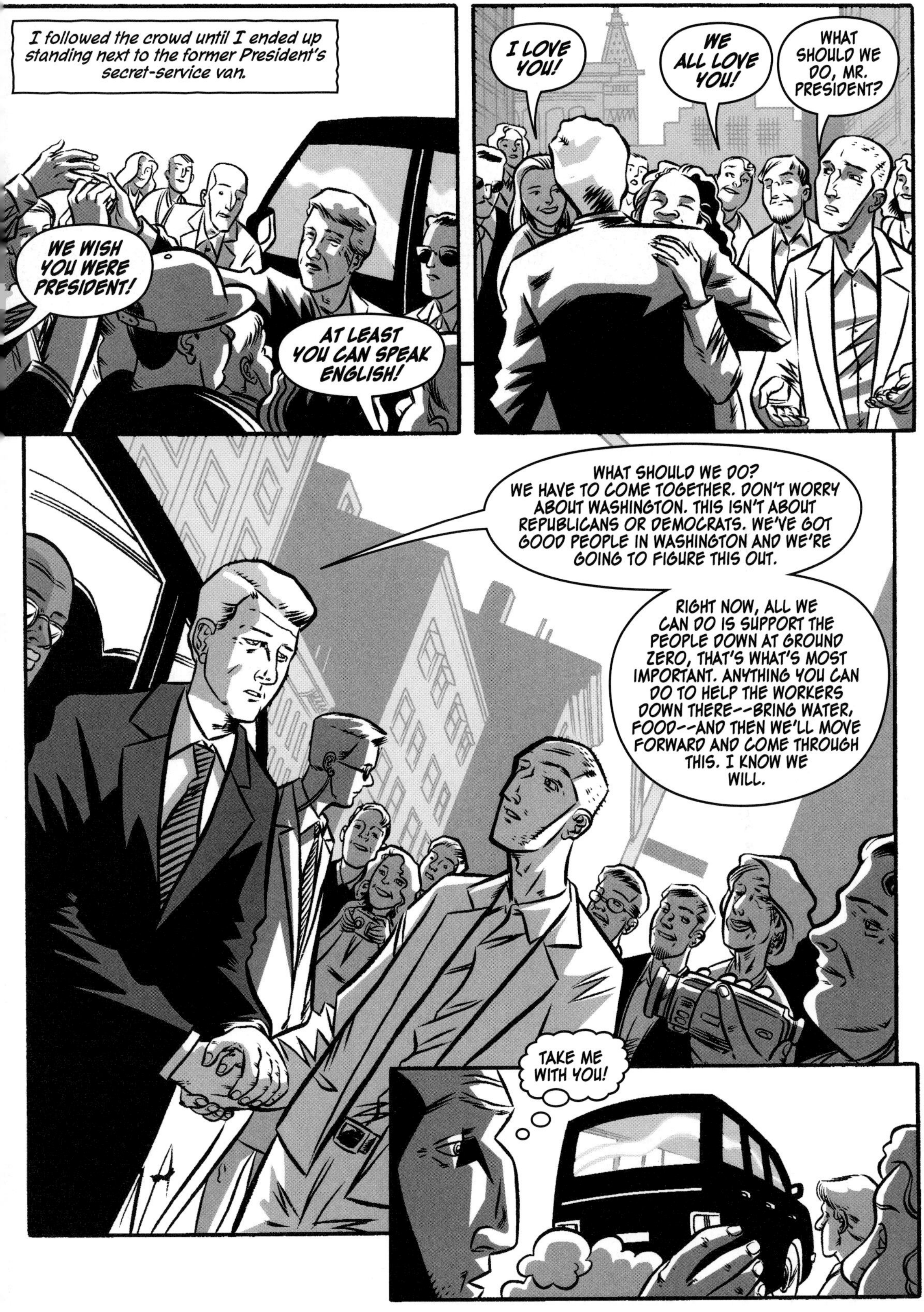

I followed the crowd until I ended up standing next to the former President's secret-service van.
WE WISH YOU WERE PRESIDENT!
AT LEAST YOU CAN SPEAK ENGLISH!
I LOVE YOU!
WE ALL LOVE YOU!
WHAT SHOULD WE DO, MR. PRESIDENT?
WHAT SHOULD WE DO? WE HAVE TO COME TOGETHER. DON'T WORRY ABOUT WASHINGTON. THIS ISN'T ABOUT REPUBLICANS OR DEMOCRATS. WE'VE GOT GOOD PEOPLE IN WASHINGTON AND WE'RE GOING TO FIGURE THIS OUT.
RIGHT NOW, ALL WE CAN DO IS SUPPORT THE PEOPLE DOWN AT GROUND ZERO, THAT'S WHAT'S MOST IMPORTANT. ANYTHING YOU CAN DO TO HELP THE WORKERS DOWN THERE--BRING WATER, FOOD--AND THEN WE'LL MOVE FORWARD AND COME THROUGH THIS. I KNOW WE WILL.
TAKE ME WITH YOU!

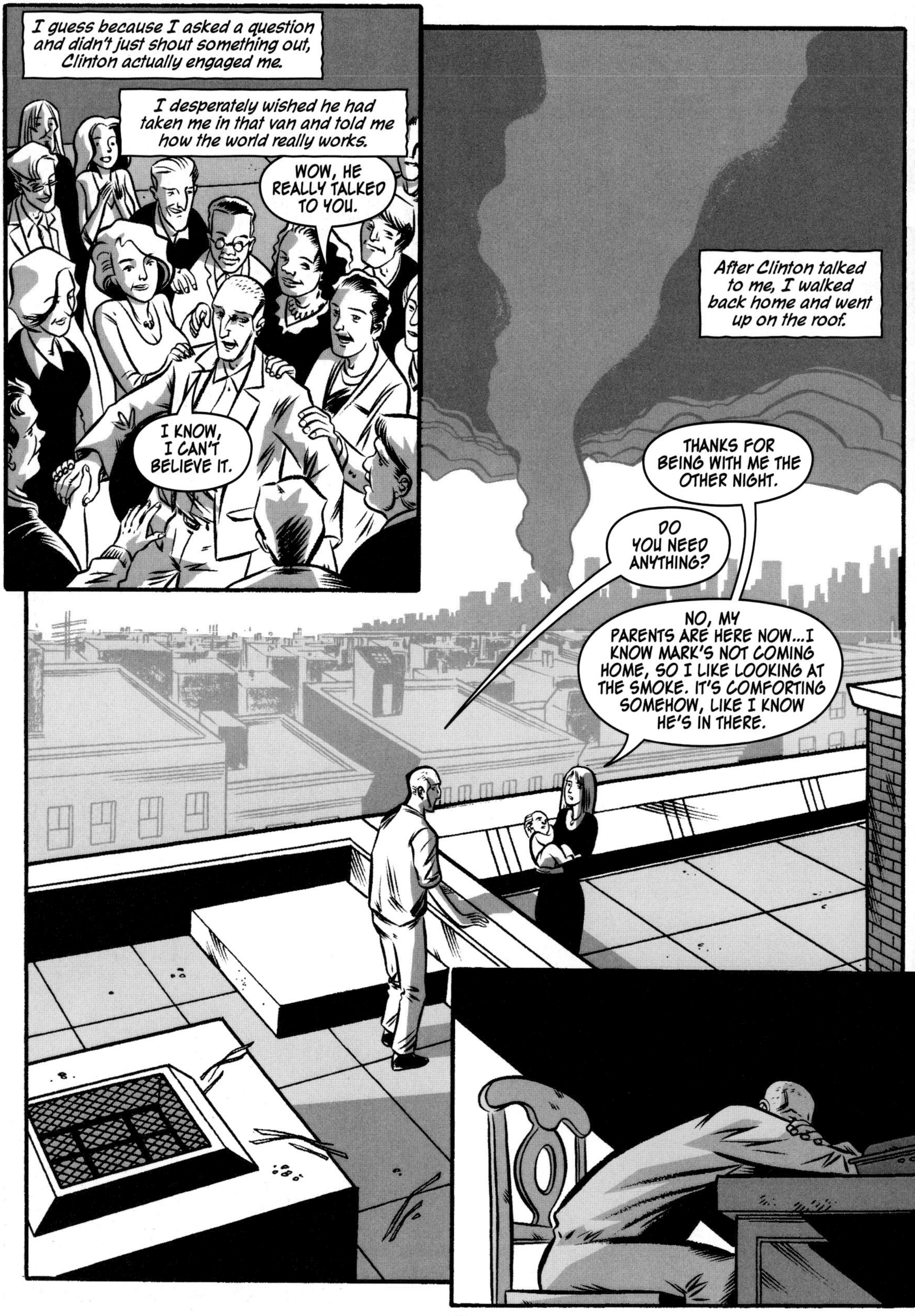

I guess because I asked a question and didn't just shout something out, Clinton actually engaged me.
I desperately wished he had taken me in that van and told me how the world really works.
WOW, HE REALLY TALKED TO YOU.
I KNOW, I CAN'T BELIEVE IT.
After Clinton talked to me, I walked back home and went up on the roof.
THANKS FOR BEING WITH ME THE OTHER NIGHT.
DO YOU NEED ANYTHING?
NO, MY PARENTS ARE HERE NOW...I KNOW MARK'S NOT COMING HOME, SO I LIKE LOOKING AT THE SMOKE. IT'S COMFORTING SOMEHOW, LIKE I KNOW HE'S IN THERE.

HELLO?

YOU SOUND TERRIBLE. WHAT'S THE MATTER?

I WAS JUST TALKING TO MY NEIGHBOR, THE ONE THAT LOST HER HUSBAND.

I'M SORRY.

YOU'RE NOT GOING TO BELIEVE THIS, BUT CLINTON WAS IN MANHATTAN, GOING AROUND HUGGING PEOPLE AND I ASKED HIM A QUESTION AND HE HELD MY HAND.

I DON'T BELIEVE YOU. WHY ARE YOU MAKING UP STORIES? THIS IS A TERRIBLE TIME.

IT'S TRUE! HE HELD MY HAND. LOOKED ME IN THE EYE!

REALLY?

YES. IT'S LIKE I WAS ZELIG OR SOMETHING.

DID YOU TELL HIM YOU'RE A WRITER? YOU COULD GET A JOB AS A SPEECHWRITER. I BET HE PAYS HIS SPEECHWRITERS A LOT OF MONEY.

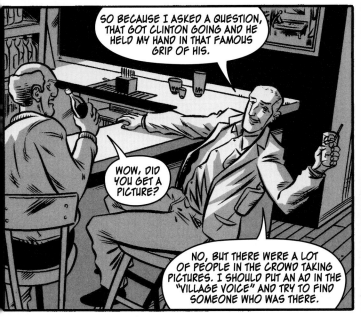

SO BECAUSE I ASKED A QUESTION, THAT GOT CLINTON GOING AND HE HELD MY HAND IN THAT FAMOUS GRIP OF HIS.

WOW, DID YOU GET A PICTURE?

NO, BUT THERE WERE A LOT OF PEOPLE IN THE CROWD TAKING PICTURES. I SHOULD PUT AN AD IN THE "VILLAGE VOICE" AND TRY TO FIND SOMEONE WHO WAS THERE.

...SO CLINTON HELD MY HAND AND LOOKED RIGHT INTO MY EYES. HIS HAIR IS REALLY WHITE. I'M AS TALL AS HE IS...IT WAS INCREDIBLE...OKAY, WELL, YOU DON'T HAVE TO CALL BACK ...I HOPE THINGS ARE GOOD IN SEATTLE...JUST SAYING HELLO...

The next day, September 14th, 2001.

OH, NO!

The girl in charge of reunions for my high school class tracked most of us down and let us know that a classmate of ours had died in the Trade Center.

I remembered sitting next to the boy in math class. He was famous for his freckles and his sweet nature. He had helped me with algebra-- he was better at it than me.

WHAT'S THE ANSWER TO NUMBER TEN?

We played tennis together a few times.

He had been sitting at his desk when one of the planes plowed through his office.

After I read the mass e-mail from the high school girl, there was a private one-on-one e-mail from her just for me.

OH, GOD. I CAN'T BELIEVE IT.

She knew I was friends with Sal and she had learned from someone else in our class that Sal was living with his parents in Illinois and that he was dying.

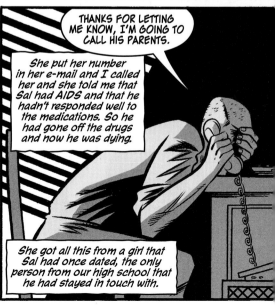

THANKS FOR LETTING ME KNOW, I'M GOING TO CALL HIS PARENTS.

She put her number in her e-mail and I called her and she told me that Sal had AIDS and that he hadn't responded well to the medications. So he had gone off the drugs and now he was dying.

She got all this from a girl that Sal had once dated, the only person from our high school that he had stayed in touch with.

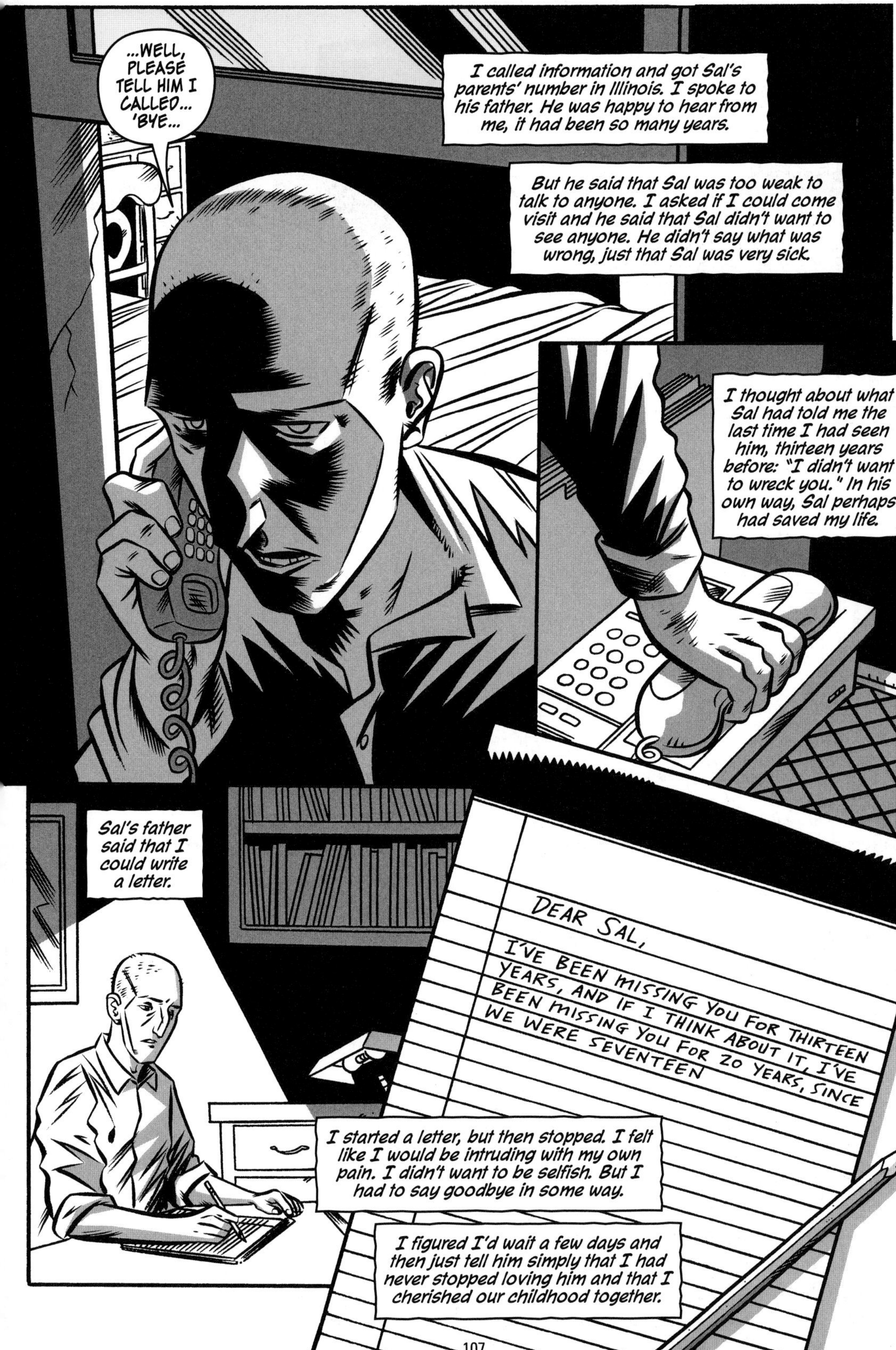

...WELL, PLEASE TELL HIM I CALLED... 'BYE...
I called information and got Sal's parents' number in Illinois. I spoke to his father. He was happy to hear from me, it had been so many years.
But he said that Sal was too weak to talk to anyone. I asked if I could come visit and he said that Sal didn't want to see anyone. He didn't say what was wrong, just that Sal was very sick.
I thought about what Sal had told me the last time I had seen him, thirteen years before: "I didn't want to wreck you." In his own way, Sal perhaps had saved my life.
Sal's father said that I could write a letter.
DEAR SAL,
I'VE BEEN MISSING YOU FOR THIRTEEN YEARS, AND IF I THINK ABOUT IT, I'VE BEEN MISSING YOU FOR 20 YEARS, SINCE WE WERE SEVENTEEN
I started a letter, but then stopped. I felt like I would be intruding with my own pain. I didn't want to be selfish. But I had to say goodbye in some way.
I figured I'd wait a few days and then just tell him simply that I had never stopped loving him and that I cherished our childhood together.

When Bill's bar closed, it became an after-hours joint and the drugs came out. I'd give him a little money, but he didn't seem to want much.

I was really losing control. I started doing that classic thing of waking up each day and swearing that I would stay sober and by nighttime I'd be in a bar, and by the end of the night I'd go to Bill's.

COKE IS FOR SHARING.

So I'd wait for my turn to snort a line. I was hungry for the stuff. I felt like a rat.

As I would do the coke, I'd think of those tests they did, where rats would keep going back to the cocaine dropper until they died.

I didn't really even like the stuff. I liked the first line, maybe, and then after that you just had to keep doing it.

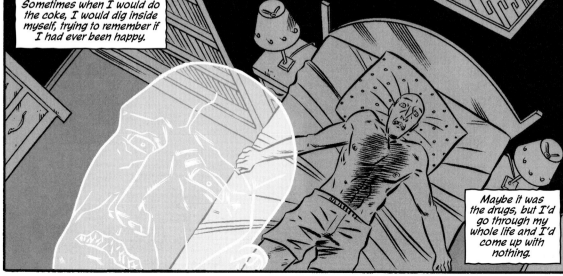

Sometimes when I would do the coke, I would dig inside myself, trying to remember if I had ever been happy.

Maybe it was the drugs, but I'd go through my whole life and I'd come up with nothing.

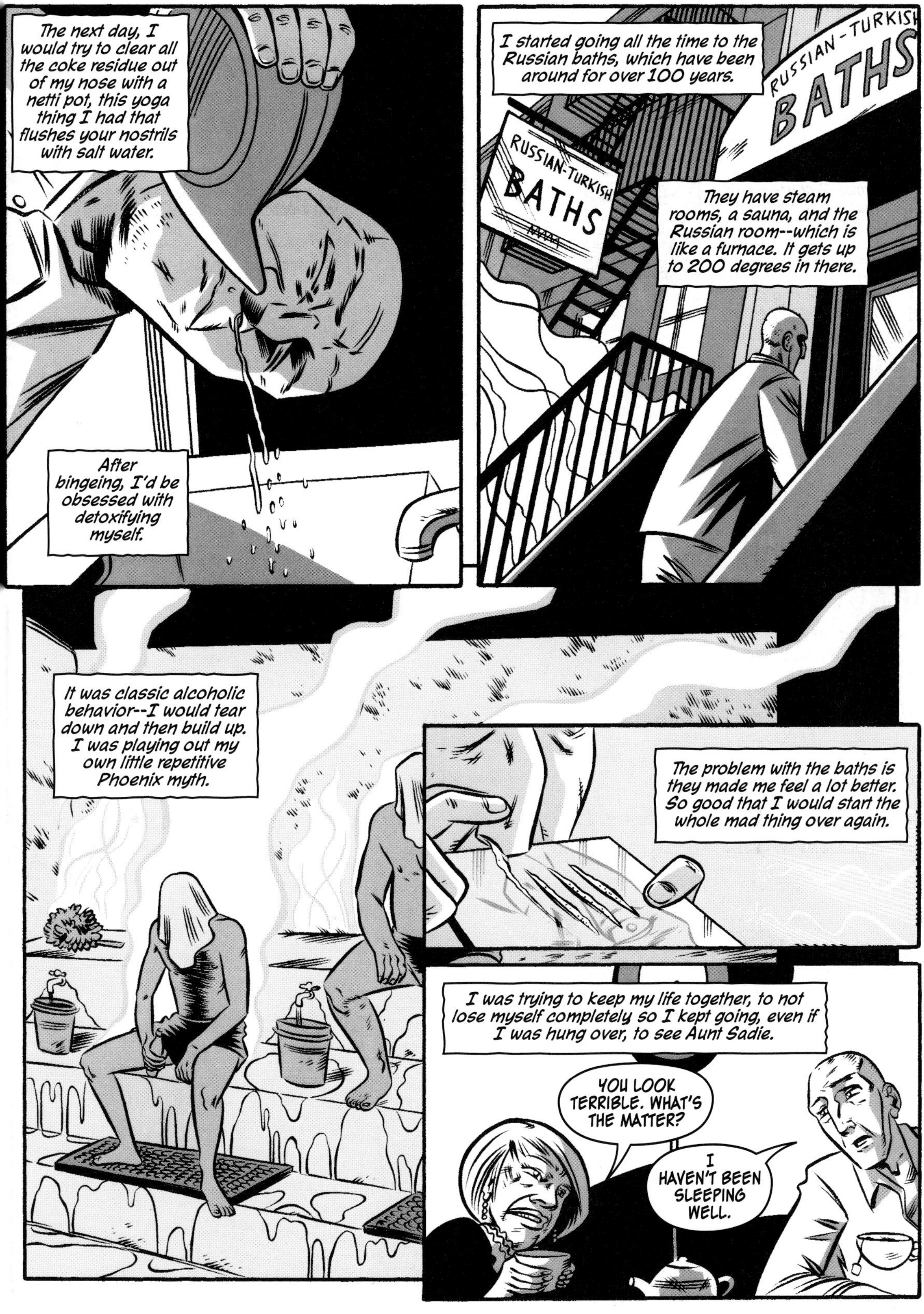
The next day, I would try to clear all the coke residue out of my nose with a netti pot, this yoga thing I had that flushes your nostrils with salt water.
After bingeing, I'd be obsessed with detoxifying myself.
I started going all the time to the Russian baths, which have been around for over 100 years.
RUSSIAN-TURKISH BATHS
RUSSIAN-TURKISH BATHS
They have steam rooms, a sauna, and the Russian room--which is like a furnace. It gets up to 200 degrees in there.
It was classic alcoholic behavior--I would tear down and then build up. I was playing out my own little repetitive Phoenix myth.
The problem with the baths is they made me feel a lot better. So good that I would start the whole mad thing over again.
I was trying to keep my life together, to not lose myself completely so I kept going, even if I was hung over, to see Aunt Sadie.
YOU LOOK TERRIBLE. WHAT'S THE MATTER?
I HAVEN'T BEEN SLEEPING WELL.

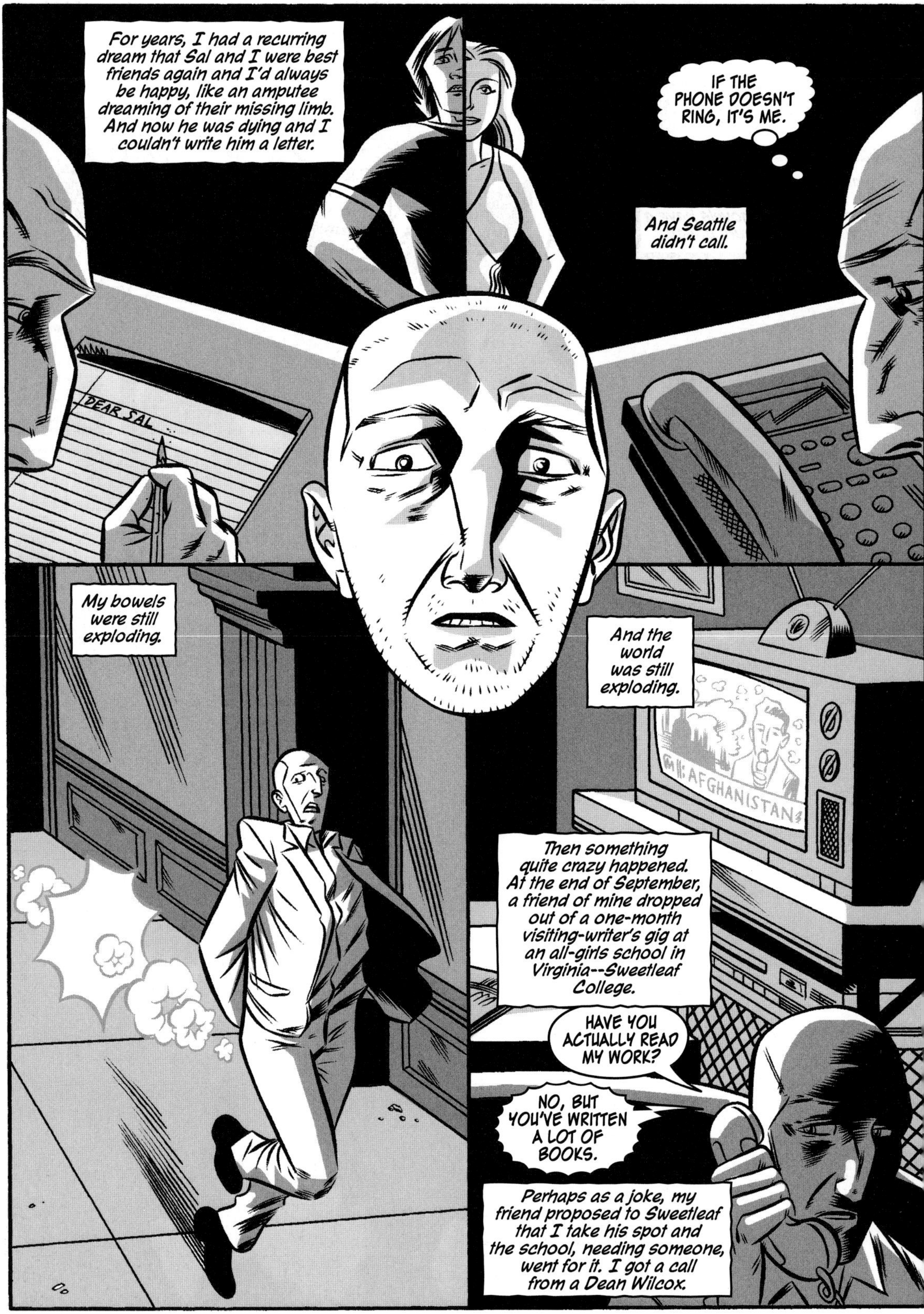

For years, I had a recurring dream that Sal and I were best friends again and I'd always be happy, like an amputee dreaming of their missing limb. And now he was dying and I couldn't write him a letter.
IF THE PHONE DOESN'T RING, IT'S ME.
And Seattle didn't call.
DEAR SAL
My bowels were still exploding.
And the world was still exploding.
AFGHANISTAN
Then something quite crazy happened. At the end of September, a friend of mine dropped out of a one-month visiting-writer's gig at an all-girls school in Virginia--Sweetleaf College.
HAVE YOU ACTUALLY READ MY WORK?
NO, BUT YOU'VE WRITTEN A LOT OF BOOKS.
Perhaps as a joke, my friend proposed to Sweetleaf that I take his spot and the school, needing someone, went for it. I got a call from a Dean Wilcox.

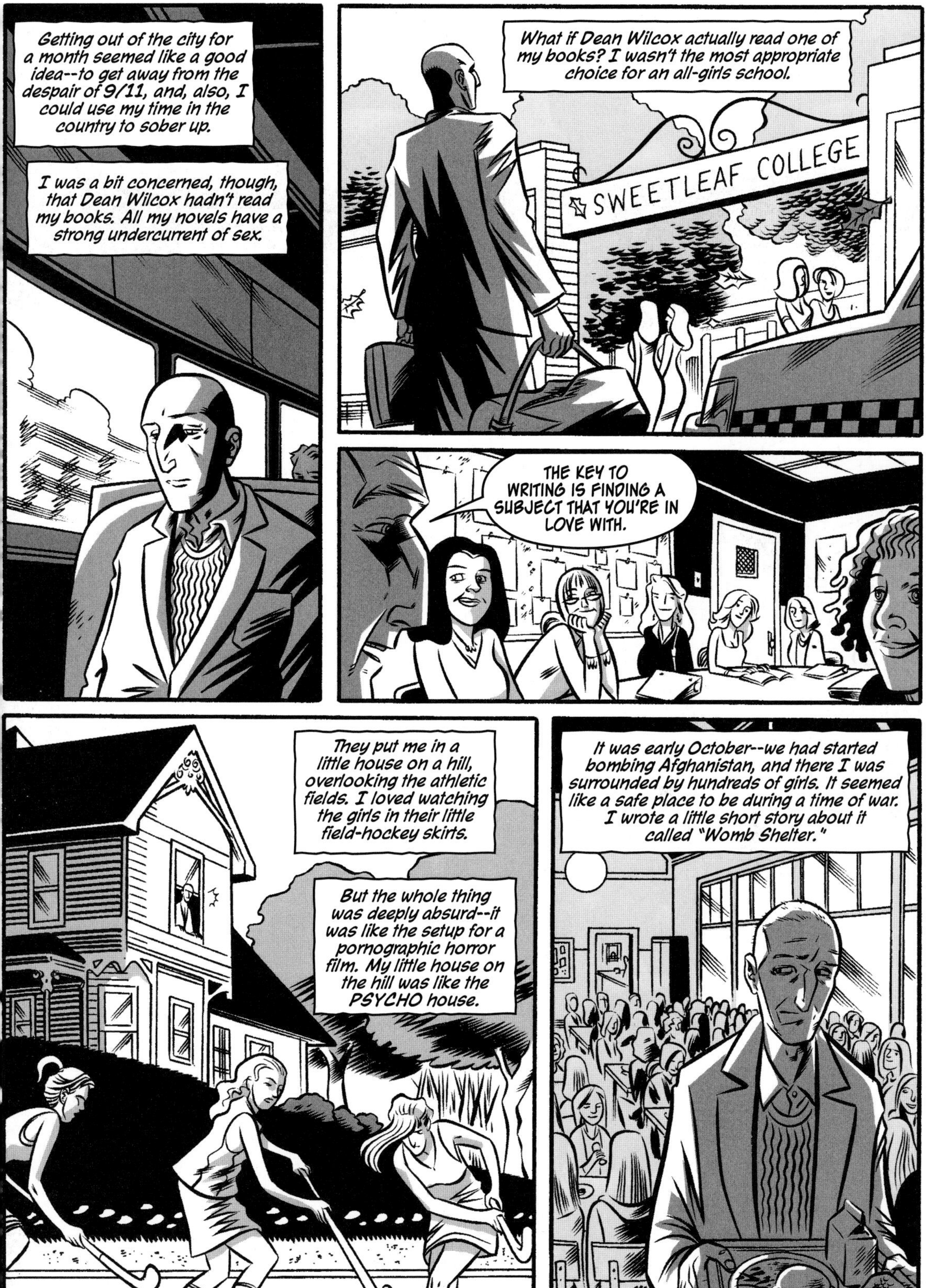
Getting out of the city for a month seemed like a good idea--to get away from the despair of 9/11, and, also, I could use my time in the country to sober up.
I was a bit concerned, though, that Dean Wilcox hadn't read my books. All my novels have a strong undercurrent of sex.
What if Dean Wilcox actually read one of my books? I wasn't the most appropriate choice for an all-girls school.
SWEETLEAF COLLEGE
THE KEY TO WRITING IS FINDING A SUBJECT THAT YOU'RE IN LOVE WITH.
They put me in a little house on a hill, overlooking the athletic fields. I loved watching the girls in their little field-hockey skirts.
But the whole thing was deeply absurd--it was like the setup for a pornographic horror film. My little house on the hill was like the PSYCHO house.
It was early October--we had started bombing Afghanistan, and there I was surrounded by hundreds of girls. It seemed like a safe place to be during a time of war. I wrote a little short story about it called "Womb Shelter."

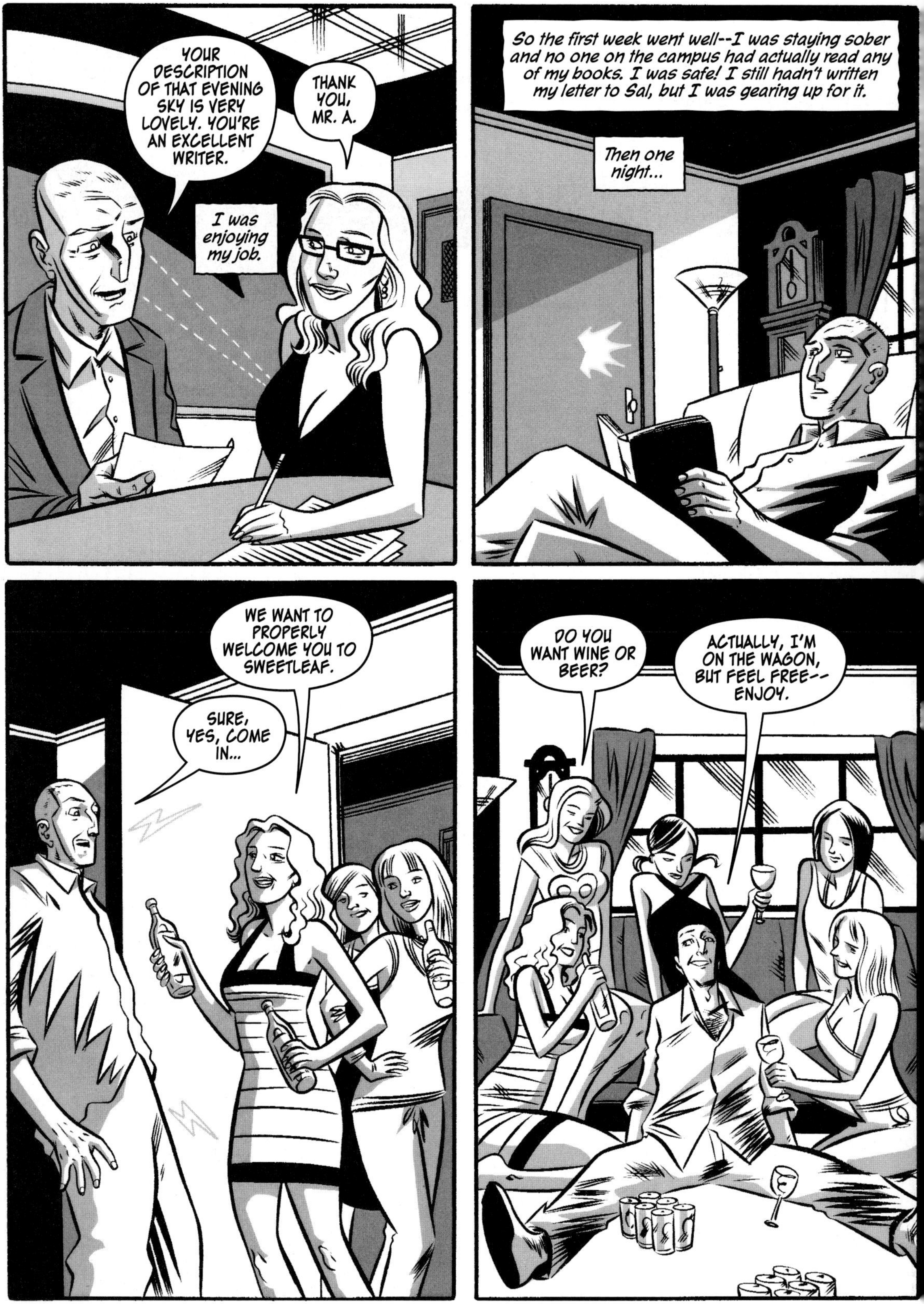
YOUR DESCRIPTION OF THAT EVENING SKY IS VERY LOVELY. YOU'RE AN EXCELLENT WRITER.
THANK YOU, MR. A.
I was enjoying my job.
So the first week went well--I was staying sober and no one on the campus had actually read any of my books. I was safe! I still hadn't written my letter to Sal, but I was gearing up for it.
Then one night...
WE WANT TO PROPERLY WELCOME YOU TO SWEETLEAF.
SURE, YES, COME IN...
DO YOU WANT WINE OR BEER?
ACTUALLY, I'M ON THE WAGON, BUT FEEL FREE--ENJOY.

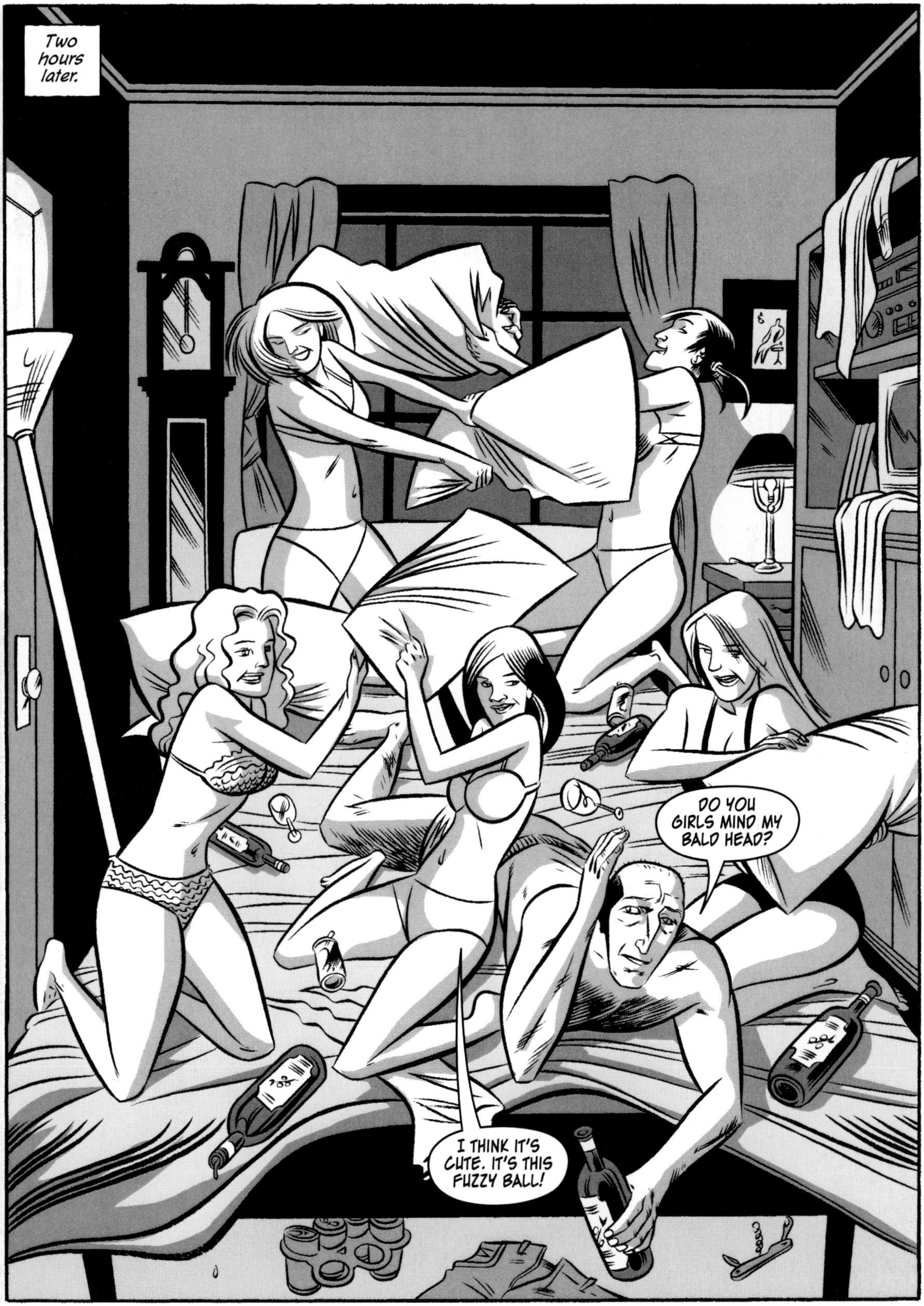
Two hours later.
DO YOU GIRLS MIND MY BALD HEAD?
I THINK IT'S CUTE. IT'S THIS FUZZY BALL!

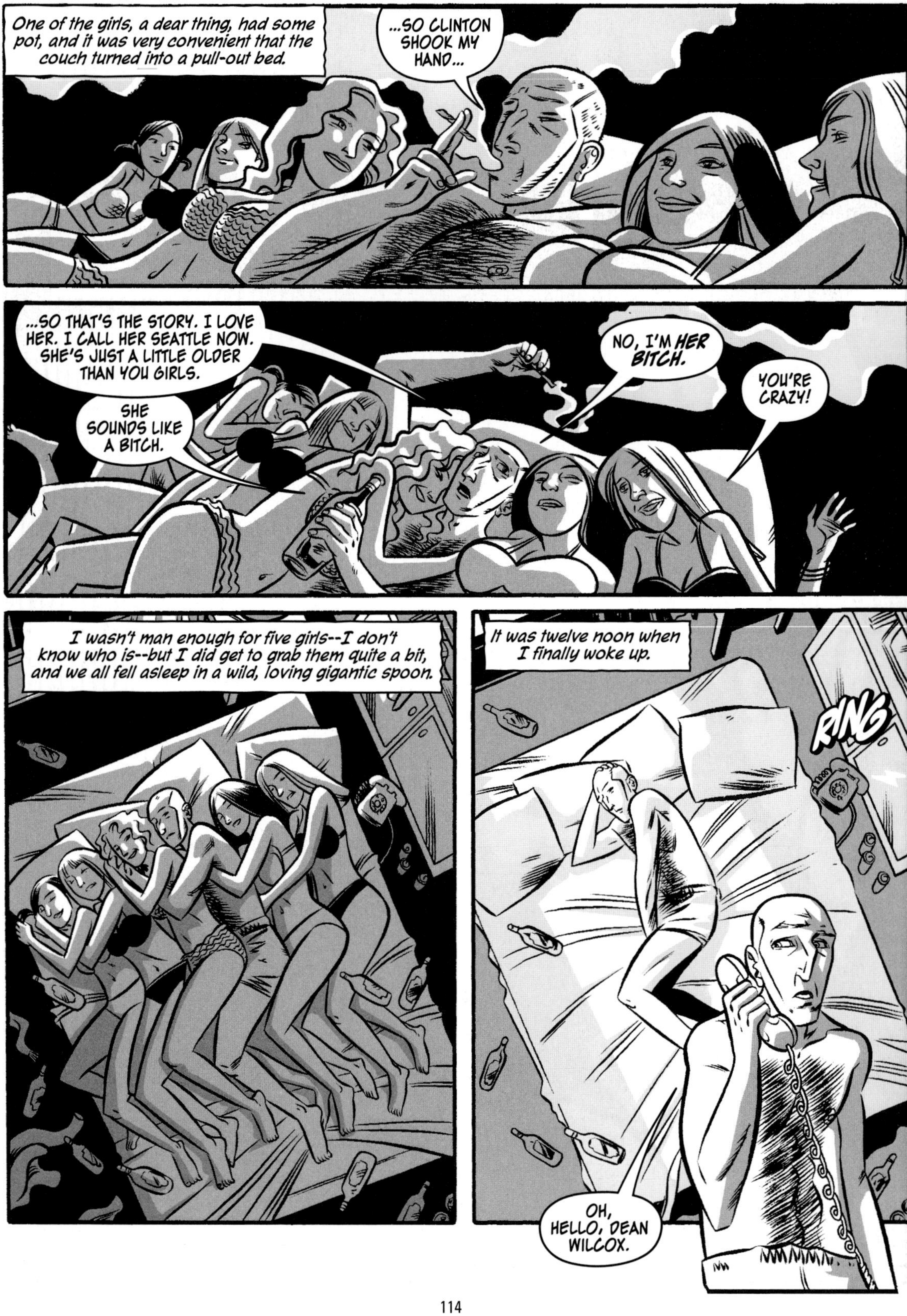
One of the girls, a dear thing, had some pot, and it was very convenient that the couch turned into a pull-out bed.
...SO CLINTON SHOOK MY HAND...
...SO THAT'S THE STORY. I LOVE HER. I CALL HER SEATTLE NOW. SHE'S JUST A LITTLE OLDER THAN YOU GIRLS.
SHE SOUNDS LIKE A BITCH.
NO, I'M HER BITCH.
YOU'RE CRAZY!
I wasn't man enough for five girls--I don't know who is--but I did get to grab them quite a bit, and we all fell asleep in a wild, loving gigantic spoon.
It was twelve noon when I finally woke up.
RING
OH, HELLO, DEAN WILCOX.

I was fired and told to leave immediately. Word had spread to Dean Wilcox that I had held an orgy with ten girls. It was a small campus, and the girls had talked.

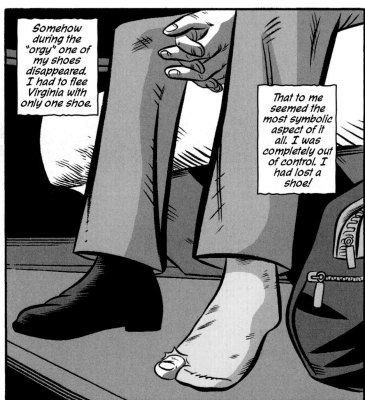

Somehow during the "orgy" one of my shoes disappeared. I had to flee Virginia with only one shoe.

That to me seemed the most symbolic aspect of it all. I was completely out of control. I had lost a shoe!

A few hours before.

THIS IS DISGRACEFUL! NOTHING LIKE THIS HAS EVER HAPPENED BEFORE.

I'M SORRY.

WHY ARE YOU ONLY WEARING ONE SHOE?

I DON'T KNOW.

When I got home there were no messages from Seattle. It looked like it was finally over.

I didn't blame her for anything. She was young and confused. What was my excuse? I was old and confused. I was sick to want it, but I wished she had called.

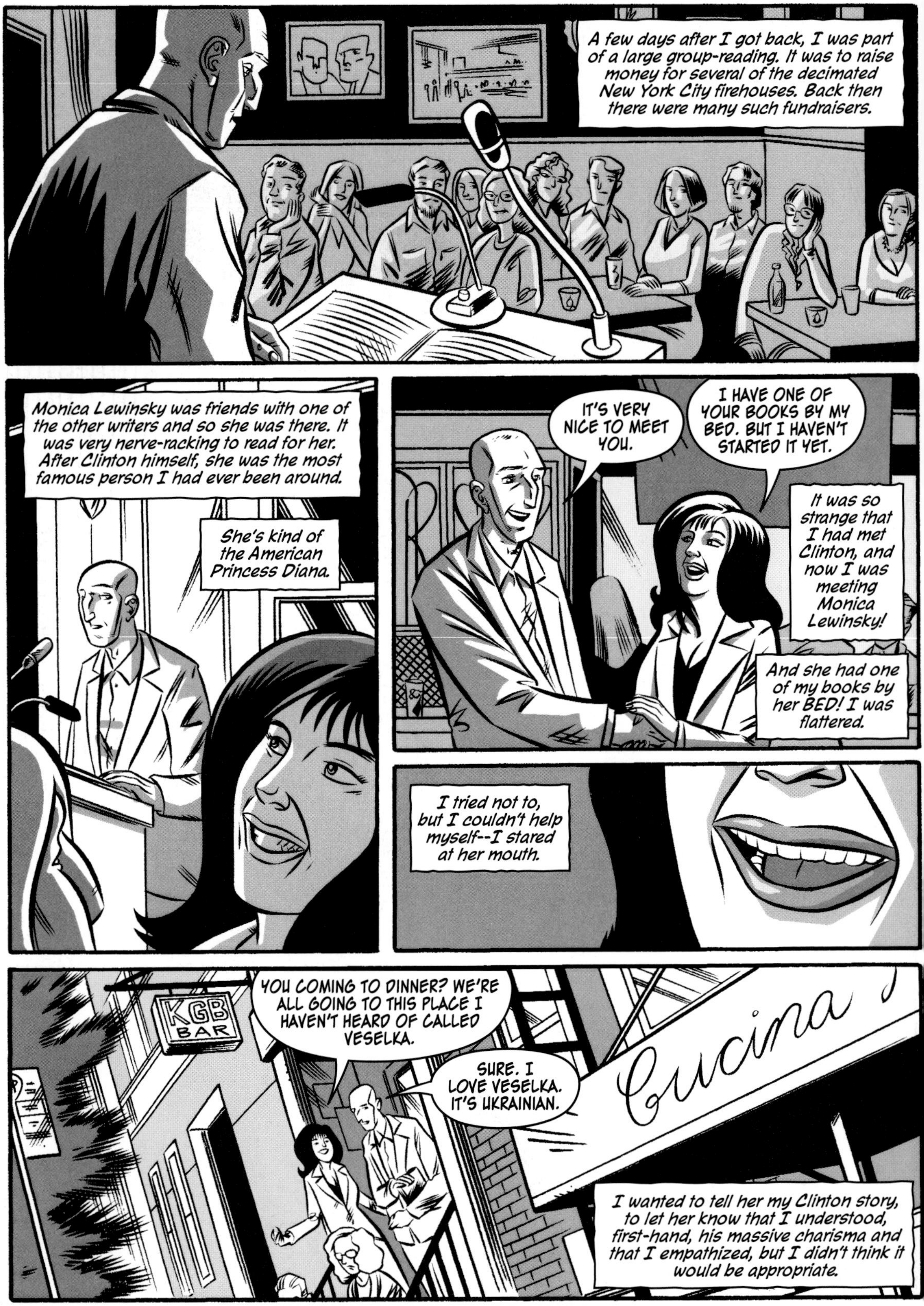
A few days after I got back, I was part of a large group-reading. It was to raise money for several of the decimated New York City firehouses. Back then there were many such fundraisers.
Monica Lewinsky was friends with one of the other writers and so she was there. It was very nerve-racking to read for her. After Clinton himself, she was the most famous person I had ever been around.
She's kind of the American Princess Diana.
IT'S VERY NICE TO MEET YOU.
I HAVE ONE OF YOUR BOOKS BY MY BED. BUT I HAVEN'T STARTED IT YET.
It was so strange that I had met Clinton, and now I was meeting Monica Lewinsky!
And she had one of my books by her BED! I was flattered.
I tried not to, but I couldn't help myself--I stared at her mouth.
KGB BAR
YOU COMING TO DINNER? WE'RE ALL GOING TO THIS PLACE I HAVEN'T HEARD OF CALLED VESELKA.
SURE. I LOVE VESELKA. IT'S UKRAINIAN.
Cucina
I wanted to tell her my Clinton story, to let her know that I understood, first-hand, his massive charisma and that I empathized, but I didn't think it would be appropriate.

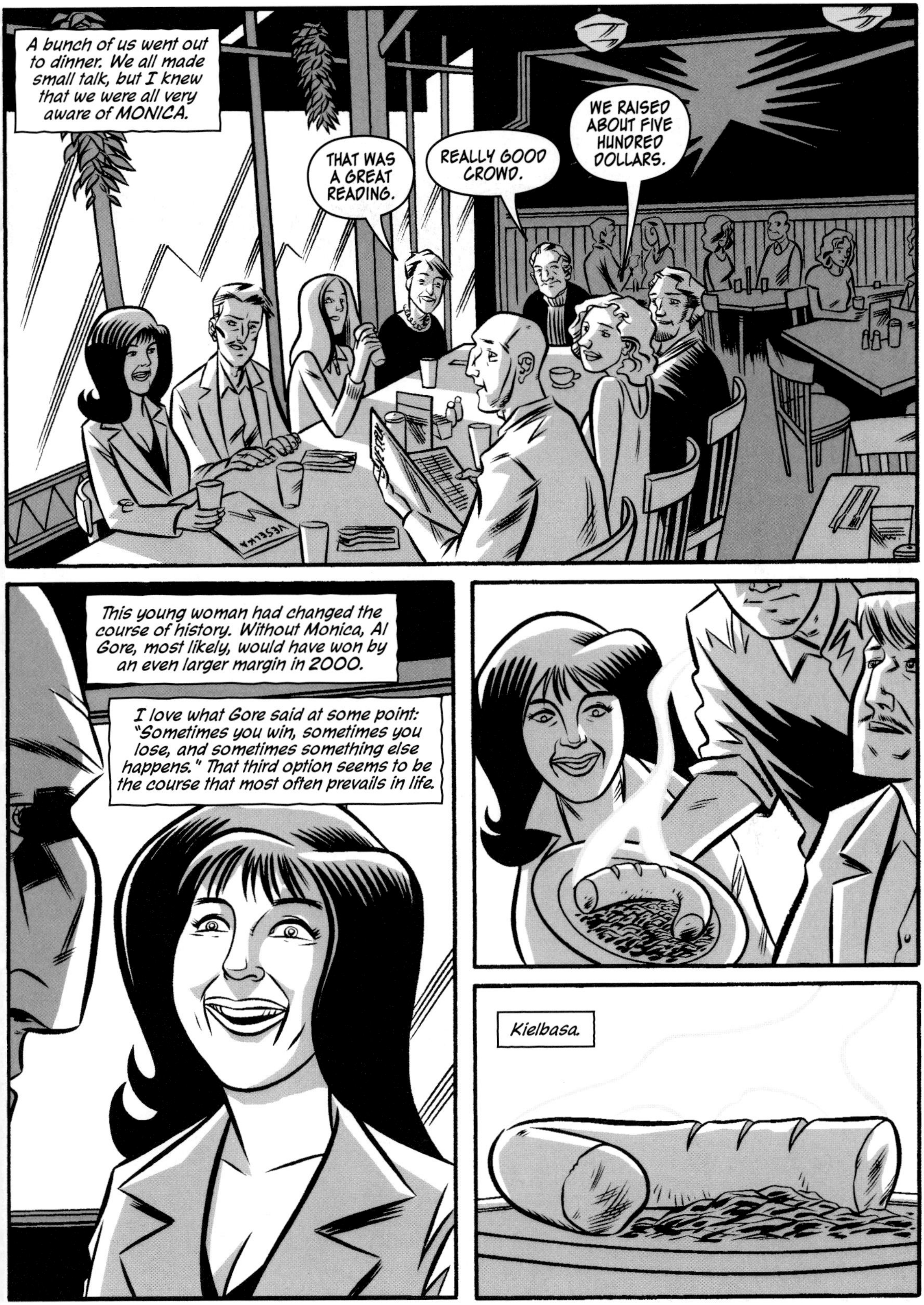
A bunch of us went out to dinner. We all made small talk, but I knew that we were all very aware of MONICA.
THAT WAS A GREAT READING.
REALLY GOOD CROWD.
WE RAISED ABOUT FIVE HUNDRED DOLLARS.
This young woman had changed the course of history. Without Monica, Al Gore, most likely, would have won by an even larger margin in 2000.
I love what Gore said at some point: "Sometimes you win, sometimes you lose, and sometimes something else happens." That third option seems to be the course that most often prevails in life.
Kielbasa.

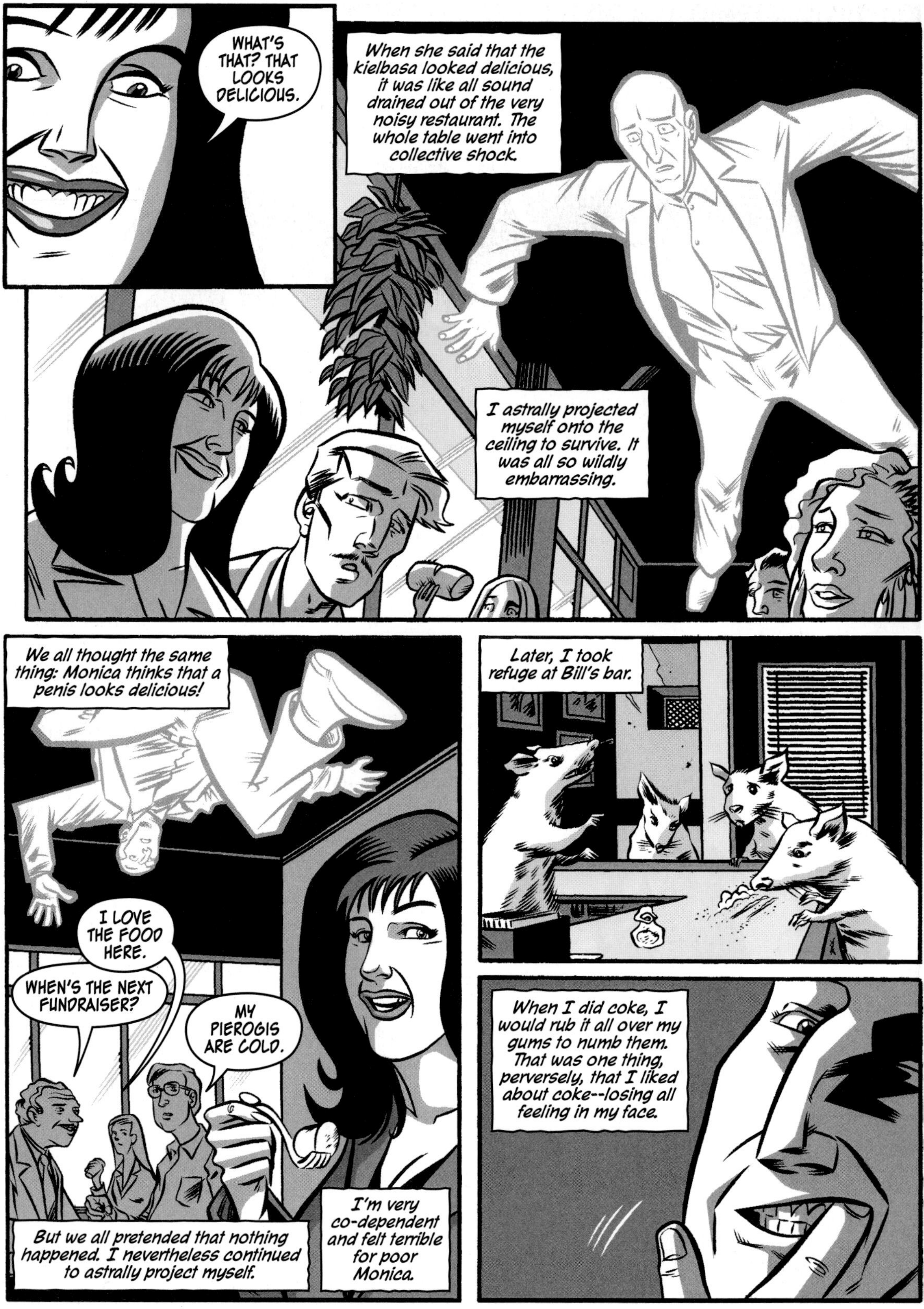
WHAT'S THAT? THAT LOOKS DELICIOUS.
When she said that the kielbasa looked delicious, it was like all sound drained out of the very noisy restaurant. The whole table went into collective shock.
I astrally projected myself onto the ceiling to survive. It was all so wildly embarrassing.
We all thought the same thing: Monica thinks that a penis looks delicious!
I LOVE THE FOOD HERE.
WHEN'S THE NEXT FUNDRAISER?
MY PIEROGIS ARE COLD.
But we all pretended that nothing happened. I nevertheless continued to astrally project myself.
I'm very co-dependent and felt terrible for poor Monica.
Later, I took refuge at Bill's bar.
When I did coke, I would rub it all over my gums to numb them. That was one thing, perversely, that I liked about coke--losing all feeling in my face.

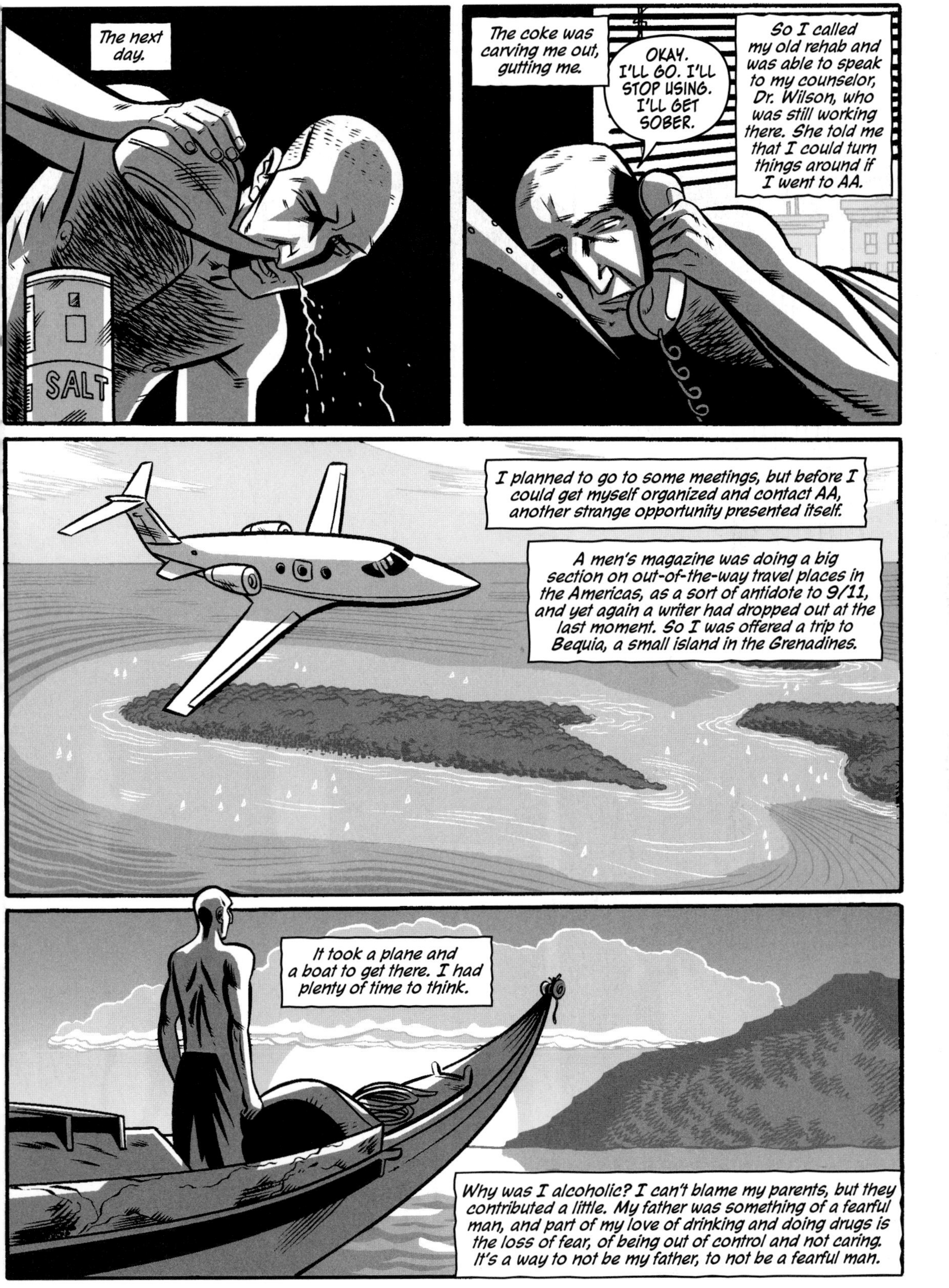
The next day.
SALT
The coke was carving me out, gutting me.
OKAY. I'LL GO. I'LL STOP USING. I'LL GET SOBER.
So I called my old rehab and was able to speak to my counselor, Dr. Wilson, who was still working there. She told me that I could turn things around if I went to AA.
I planned to go to some meetings, but before I could get myself organized and contact AA, another strange opportunity presented itself.
A men's magazine was doing a big section on out-of-the-way travel places in the Americas, as a sort of antidote to 9/11, and yet again a writer had dropped out at the last moment. So I was offered a trip to Bequia, a small island in the Grenadines.
It took a plane and a boat to get there. I had plenty of time to think.
Why was I alcoholic? I can't blame my parents, but they contributed a little. My father was something of a fearful man, and part of my love of drinking and doing drugs is the loss of fear, of being out of control and not caring. It's a way to not be my father, to not be a fearful man.

And my mother was a perfectionist and I could never really live up to her standards, at least in my mind, and so drinking always felt like a relief--I didn't have to be perfect anymore.

And then, nothing to do with my parents, there has always been this germ of self-loathing in me, this desire deep down to destroy myself.

I read this line in a book once: "Alcoholics think they're bad and deserve to be punished."

Plus, there is the physical side to alcoholism, the allergy part--I've almost never been able to stop at one or two drinks. Once I get a taste for booze or drugs, I simply want MORE.

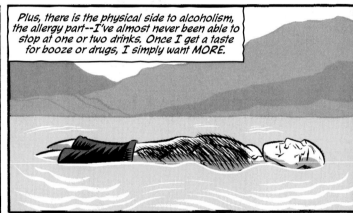

And I've never wanted to be a social drinker. I've just wanted to drink and not get in trouble, not feel in pain afterwards.

But there's always pain, because as Tony, my old friend from rehab said, you can't stay intoxicated forever. Eventually you come down and your body feels destroyed.

And for me there's also this terrible guilt. A feeling of shame for what I've done.

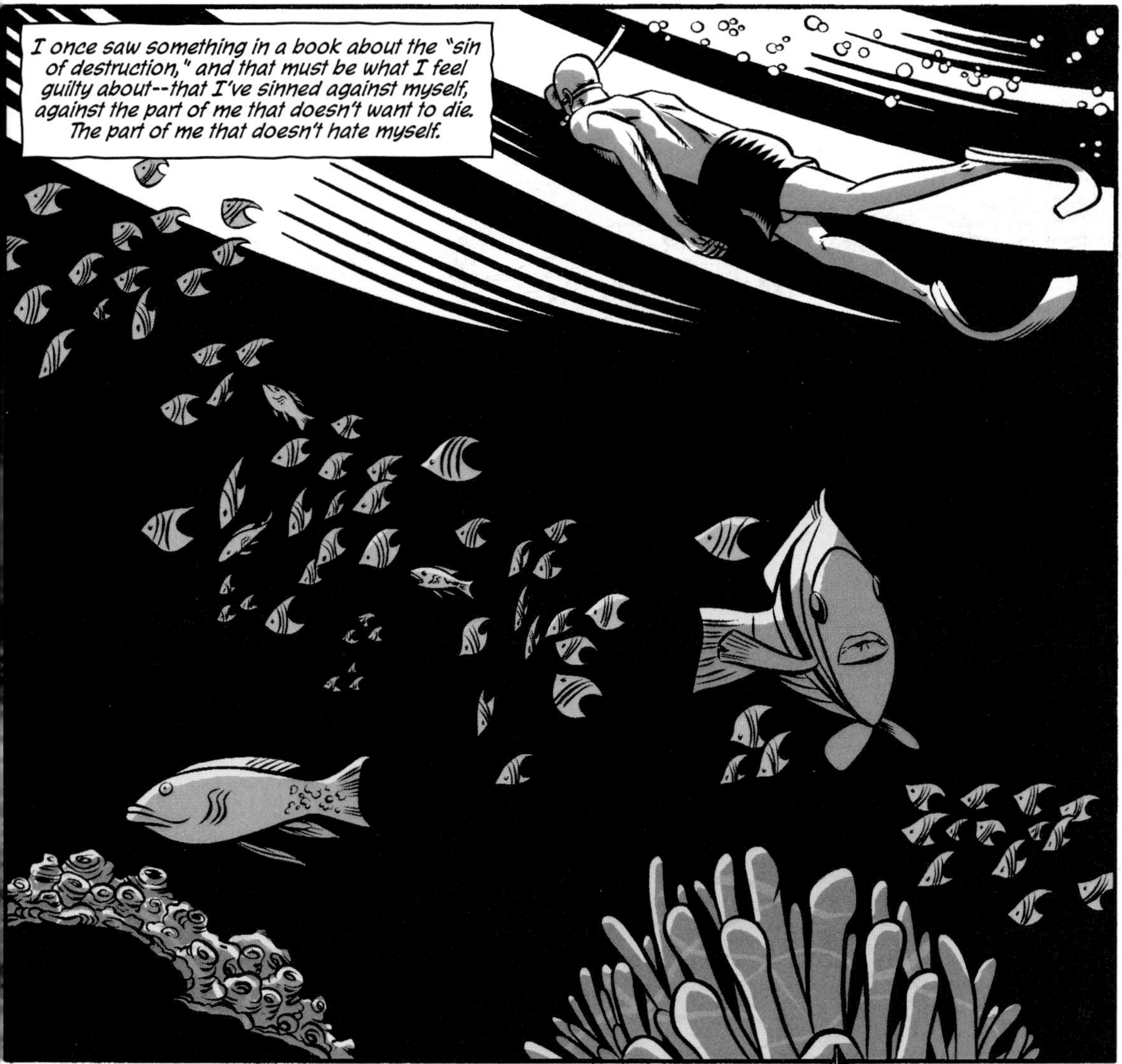
I once saw something in a book about the "sin of destruction," and that must be what I feel guilty about--that I've sinned against myself, against the part of me that doesn't want to die. The part of me that doesn't hate myself.

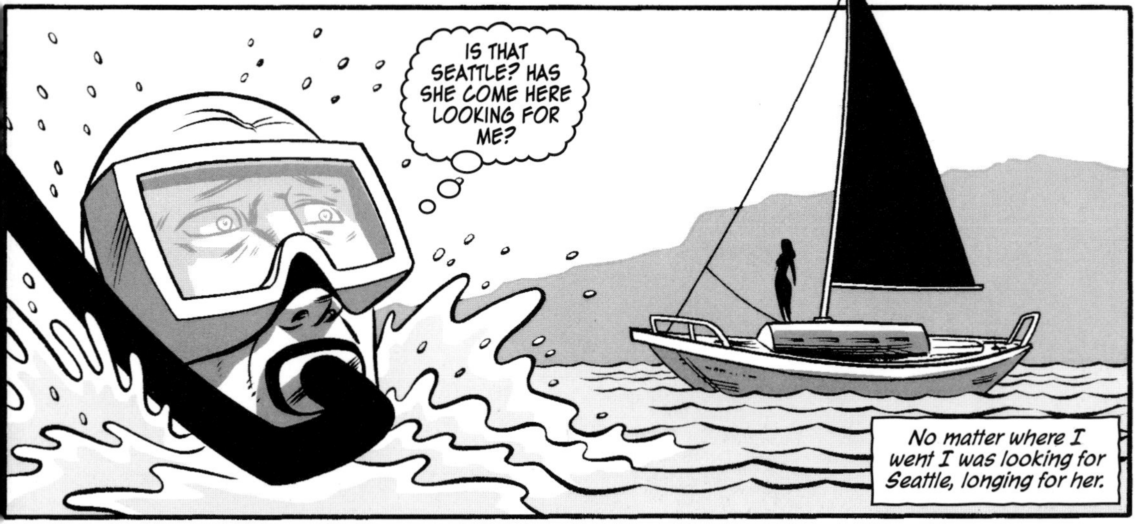
IS THAT SEATTLE? HAS SHE COME HERE LOOKING FOR ME?
No matter where I went I was looking for Seattle, longing for her.

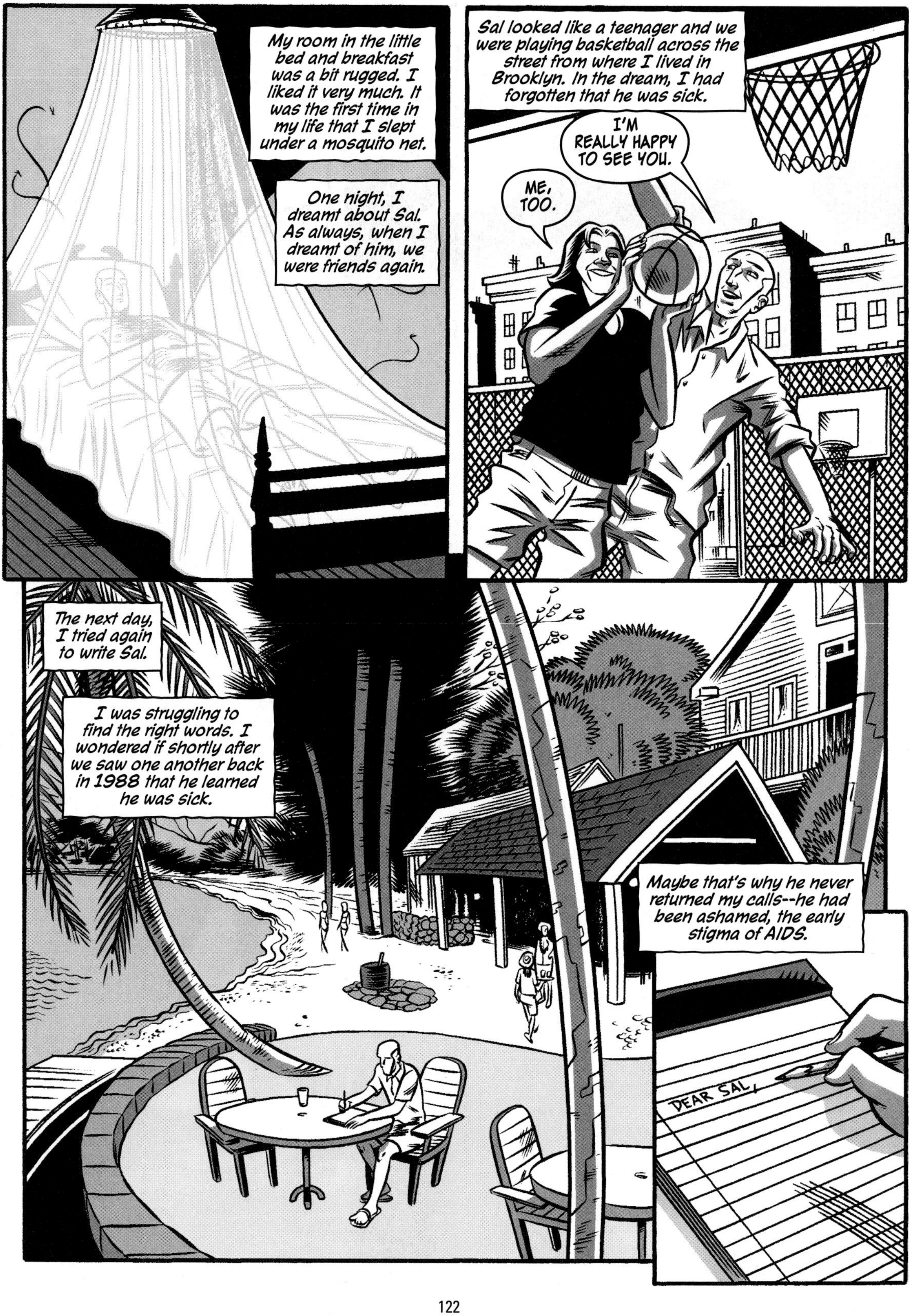
My room in the little bed and breakfast was a bit rugged. I liked it very much. It was the first time in my life that I slept under a mosquito net.
One night, I dreamt about Sal. As always, when I dreamt of him, we were friends again.
Sal looked like a teenager and we were playing basketball across the street from where I lived in Brooklyn. In the dream, I had forgotten that he was sick.
I'M REALLY HAPPY TO SEE YOU.
ME, TOO.
The next day, I tried again to write Sal.
I was struggling to find the right words. I wondered if shortly after we saw one another back in 1988 that he learned he was sick.
Maybe that's why he never returned my calls--he had been ashamed, the early stigma of AIDS.
DEAR SAL,

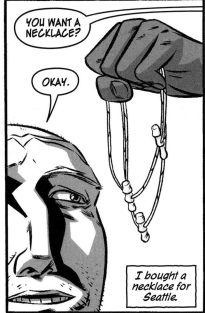

YOU WANT A NECKLACE?

OKAY.

I bought a necklace for Seattle.

I had been in Bequia four days and hadn't taken a drink. My last night I was feeling lonely and wished I could drink, but I fought the temptation.

The man who sold me the necklace sat at my table. His name was Desmond.

WHERE YOU FROM?

NEW YORK.

BAD THINGS THERE NOW. YOU SHOULD LIVE HERE. MORE BEAUTIFUL.

I KNOW.

DO YOU SMOKE GANJA?

I'M NOT SUPPOSED TO.

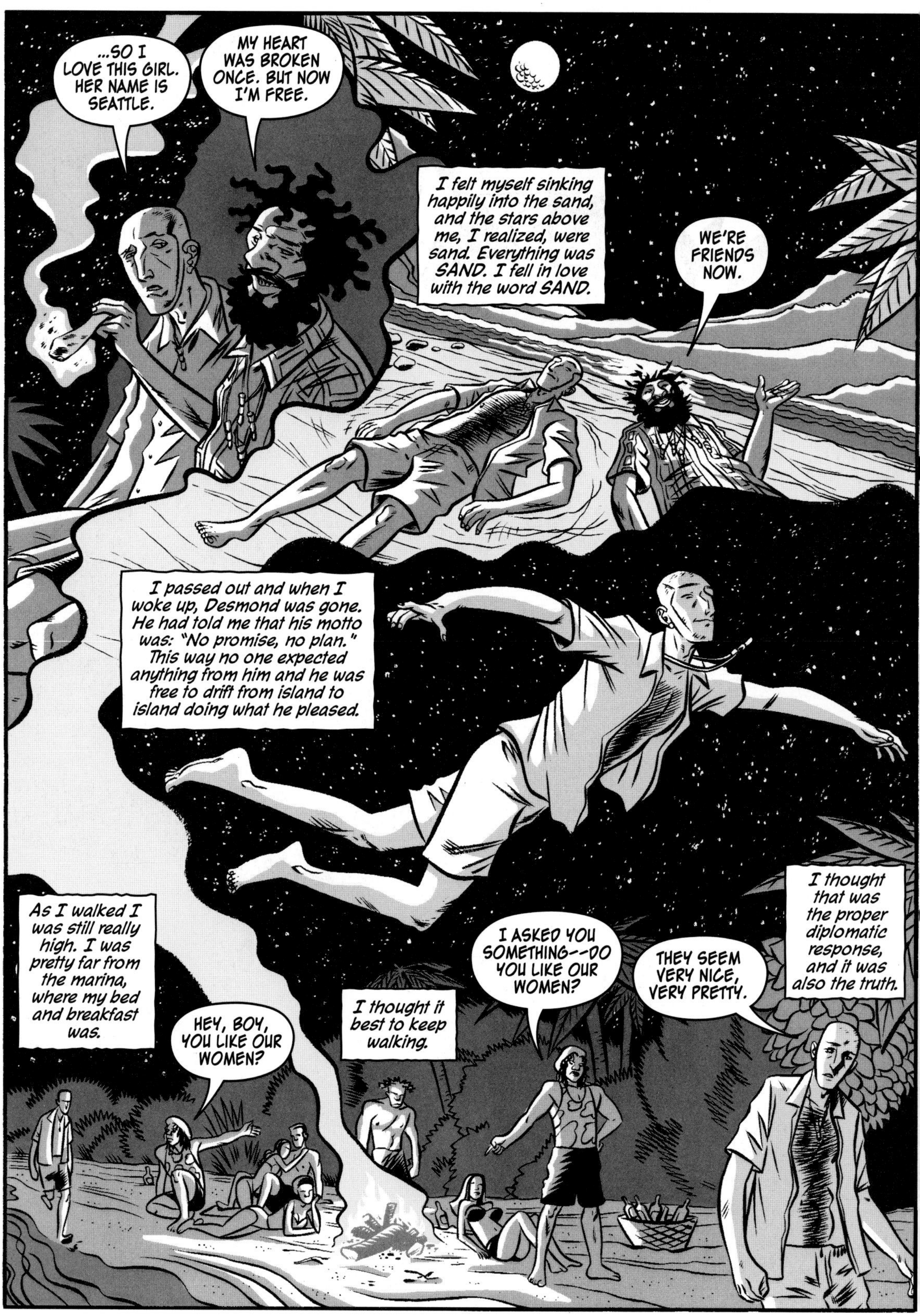
...SO I LOVE THIS GIRL. HER NAME IS SEATTLE.
MY HEART WAS BROKEN ONCE. BUT NOW I'M FREE.
I felt myself sinking happily into the sand, and the stars above me, I realized, were sand. Everything was SAND. I fell in love with the word SAND.
WE'RE FRIENDS NOW.
I passed out and when I woke up, Desmond was gone. He had told me that his motto was: "No promise, no plan." This way no one expected anything from him and he was free to drift from island to island doing what he pleased.
As I walked I was still really high. I was pretty far from the marina, where my bed and breakfast was.
HEY, BOY, YOU LIKE OUR WOMEN?
I thought it best to keep walking.
I ASKED YOU SOMETHING--DO YOU LIKE OUR WOMEN?
THEY SEEM VERY NICE, VERY PRETTY.
I thought that was the proper diplomatic response, and it was also the truth.

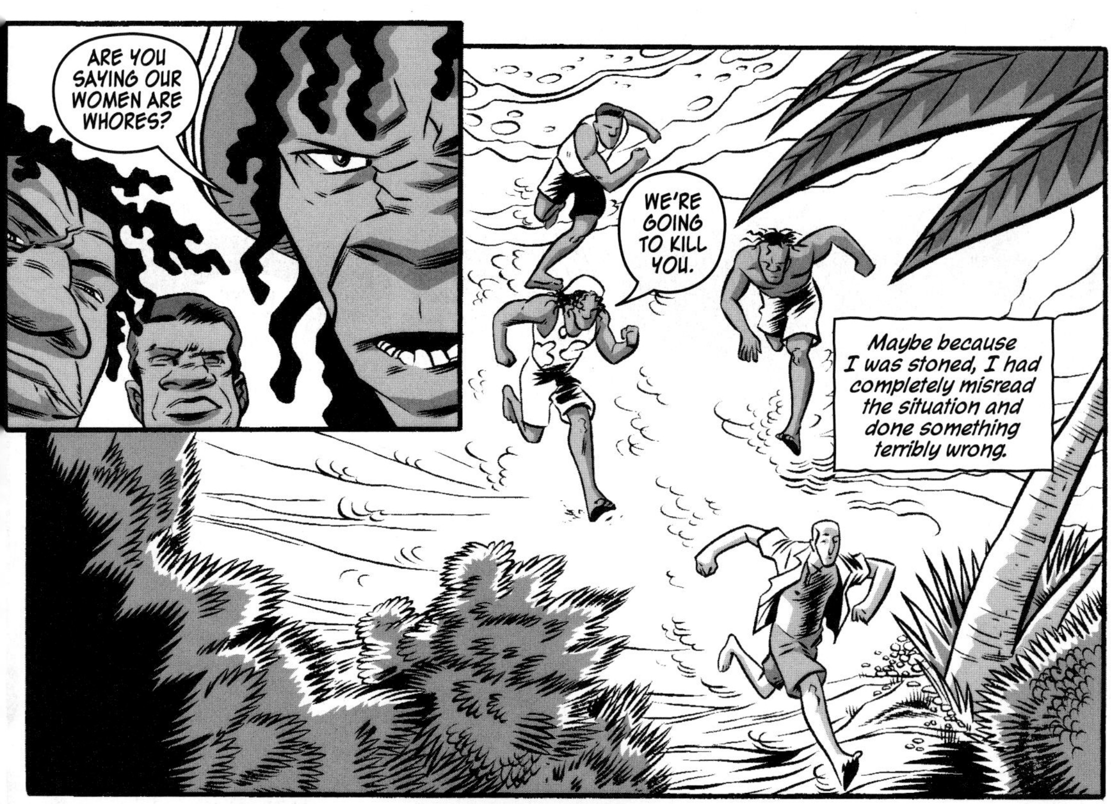
ARE YOU SAYING OUR WOMEN ARE WHORES?
WE'RE GOING TO KILL YOU.
Maybe because I was stoned, I had completely misread the situation and done something terribly wrong.

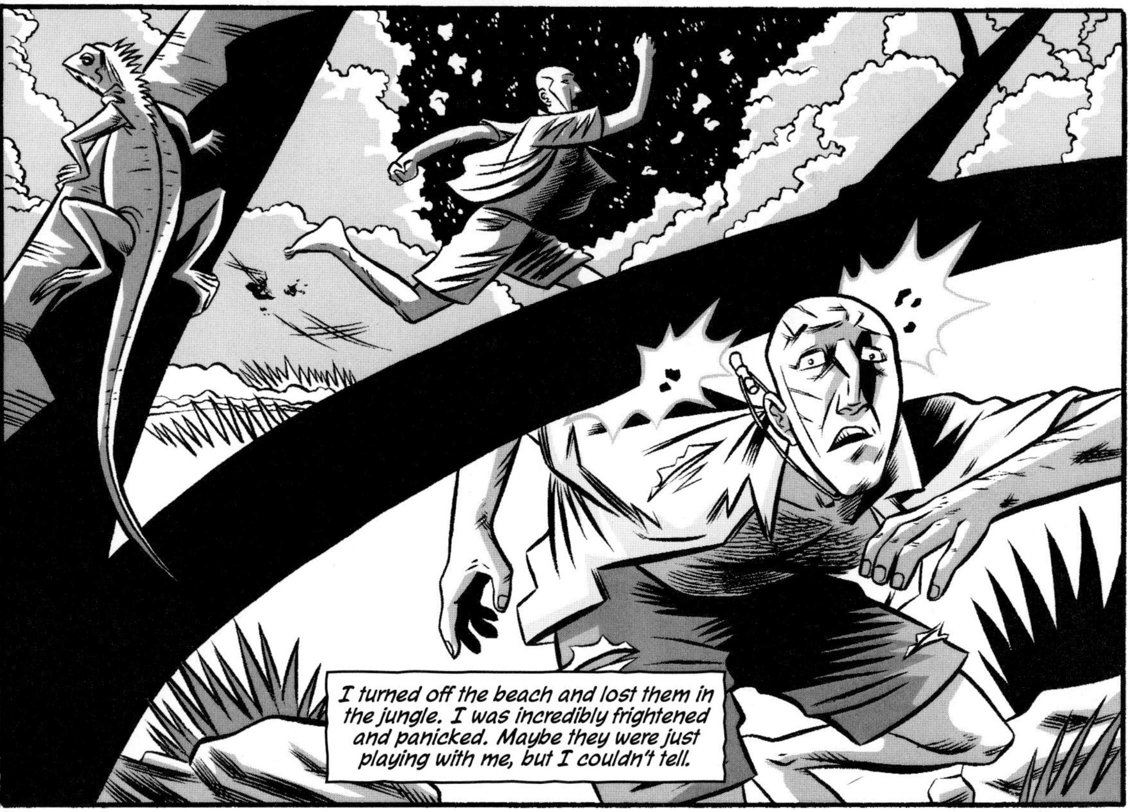
I turned off the beach and lost them in the jungle. I was incredibly frightened and panicked. Maybe they were just playing with me, but I couldn't tell.

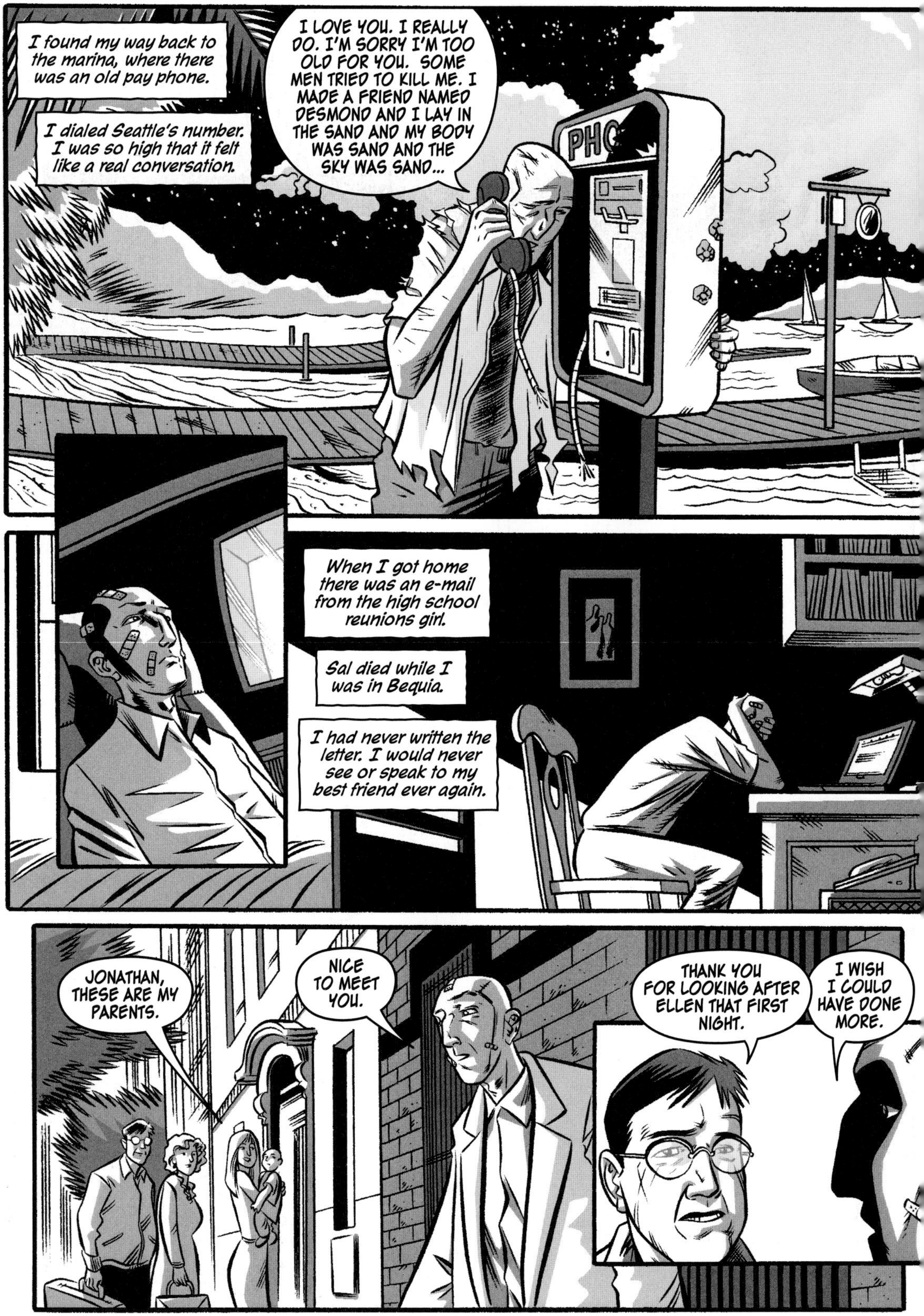
I found my way back to the marina, where there was an old pay phone.
I dialed Seattle's number. I was so high that it felt like a real conversation.
I LOVE YOU. I REALLY DO. I'M SORRY I'M TOO OLD FOR YOU. SOME MEN TRIED TO KILL ME. I MADE A FRIEND NAMED DESMOND AND I LAY IN THE SAND AND MY BODY WAS SAND AND THE SKY WAS SAND...
PHO
When I got home there was an e-mail from the high school reunions girl.
Sal died while I was in Bequia.
I had never written the letter. I would never see or speak to my best friend ever again.
JONATHAN, THESE ARE MY PARENTS.
NICE TO MEET YOU.
THANK YOU FOR LOOKING AFTER ELLEN THAT FIRST NIGHT.
I WISH I COULD HAVE DONE MORE.

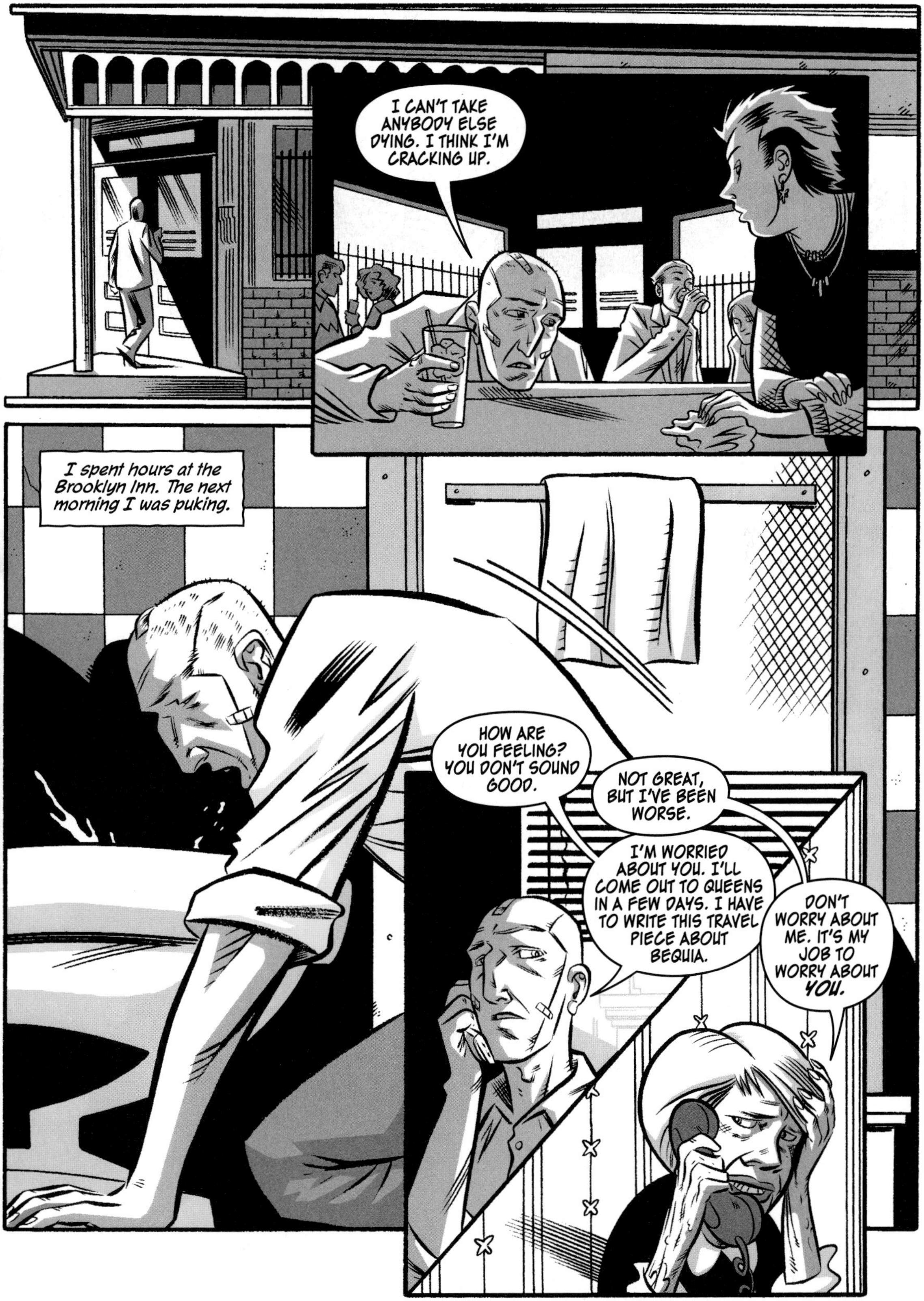

I CAN'T TAKE ANYBODY ELSE DYING. I THINK I'M CRACKING UP.
I spent hours at the Brooklyn Inn. The next morning I was puking.
HOW ARE YOU FEELING? YOU DON'T SOUND GOOD.
NOT GREAT, BUT I'VE BEEN WORSE.
I'M WORRIED ABOUT YOU. I'LL COME OUT TO QUEENS IN A FEW DAYS. I HAVE TO WRITE THIS TRAVEL PIECE ABOUT BEQUIA.
DON'T WORRY ABOUT ME. IT'S MY JOB TO WORRY ABOUT YOU.

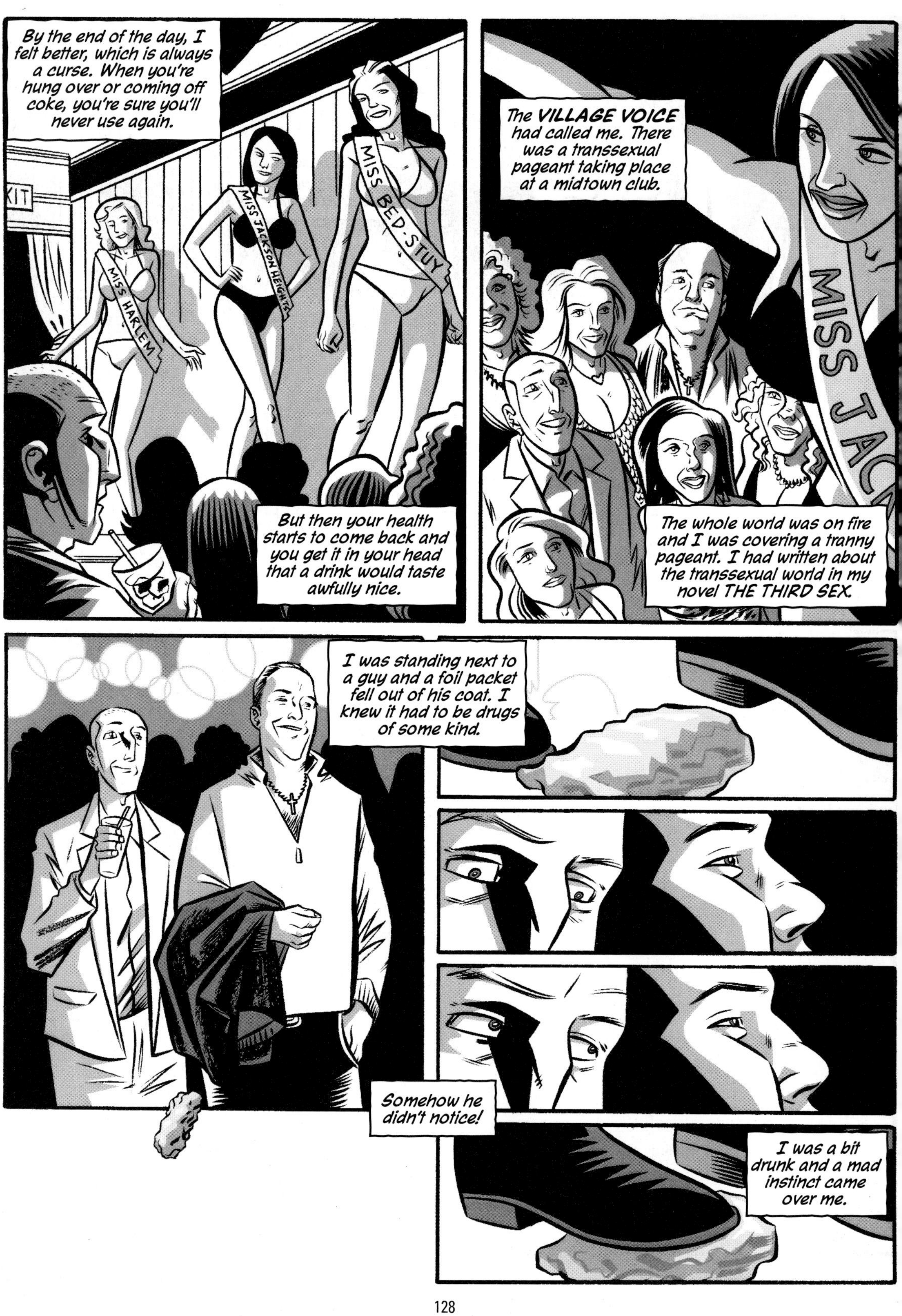
By the end of the day, I felt better, which is always a curse. When you're hung over or coming off coke, you're sure you'll never use again.
EXIT
MISS HARLEM
MISS JACKSON HEIGHTS
MISS BED-STUY
But then your health starts to come back and you get it in your head that a drink would taste awfully nice.
The VILLAGE VOICE had called me. There was a transsexual pageant taking place at a midtown club.
MISS JACK
The whole world was on fire and I was covering a tranny pageant. I had written about the transsexual world in my novel THE THIRD SEX.
I was standing next to a guy and a foil packet fell out of his coat. I knew it had to be drugs of some kind.
Somehow he didn't notice!
I was a bit drunk and a mad instinct came over me.

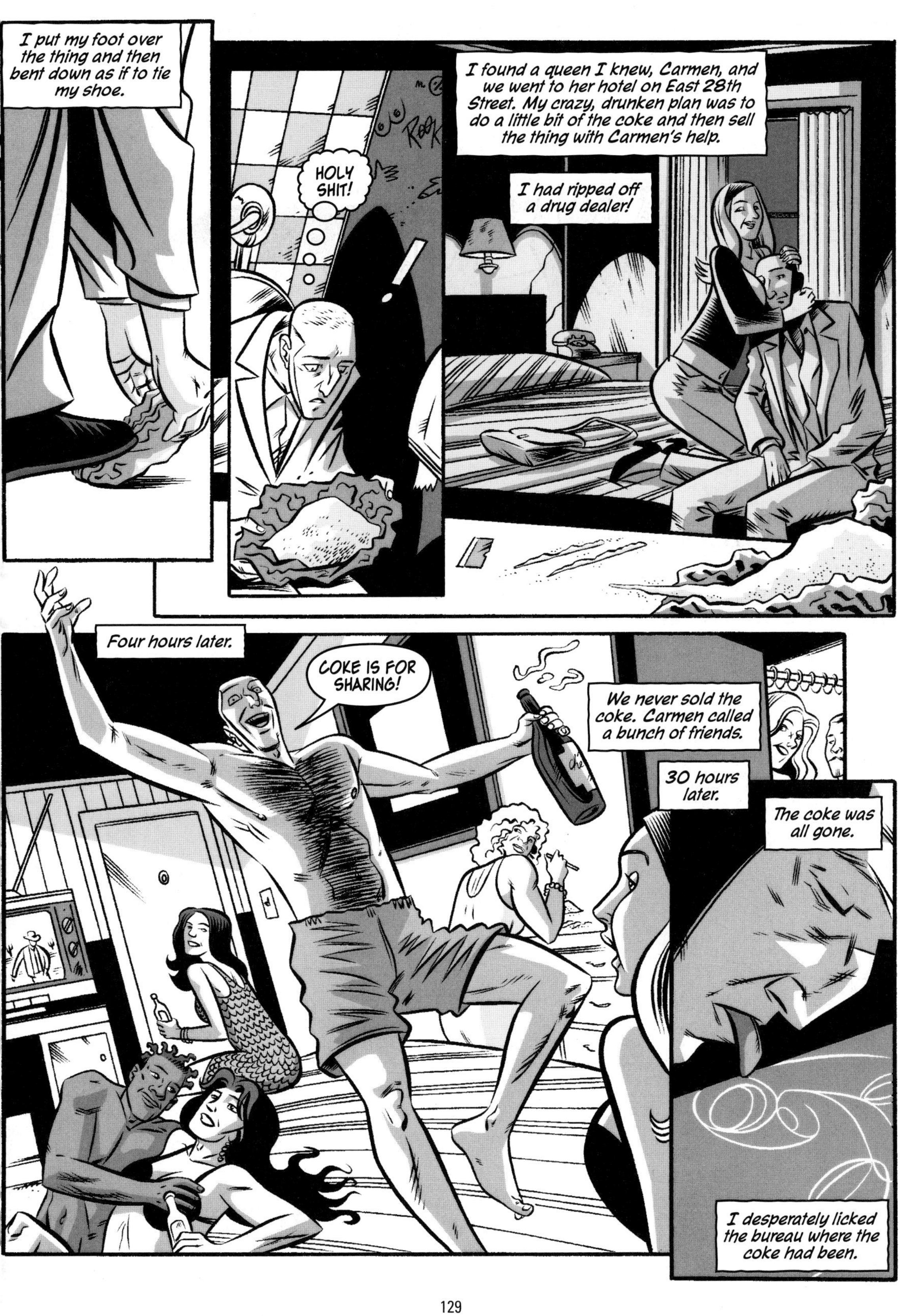
I put my foot over the thing and then bent down as if to tie my shoe.
HOLY SHIT!
!
I found a queen I knew, Carmen, and we went to her hotel on East 28th Street. My crazy, drunken plan was to do a little bit of the coke and then sell the thing with Carmen's help.
I had ripped off a drug dealer!
Four hours later.
COKE IS FOR SHARING!
We never sold the coke. Carmen called a bunch of friends.
30 hours later.
The coke was all gone.
I desperately licked the bureau where the coke had been.

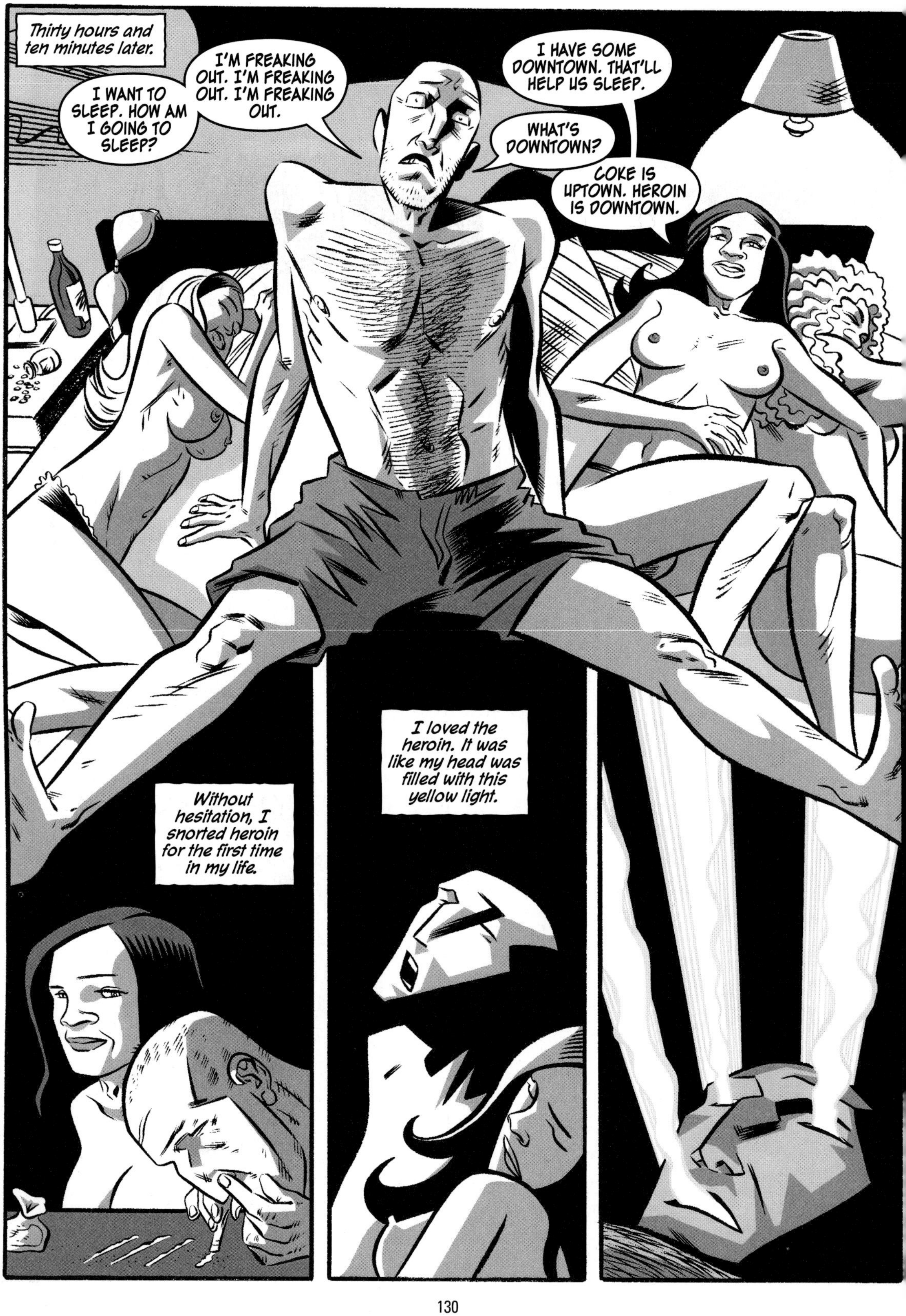
Thirty hours and ten minutes later.
I WANT TO SLEEP. HOW AM I GOING TO SLEEP?
I'M FREAKING OUT. I'M FREAKING OUT. I'M FREAKING OUT.
I HAVE SOME DOWNTOWN. THAT'LL HELP US SLEEP.
WHAT'S DOWNTOWN?
COKE IS UPTOWN. HEROIN IS DOWNTOWN.
Without hesitation, I snorted heroin for the first time in my life.
I loved the heroin. It was like my head was filled with this yellow light.

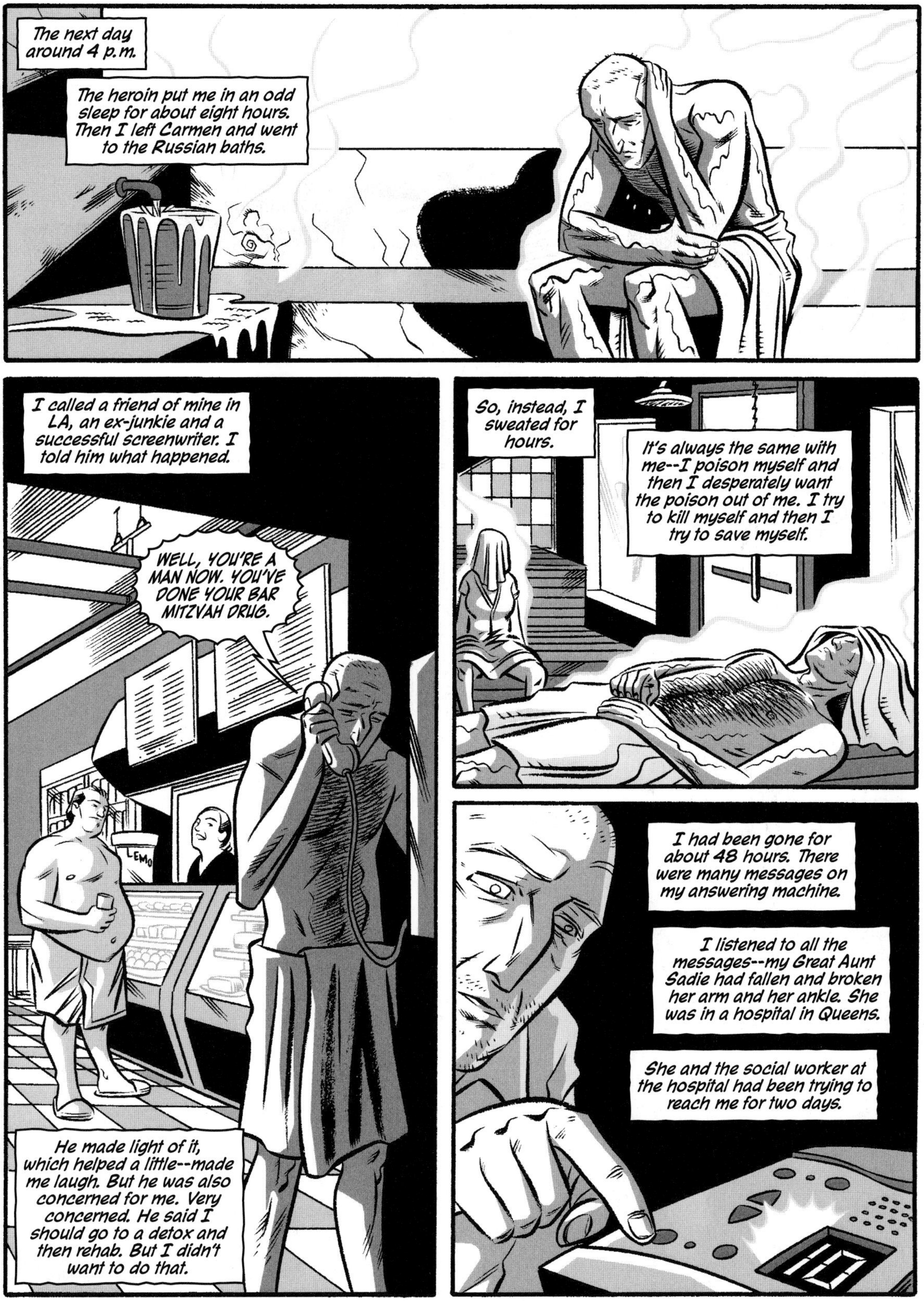
The next day around 4 p.m.
The heroin put me in an odd sleep for about eight hours. Then I left Carmen and went to the Russian baths.
I called a friend of mine in LA, an ex-junkie and a successful screenwriter. I told him what happened.
WELL, YOU'RE A MAN NOW. YOU'VE DONE YOUR BAR MITZVAH DRUG.
He made light of it, which helped a little--made me laugh. But he was also concerned for me. Very concerned. He said I should go to a detox and then rehab. But I didn't want to do that.
So, instead, I sweated for hours.
It's always the same with me--I poison myself and then I desperately want the poison out of me. I try to kill myself and then I try to save myself.
I had been gone for about 48 hours. There were many messages on my answering machine.
I listened to all the messages--my Great Aunt Sadie had fallen and broken her arm and her ankle. She was in a hospital in Queens.
She and the social worker at the hospital had been trying to reach me for two days.

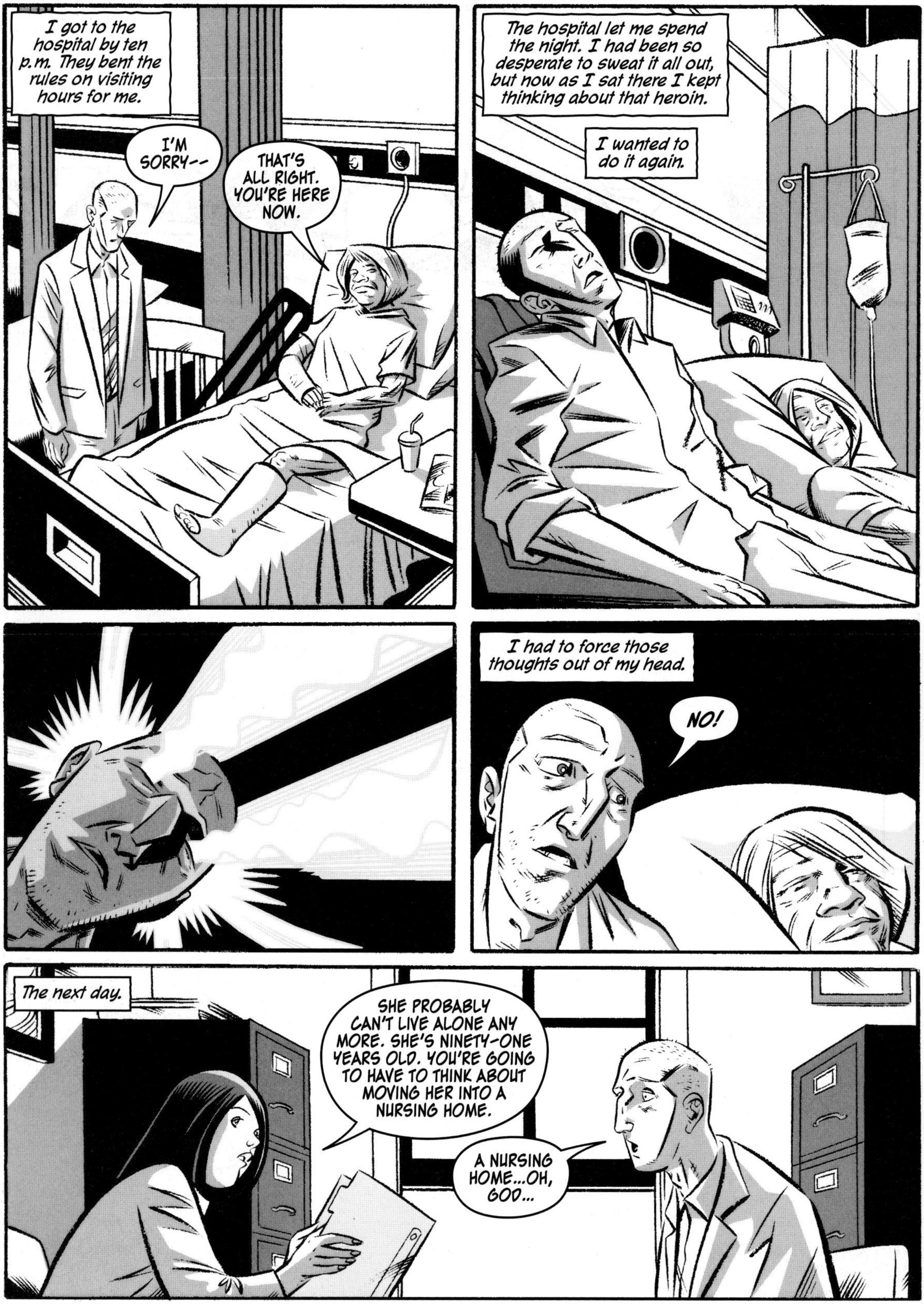

I got to the hospital by ten p.m. They bent the rules on visiting hours for me.
I'M SORRY--
THAT'S ALL RIGHT. YOU'RE HERE NOW.
The hospital let me spend the night. I had been so desperate to sweat it all out, but now as I sat there I kept thinking about that heroin.
I wanted to do it again.
I had to force those thoughts out of my head.
NO!
The next day.
SHE PROBABLY CAN'T LIVE ALONE ANY MORE. SHE'S NINETY-ONE YEARS OLD. YOU'RE GOING TO HAVE TO THINK ABOUT MOVING HER INTO A NURSING HOME.
A NURSING HOME...OH, GOD...

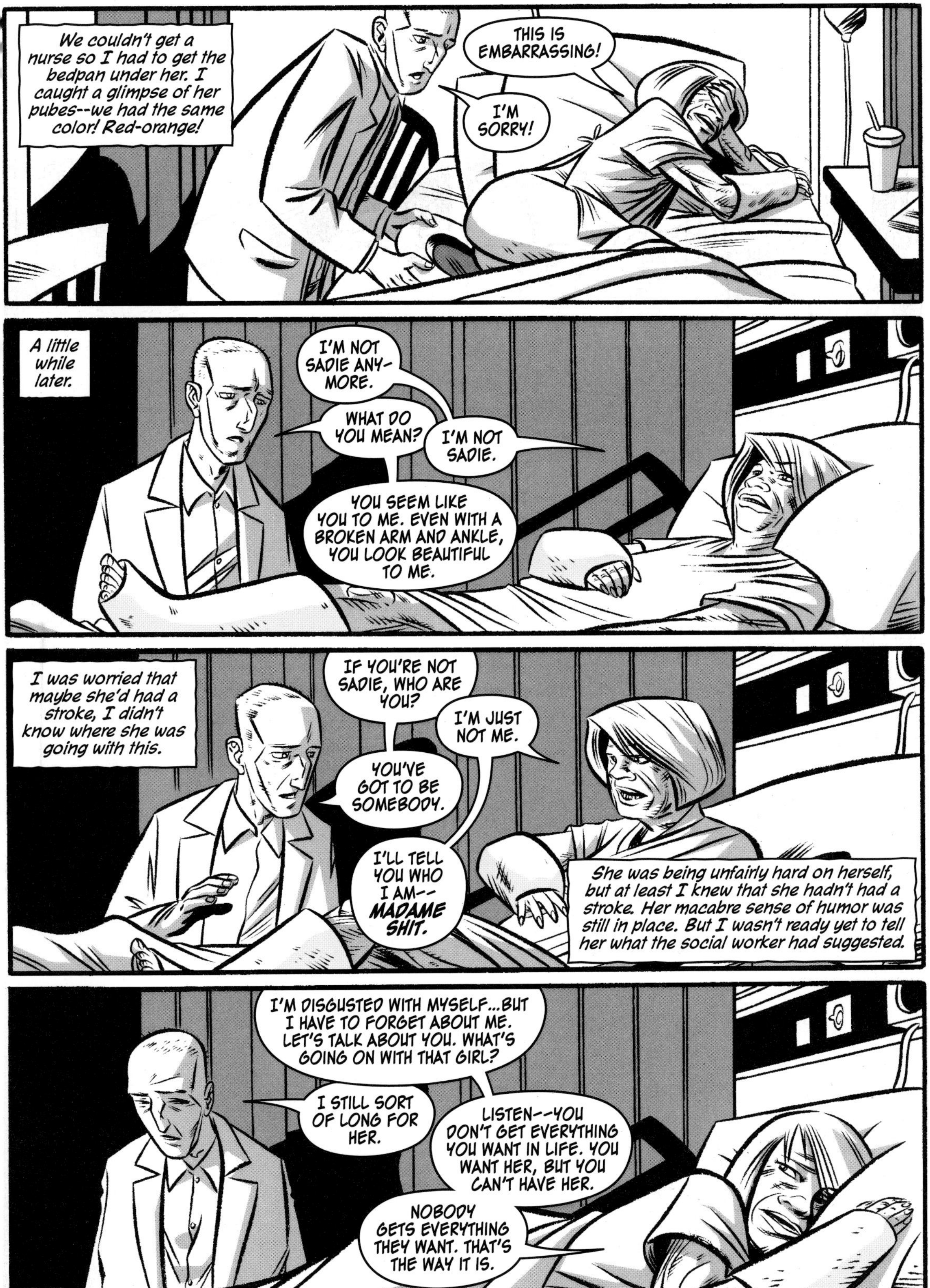
We couldn't get a nurse so I had to get the bedpan under her. I caught a glimpse of her pubes--we had the same color! Red-orange!
THIS IS EMBARRASSING!
I'M SORRY!
A little while later.
I'M NOT SADIE ANY-MORE.
WHAT DO YOU MEAN?
I'M NOT SADIE.
YOU SEEM LIKE YOU TO ME. EVEN WITH A BROKEN ARM AND ANKLE, YOU LOOK BEAUTIFUL TO ME.
I was worried that maybe she'd had a stroke, I didn't know where she was going with this.
IF YOU'RE NOT SADIE, WHO ARE YOU?
I'M JUST NOT ME.
YOU'VE GOT TO BE SOMEBODY.
I'LL TELL YOU WHO I AM-- MADAME SHIT.
She was being unfairly hard on herself, but at least I knew that she hadn't had a stroke. Her macabre sense of humor was still in place. But I wasn't ready yet to tell her what the social worker had suggested.
I'M DISGUSTED WITH MYSELF...BUT I HAVE TO FORGET ABOUT ME. LET'S TALK ABOUT YOU. WHAT'S GOING ON WITH THAT GIRL?
I STILL SORT OF LONG FOR HER.
LISTEN--YOU DON'T GET EVERYTHING YOU WANT IN LIFE. YOU WANT HER, BUT YOU CAN'T HAVE HER.
NOBODY GETS EVERYTHING THEY WANT. THAT'S THE WAY IT IS.

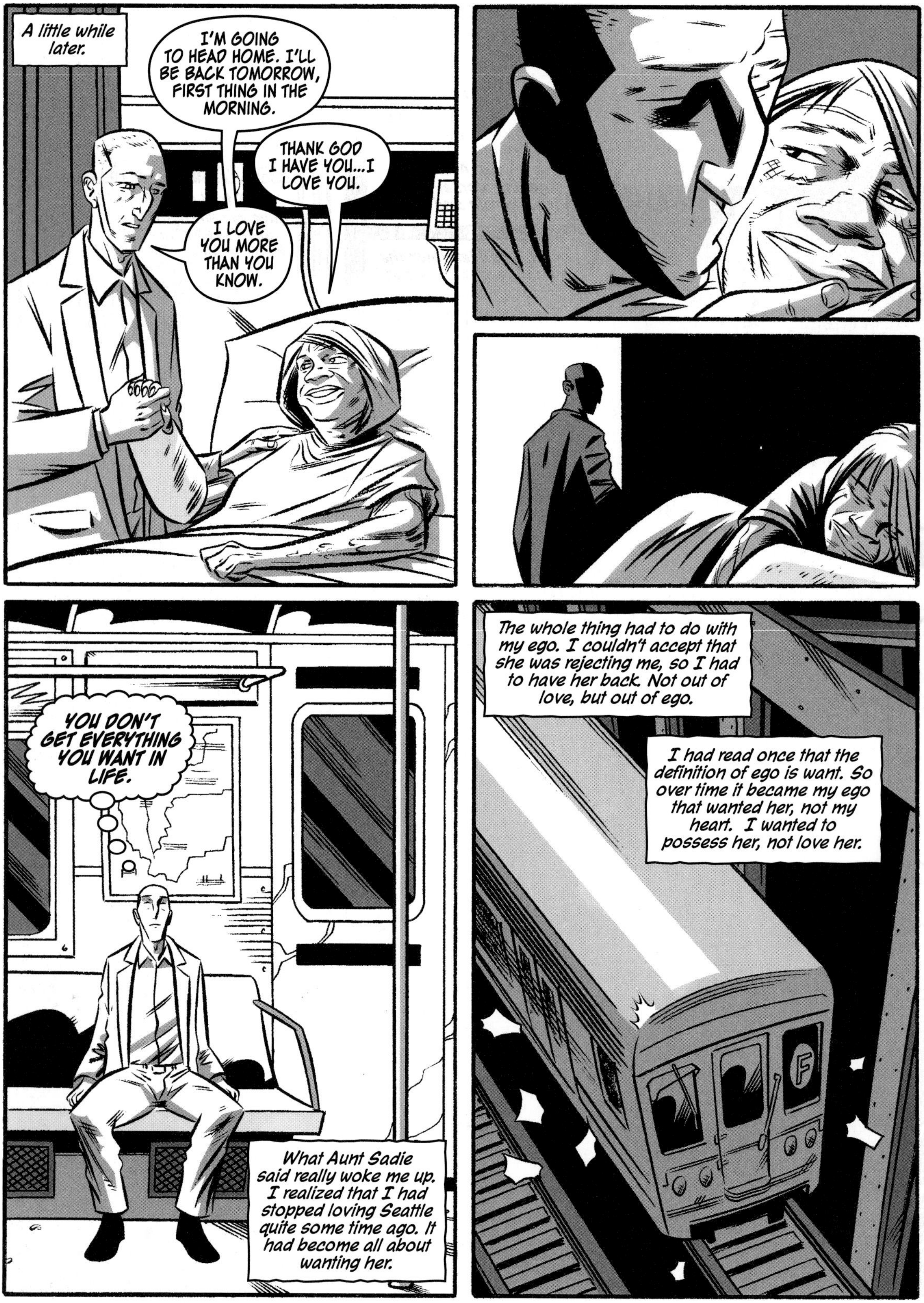

A little while later.
I'M GOING TO HEAD HOME. I'LL BE BACK TOMORROW, FIRST THING IN THE MORNING.
THANK GOD I HAVE YOU...I LOVE YOU.
I LOVE YOU MORE THAN YOU KNOW.
YOU DON'T GET EVERYTHING YOU WANT IN LIFE.
What Aunt Sadie said really woke me up. I realized that I had stopped loving Seattle quite some time ago. It had become all about wanting her.
The whole thing had to do with my ego. I couldn't accept that she was rejecting me, so I had to have her back. Not out of love, but out of ego.
I had read once that the definition of ego is want. So over time it became my ego that wanted her, not my heart. I wanted to possess her, not love her.
F

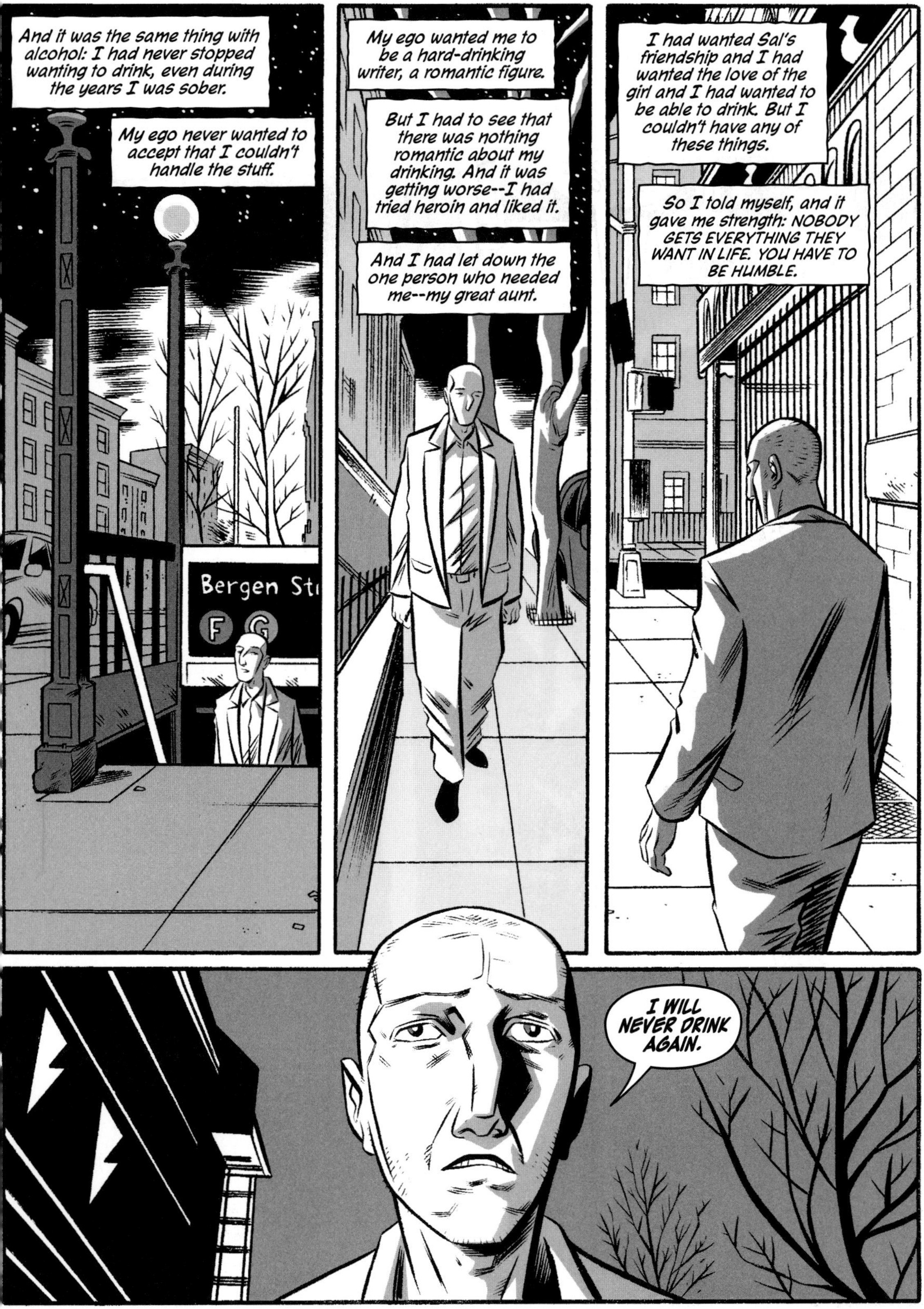

And it was the same thing with alcohol: I had never stopped wanting to drink, even during the years I was sober.
My ego never wanted to accept that I couldn't handle the stuff.
Bergen St
F G
My ego wanted me to be a hard-drinking writer, a romantic figure.
But I had to see that there was nothing romantic about my drinking. And it was getting worse--I had tried heroin and liked it.
And I had let down the one person who needed me--my great aunt.
I had wanted Sal's friendship and I had wanted the love of the girl and I had wanted to be able to drink. But I couldn't have any of these things.
So I told myself, and it gave me strength: NOBODY GETS EVERYTHING THEY WANT IN LIFE. YOU HAVE TO BE HUMBLE.
I WILL NEVER DRINK AGAIN.

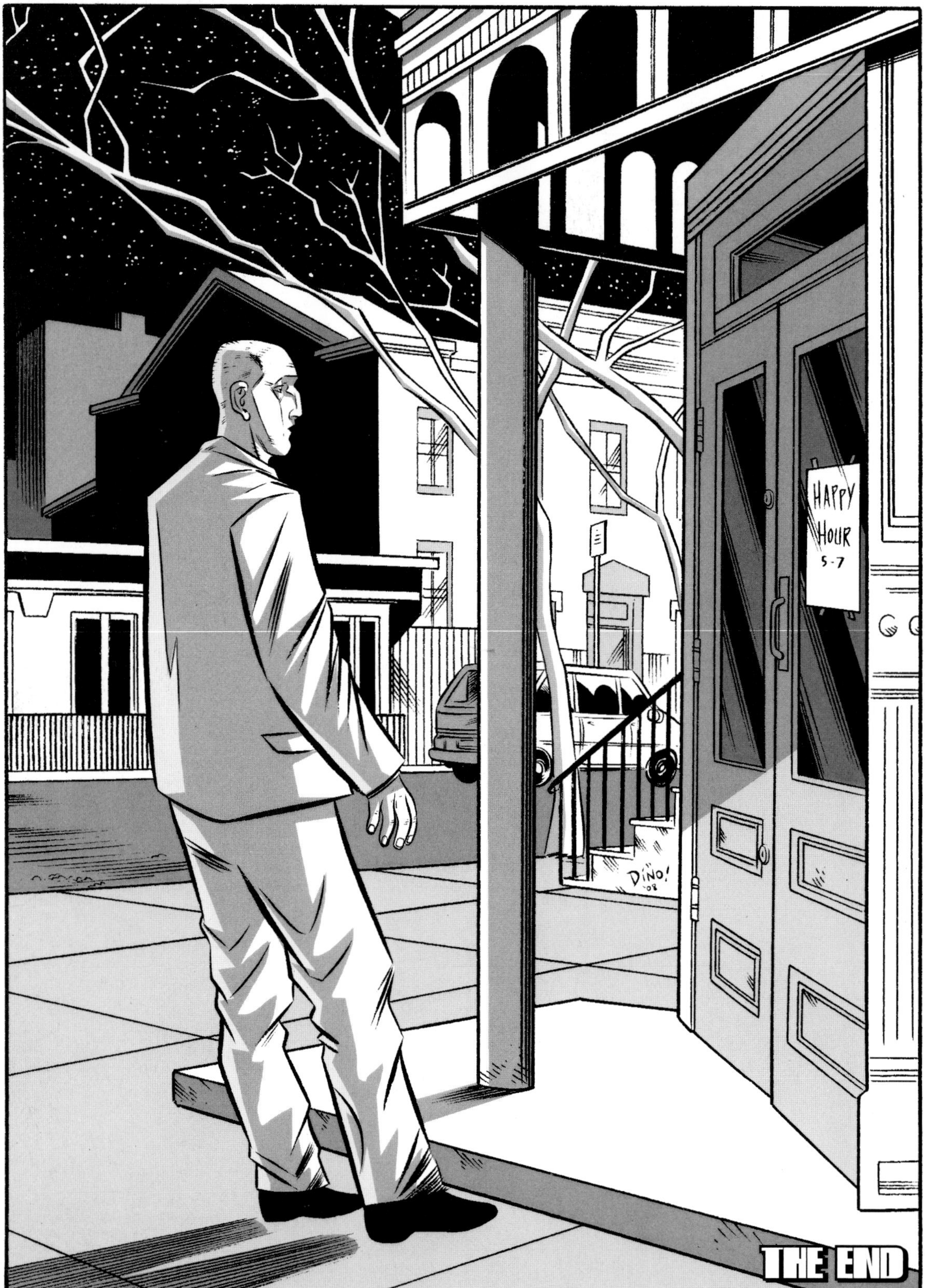
HAPPY
HOUR
5-7
DINO! '08
THE END